Essential Aspects of Physical Design and Implementation of Relational Databases

Tatiana Malyuta and Ashwin Satyanarayana

ISBN: 0692281886
ISBN-13: 9780692281888

DEDICATION

*This book is dedicated to all our students of
New York City College of Technology.
We appreciate and admire their perseverance and determination, and wish
them further successes in pursuing their careers.*

CONTENTS

Chapter 1.   User Requirements and Relational Databases......................................6

    1.1.   Introduction.. 6

    1.2.   User Requirements and the Conceptual Data Model....................... 13

    1.3.   User Requirements and the Relational Model 16

    1.4.   User Requirements and the Database 18

    1.5.   Structure of the Book 20

Chapter 2.   The Physical Data Model **22**

    2.1.   Goals of Physical Modeling 22

    2.2.   Tables... 23

    2.3.   Data Storage 26

    2.4.   Indices 32

    2.5.   Transparency of the Physical Model 34

    2.6.   The Physical Data Model in Oracle.. 37

    2.7.   Distributed Data Storage... 44

    2.8.   Example: Building the Physical Model of Data............................. 51

    2.9.   Summary 54

    Review Questions... 55

    Practical Assignments... 55

Chapter 3.   Distributed Database Design **57**

    3.1.   Prerequisites of the Distributed Design.. 58

    3.2.   Review of Basic Features of the Distributed Database 59

    3.3.   General Approaches to Distribution.. 59

    3.4.   Horizontal fragmentation... 61

    3.5.   Vertical Fragmentation 69

3.6.   Hybrid Fragmentation 70

3.7.   Allocation and Replication 73

3.8.   Preserving Semantics of the Relational Model 75

3.9.   Examples: Implementing a Distributed Database in Oracle 81

3.10.   Summary 85

Review Questions 86

Practical Assignments 86

Chapter 4.   Security **89**

4.1.   Database Security 89

4.2.   The Basic Tools for Implementing Security 92

4.3.   Database Objects and Security 98

4.4.   Security in the Distributed Database 103

4.5.   Security Measures in Oracle 105

4.6.   Security in the Distributed Oracle Database 116

4.7.   Examples: Implementing Security Measures in the Centralized and Distributed
Databases 121

4.8.   Summary 124

Review Questions 125

Practical Assignments 126

Chapter 5.   Query Processing and Performance **127**

5.1.   Problems of Query Processing 127

5.2.   Types of Optimization 131

5.3.   Factors That Influence Performance 133

5.4.   Examples of Influence of Different Factors on Performance 145

5.5.   Database Tuning 147

5.6.   Performance in Distributed Databases 148

5.7.   Query Processing in Oracle 154

5.8.   Examples: Tuning Query Processing 165

5.9.   Summary 167

Review Questions 168

Practical Assignments 169

Chapter 6.   Transaction Management 171

6.1.   Problems of Concurrent Access and Failures 171

6.2.   The Concept of a Transaction 176

6.3.   Properties of Transactions 180

6.4.   Serializability Theory 183

6.5.   Concurrency Control Approaches 187

6.6.   Transaction Management in the Distributed Database 204

6.7.   Transactions and Performance 205

6.8.   How Oracle Manages Data Concurrency and Consistency 208

6.9.   Preventing Phenomena in Oracle Transactions 217

6.10.   Examples: Implementation of Transactions and the Design of the Database for Performance and Consistency 217

6.11.   Summary 219

Review Questions 220

Practical Assignments 221

Chapter 7.   Transactions and the Database Recovery 223

7.1.   Recovery from a System Failure 223

7.2.   Recovery from a System Failure in a Distributed Database 229

7.3.   Recovery from a System Failure in a Replicated Database 234

7.4.   Recovery from a Media Failure 234

7.5.   Summary 235

Review Questions...235

Appendix 1. Case Studies... **237**

Appendix 2. Operations of Relational Algebra....................................... **243**

Appendix 3. Architecture of the Oracle Database **249**

Appendix 4. Oracle Database Vault.. **254**

Appendix 5. Analysis of Performance in Oracle **257**

Appendix 6. Example of Concurrent Execution of Transactions **261**

References...**267**

ACKNOWLEDGMENTS

The authors want to thank our former colleague, Prof. R. Guidone, for his contribution to the earlier version of the manuscript.

Chapter 1. User Requirements and Relational Databases

1.1. Introduction

This book is dedicated to the physical design and implementation of relational databases which are the two phases in the building of databases that do not get enough attention in most of the textbooks on database design and management. The physical design and implementation phases involve the Database Management System (DBMS), and our goal is to demonstrate how to combine data design and functionality of the DBMS to achieve the most effective database and database applications.

The first two steps in database design – conceptual and logical – are aimed at correctly modeling the users' information needs and do not address the issues of the actual utilization of data, such as where data will be stored, how data storage will be organized, whether the future database will allow for concurrent access of multiple users, and similar considerations. The physical design and implementation of the database is more application-oriented and is concerned with producing successful and efficient data usage in the designed structure.

The methodology of designing relational databases (building the relational model of data) is relatively straightforward and is described in numerous database books: [Connolly 2004], [Connolly 2010], [Hoffer], [Kifer], [Mannino], [Silberschatz]. However, getting from the relational data model to the physical model for a particular DBMS and implementing the database is less direct and often require trying different approaches.

For practically any given business requirement described by the future users of a database, an experienced database designer can build the relational data model that takes into account the most important requirements regarding the data contents without sacrificing any of the requirements for the sake of others. The creation of the physical model of the database and the model's subsequent implementation, on the other hand, are much less straightforward processes. The user requirements that the database developers have to deal with often conflict with each other – support of some requirements may make it difficult or impossible to support others. Furthermore, the support of a new requirement may jeopardize the already successfully implemented ones. In addition, when performing the physical design and implementation of the database, professionals are dependent on the chosen hardware, software and the specific DBMS. They have to know about these products' capabilities on the one hand, and their limitations on the other.

It is difficult, therefore, to talk about the *methodology* for the physical design and implementation of relational databases. It is more appropriate to try to define the goals of the physical modeling and implementation of the database, to suggest various solutions for the support of particular user requirements with the help of the DBMS, and to describe the possible impact of these solutions on other requirements and the database as a whole. The scheme for decision making about the physical design and implementation of a database is shown in Figure 1-1.

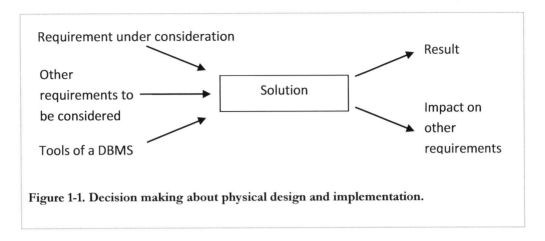

Figure 1-1. Decision making about physical design and implementation.

This chapter gives an overview of the entire process of database design and implementation. The database is supposed to support information needs of its potential users. That is why it is important to understand how different user needs and requirements are realized by our decisions. The better the model reflects the users' needs and the better the database satisfies users, the more effectively it will be utilized and maintained.

1.1.1 The Database Life Cycle

The database project, as any other information system (IS) project, goes through the following steps known as the life cycle of the IS:

1. Initiation and Planning
2. Analysis
3. Design
   - Conceptual
   - Logical
   - Physical
4. Implementation
5. Maintenance.

The project is initiated in response to particular needs of a group of people who are called users (potential) of the future system. The users express their needs in different ways, e.g. they may say "We want the database to support data about employees of our company." Descriptions of users' needs are called user requirements or business rules.

The generic user requirements (what every user expects from the database regardless of its specific purpose) can be defined as:

- Support of all necessary data
- Maintenance of data consistency in accordance with the business rules
- Acceptable performance (user defined) for database applications and requests
- Availability of data manipulations to authorized users
- Reliability and ability to recover from various failures.

It is also very important that the support of the database be as easy as possible.

These generic requirements define properties by which users decide how good the database is:

- Completeness of data
- Consistency of data
- Performance
- Security
- Reliability
- Ease of use and maintenance.

The life of the information system is said to be a cycle because at any moment user requirements may change, and therefore the system has to be modified. Depending on the nature of the change, the modification of the system and resultant changes to the database may happen at any step of the life cycle. For example:

- *Implementation.* Users may want faster execution of some applications, and the designer would then have to add several indices to enhance the performance of these applications.
- *Physical design.* If indices from the previous step do not resolve the performance issue, then the designer may consider reorganizing the data storage.
- *Logical design.* If neither indices, nor reorganizing the data storage improve performance to the required level, then the redesign of the database may be required, e.g. performing denormalization of the data model.
- *Conceptual design.* Users may decide to expand the database application's functionality and require that additional data be placed in the database leading to redesigning of the database.
- *Initiation.* Reorganization of the enterprise's IS may necessitate reinitiating the whole project.

Though traditionally the term *cycle* is used to describe the life of the system, in the case of the development of the database it is more like a *spiral* development: the system goes through the same steps, but each turn leads to a higher level of development ("higher" level means that the results of the steps of the previous spiral turn are used with some changes or additions). Of course, changes on a particular step may affect all the subsequent steps of the system's life cycle.

Figure 1-2 shows the finished first cycle of the database development, and changes in the requirements that cause the redesign of the database and take the project to the second turn of the life spiral. The conceptual, logical, and physical designs of the database are affected, as well as the implementation and maintenance.

This book concentrates on the physical design and implementation of relational databases. The discussion assumes that the relational data model appropriately reflects the user requirements. The conceptual and logical (relational) data design steps are covered in numerous database books, e.g. [Connolly 2010], [Hoffer], [Kifer], [Mannino],[Silberschatz] and are briefly reviewed in this chapter.

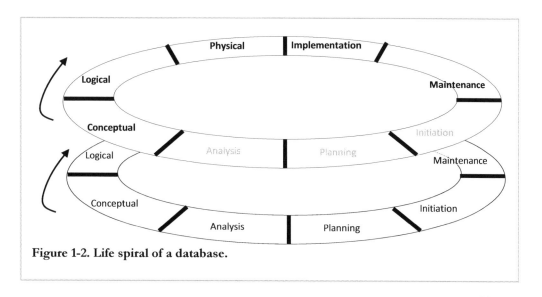

Figure 1-2. Life spiral of a database.

We also want to discuss terms such as "design of data" and "design of the database" that are often used interchangeably. From the point of view of this book, the conceptual and logical (relational) design steps deal with the data and its design. The resulting design is reflected in the relational data model. The following step, physical design, continues to develop the data model and enriches it with physical features. This step, however, involves the DBMS and the database – *data design evolves into database design*. The database is much more than just the data. It includes a collection of objects, routines, and settings that support the data and data maintenance, and it implements some user requirements, e.g. data security, that go beyond the data model. The physical design and implementation of the database are tightly related, and the implementation of the database involves the design of indices, security measures, and reliability support. Figure 1-3 shows how the conceptual and logical design supports different generic requirements of the physical design and implementation. The database professional defines the completeness of the data during the initial steps of the conceptual design. Data consistency and ease of use result from following the design methodology in the conceptual and logical design. Other requirements (security, performance, reliability, ease of use) are supported in the physical data model and implemented in the database through the utilization of features of the DBMS.

However, the conceptual and logical data design also play a role in the successful realization of some of these requirements. For example, if a conceptual data model is built without understanding how the data will be used and maintained, then during the physical design and implementation steps, database professionals cannot compensate for the flaws in the data model and cannot achieve the desired performance levels and ease of use.

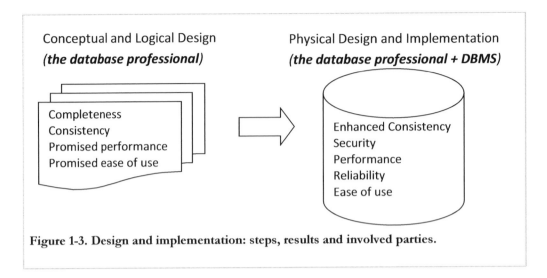

Figure 1-3. Design and implementation: steps, results and involved parties.

1.1.2 System Analysis and User Requirements

The design, implementation, and maintenance of the database are provided by the database specialists: designers, developers and programmers. They base all their decisions on the requirements of the potential users of the database. Obviously, requirements like the one mentioned above – "We want the database to support data about employees of our company" – are not useful for the design and implementation of the database. There are different methodologies and techniques for gathering and preparing user requirements [Whitten]. Requirements are collected, systematized and formulated by groups of analysts in the initial phases of a database project: initiation, planning, and analysis.

Database specialists use the requirements developed by the analysts and apply them for the design and implementation of the database. The specialists must understand the nature of the requirements, know which of them have to be considered at the design and implementation steps and decide how to support the requirements.

As an example, consider these business rules, which are relevant for the database about employees:

1. Data about each employee must be kept in the database for three years after the employee stops working for the company.
2. The company has several thousand employees.
3. It is expected that the number of employees will increase by 3% each year.
4. Users of the Payroll department cannot see some personal information of employees.
5. Users of the Personnel department cannot see the financial information of employees.
6. For each employee, it is necessary to store the employee's company identification number, name, date of birth, age, and title.
7. The identification number of an employee is unique.
8. Each employee is assigned to a department.
9. The database has to store a department's code and location.
10. Retrieval of data about a particular employee should not take more than 5 seconds.

11. Data about employees have to be available from 9 a.m. to 6 p.m. every weekday.

These rules specify the generic user requirements:

- Completeness of data (6 and 9)
- Consistency of data (7 and 8)
- Performance (10)
- Security (4 and 5)
- Reliability and availability (11).

Requirements 1, 2, and 3 additionally define the expected size of the database.

The completeness of data requirements and some of the consistency requirements are implemented in the conceptual data model. The logical model (in our case, it is the relational model) is the result of mapping of the conceptual model on the set of relations. The logical model merely reflects the particular data structure (in our case, relations) of the requirements presented in the conceptual model (some of the consistency requirements may even be lost, e.g. whether a relationship is mandatory or optional). During the physical data design, data types and additional constraints supported by the DBMS enhance data consistency and define to a large extent the performance of database applications, the reliability, the ease of use and the ease of maintenance requirements of the database. The implementation of the database finalizes the realization of the complicated consistency requirements with the help of triggers[1], improves the performance through indices[2], establishes security policies and defines the reliability of the database.

The conceptual design, therefore, lays the foundation for the successful fulfillment of the database's goals, while the physical design and implementation are supposed to realize the potential of the conceptual model and guarantee the required properties of the database with the help of the DBMS.

Let us take a closer look at user requirements. In database literature, there are multiple classifications of them. For a more detailed discussion of the types of user requirements and their relationships to the database we will use the classification from one of the previous editions of [Hoffer].

User requirements are divided into *structural* and *action* requirements (see Figure 1-4). Structural requirements, such as attributes (base and derived), terms, and relationships define both the data structure and the relationships between different data. Most of them are implemented in the conceptual and logical models of the database.

---

[1] Triggers are special database procedures defined on events (INSERT, DELETE, UPDATE) on a table. Every time the event defined in the trigger occurs, the trigger is initiated and executed.

[2] An index is a data structure used to determine the location of rows in a table that satisfy a certain condition.

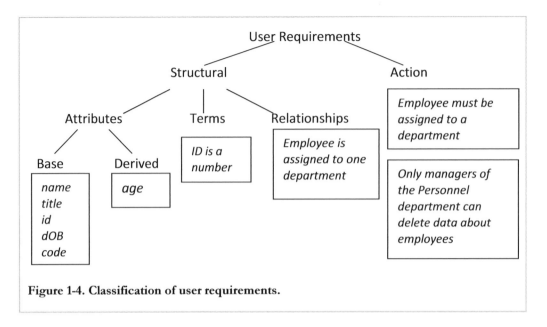

Figure 1-4. Classification of user requirements.

Action requirements specify how data are used, and what the rules and restrictions of using data are. For example, access to particular data by some users may be restricted, or the response time of an important request has to be within specific limits. Some action requirements are reflected in the conceptual and logical models of a database, but most of them are supported in the physical model or during implementation with the help of special features of the DBMS.

1.1.3   Goals of Database Design and Implementation

The ultimate goal of database design and implementation is a database on which all or the most important user requirements are supported. Realistically, some requirements may be sacrificed to lower the cost, to provide ease of implementation and maintenance, or to support more important requirements (if support of all of them is difficult). From the initial steps of the database project, database professionals have to compromise between: cost vs. a particular feature of the database, one requirement vs. another, a particular feature of the database vs. simplicity of implementation and support. For example, indices can be created to improve the performance of particular data retrieval requests knowing that these indices may worsen the performance of modifying queries.

Not only do user requirements have to be supported, but their support has to be performed in the easiest and most natural way for the chosen tools. For example, referential integrity in relational databases has to be implemented with the help of foreign key constraints, and not with the help of triggers. Triggers require programming, decrease performance, and do not guarantee reliable support of referential integrity.   For the above data requirements about employees and departments, it is desirable to have not a single relation but two separate normalized[1] relations, because this will allow for easy data support without various modification

---

1 Normalization is the process of decomposing relations with anomalies to produce smaller, well-structured relations.

anomalies.

In addition, the support of requirements has to be reliable and independent of particular states of a database. For example, for the above mentioned situation with the foreign key constraint implementation with the help of triggers, referential integrity may be violated by concurrent transactions (explained in Chapter 6).

1.2. User Requirements and the Conceptual Data Model

The discussion of the employees' database continues. The design of the database starts with the conceptual modeling, which is the first formalization of user requirements related to data and is aimed to reflect the necessary data and relationships between the data. The most popular tools for conceptual modeling are the Entity-Relationship Diagram (ERD) and Unified Modeling Language (UML). Further discussion in this book is based on the ERD. Detailed coverage of ERD and conceptual design can be found in most of the books on database concepts, e.g. [Hoffer].

On the ERD, designers show entities of the business, the required data for each entity and relationships between entities. Analyzing the requirements of the employees database case, the designer can decide on two entities: Employee and Department. Employee has ID, name, and title as attributes, and Department has code and location as attributes. ID and code are the identifiers of the entities Employee and Department, respectively. Figure 1-5 shows these entities and the binary one-to-many relationship Assigned between them – an employee is assigned to one department and in one department there can be more than one employee. With the help of another relationship – unary one-to-many Manages – an additional requirement is shown, stating that some of the employees are managers: each employee has one manager and a manager can supervise more than one employee.

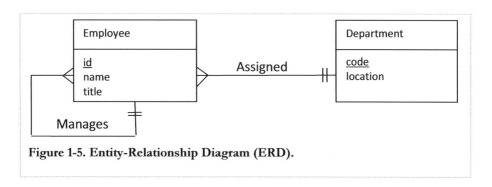

Figure 1-5. Entity-Relationship Diagram (ERD).

The conceptual model of data is very general; it does not show the structure of the data in the future database (e.g. records, or objects, or hierarchies), nor does it describe the physical features of the data (where or how data are stored).

1.2.1 Structural User Requirements

The ERD for the discussed database about employees was built using the following structural requirements:

- ID, name, title, code, and location are *attributes*.
- ID is a number, which has a unique value for each employee and is used for identification. Code is an alphanumerical string three symbols long that starts with a letter. The value of code is unique for each department and is used for the identification of departments.
- ID and code are *business terms* and their role and possible values were described above. Name, title and location are *common terms* and they do not need to be defined further.
- Employees are assigned to departments of the company. One employee is assigned to one department only. In a department, there can be many employees. An employee has one manager, who is another employee. One employee can manage several employees. These business rules specify *relationships* between instances of employees and departments, and between different instances of employees, respectively.

Most of these requirements are shown on the conceptual data model implemented with the help of ERD in Figure 1-5:

- Attributes are grouped in two entities: Employee and Department.
- The uniqueness of attributes ID and Code is shown by using these attributes as identifiers of their entities.
- The relationship requirements are shown as relationships of the conceptual model. The relationship Assigned between instances of the entities Employee and Department shows cardinalities of participation of Employee (many) and Department (one) in this relationship. The relationship Manages between different instances of Employee shows cardinalities of participation of employee-manager (one) and employee-managed (many).

However, the ERD does *not* reflect the details of term definitions (e.g. their possible values).

Suppose that additional information becomes available about different types of employees: full-time employees have an annual salary; part-time employees have an hourly rate, hours per week, and weekly pay; and consultants have a billing rate. To model the data under these conditions an enhanced ERD (EERD) with a *supertype-subtype relationship* should be considered (see Figure 1-6).

The supertype-subtype relationship shows that all employees share the attributes ID, name, and title (the supertype entity Employee), and that there are three types of employees, each with specific attributes (subtype entities Full-time, Part-time, and Consultant). Because the attribute weeklyPay is calculated by multiplying values of the attributes hourlyRate and hoursPerWeek, it is shown as a derived attribute. However, the rules for *calculating* derived attributes cannot be shown in the ERD or EERD.

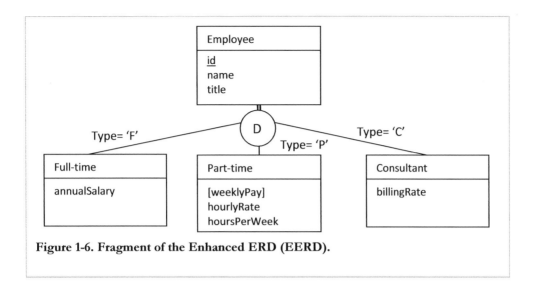

Figure 1-6. Fragment of the Enhanced ERD (EERD).

1.2.2   Action User Requirements

Action user requirements specify how data is used and how it has to be handled when used.

In [Hoffer], action requirements are classified into:

- *Conditions.* For example, if an employee has a title "Manager," then he or she can be assigned to manage other employees.
- *Integrity constraints.* For example,
    - ✓ Part-time employees cannot work more than twenty hours per week.
    - ✓ Each employee must be assigned to a department.
    - ✓ An employee cannot manage more than three people.
- *Authorization.* Only users who work in the Payroll department are entitled to access and change salary, hourly rate and billing rate data.

The following requirements of other types, which were not explicitly mentioned in [Hoffer] should also be specified:

- *Space.* The company has several thousand employees and expects the number of employees to increase by 3% each year.
- *Timing (performance).* Given an employee's ID, retrieval of data about the employee and the department the employee is assigned to, should not take more than one millisecond.
- *Accuracy.* A report of monthly payments to employees must be 99.9% accurate.
- *Reliability.* The database has to be available twenty hours a day and be protected from possible failures and data loss.
- *Concurrency.* Approximately one hundred users should be able to access and process data simultaneously.

There also may be rules that are preferences rather than requirements. For example, once a month data about all employees are updated and it would be very useful, if this operation did not take more than thirty minutes.

Some of the *conditions* and *integrity constraints* are modeled with the help of the ERD or EERD, for example in Figure 1-7:

- The constraint that an employee must be assigned to a department is shown with the help of the minimum cardinality of the relationship Assigned (the relationship is mandatory for an employee and optional for a department).
- A special element of the EERD allows the display of the maximum cardinality of the relationship Manages--an employee cannot manage more than three employees.

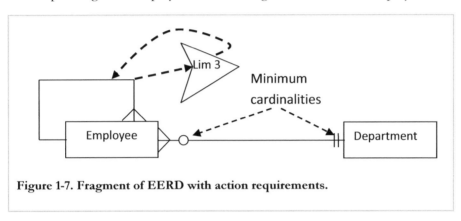

Figure 1-7. Fragment of EERD with action requirements.

1.2.3 The Expressive Capabilities of the Conceptual Model

It has been shown that the conceptual model of data is a formalization of many of the structural and some of the action business rules. Applying the enhanced ERD allows additional user requirements to be displayed. However, as it is shown later in this chapter, these enhancements are modeled partially or cannot be modeled at all in the relational data model. The expressive possibilities of the basic ERD comply with the needs of conceptual design on the one hand, and the possibilities of the relational data model on the other.

Conceptual modeling is aimed at giving a special formulation of those user requirements that describe data and relationships between data. The realization of the data model takes place in the database implementation and is affected by the capabilities of the DBMS as well as several requirements that simply go beyond data models. Such issues as security, performance, and complicated structural and action requirements not directly reflected in the *relational* data model are implemented in the *physical* data model or in the database with the help of the special tools of the DBMS.

1.3. User Requirements and the Relational Model

The logical data model is a representation of the conceptual model within a particular data structure; this presentation is obtained with the help of specific rules. In the relational model, data is structured in relations.

1.3.1   Mapping the Conceptual Model into the Relational Model

The ERD with the requirements reflected in it is mapped into the relational model of the database, where entities and relationships with their attributes are presented as relations. The relationships of the ERD are translated into the foreign keys of the relational model. The relational model accommodates most of the conceptual requirements.

Consider the relational model for the ERD of Figure 1-5.

Each of the entities of the ERD creates a separate relation, in which the identifier of an entity becomes the primary key of the respective relation (in relations in this book, primary keys are underlined):

        Department(code, location)

        Employee(ID, name, title)

The one-to-many relationship Assigned is mapped in the relation Employee with the help of the attribute code of the relation Department; the attribute code is defined as the foreign key to the relation Department (foreign keys are shown in *italic*):

        Employee(ID, name, title, *code*)

Similarly, the one-to-many relationship Manages is mapped in the relation Employee, the attribute ID_Manager is the foreign key to the relation Employee itself:

        Employee(ID, name, title, *code, ID_Manager*)

The final relational model is presented with the following two relations:

        Department(code, location)

        Employee(ID, name, title, *code, ID_Manager*)

1.3.2   The Expressive Capabilities of the Relational Model

The relational model defines the data structure, i.e. relations, for the conceptual data model. Therefore, the relations of the relational model with their primary and foreign key constraints represent the basic structural and some of the action business rules that are implemented within the conceptual model. Building the relational model is performed as a mapping of the conceptual model into relations using specific rules.

The relational model cannot reflect the minimum and maximum cardinalities of relationships of the ERD, nor the various extensions offered in the enhanced ERD, like the limitation on the number of managed employees in Figure 1-7.

1.3.3   Necessity of Following the Database Design Steps

Database professionals have to remember that it is necessary to follow the design steps. In many cases, there are numerous user requirements that have to be systematized and presented in such a way that allows construction of the database. Usually, the requirements have to be explained further and clarified by users. Database professionals then need to discuss their respective understanding of the requirements with their users. A graphical tool, like the ERD, gives a concise and clear picture of user requirements to database professionals, and is easily understood by users. Therefore, it is the best way to combine the users' less systematic and less formal – but often deep – understanding of requirements with the specific, structured perception of these requirements needed by database professionals. A discussion of requirements between users and database professionals using the relational model would be more difficult, if not impossible.

The conceptual model, which deals with the main entities of the business and relationships between the entities, can easily be mapped into a relational model. However, it is difficult to build a complete and correct relational model of data directly for a business containing tens or hundreds of business entities that are interrelated. Even in the discussed oversimplified database example, several versions of the logical model can exist, e.g.:

```
Employee(ID, name, title, code, location, ID_Manager)
```

This model is complete and accounts for all the required data. However, this model causes the duplication of data about departments, which – in addition to the overuse of computer and human resources – is prone to data inconsistencies and anomalies in update, delete and insert operations.

Though all necessary data can be supported this way, the support is complicated and it is necessary to apply significant efforts to resolve the above-mentioned issues. Understanding the problems of the relational model, on the other hand, is not always possible because the relational model is difficult to analyze in terms of completeness and consistency. Therefore, the established methodology of database design starts with conceptual design.

The data design is completed on the physical level, where the data structure that correctly and completely reflects the most important user requirements is enriched with such physical features as the location of data, the organization of data storage, and other physical features, which define how efficiently the database application will be able to process data. This step of design is less straightforward, involves many factors and is performed using various capabilities of the DBMS.

1.4. User Requirements and the Database

1.4.1   Functions of the DBMS

Most DBMSs help in maintaining various business rules by providing the following functions. The DBMS will:

- Enable users to store, update, and retrieve data
- Ensure the correctness of data according to integrity rules

- Support the database catalog with descriptions of data items and provide users access to the catalog. The catalog is a key feature of an American National Standards Institute-Standards Planning and Requirements Committee (ANSI-SPARC) database architecture; it contains information about all objects of the database – "data about data" or *metadata*. The catalog is used by both the DBMS itself and by database professionals and users
- Support query processing and optimization of query execution
- Ensure consistency of data under concurrent access to the database
- Recover data after failures
- Secure access to the database by allowing only authorized users to access data
- Support an Application Programming Interface (API) for integration with other software tools
- Provide additional utilities for database management.

In addition to these features, a *distributed* DBMS must provide access to remote sites, allow transfer of data and queries between sites, and support the main features of the DBMS in the distributed environment.

1.4.2   The Physical Model of Data

The physical model of data is based on the relational model and preserves all business rules contained in the relational model. The DBMS offers features for support of additional structural and action rules, and these features are utilized in the physical data model and the database.

The physical data model can support some *term definitions* with the help of data types for attributes. For example, the data type CHAR(3) for the attribute code of the table Department ensures that the requirement that all department codes will be alphanumeric and not longer than three symbols will be met. Additional support can be provided by the CHECK constraint on attributes of a table, e.g. a specific CHECK constraint on the attribute code can facilitate another requirement from this term's definition: that the first symbol of a department code should be a letter. Not all term definitions can be enforced by data types and CHECK constraints; some of them require more sophisticated support with the help of triggers implemented in the database.

With the help of additional integrity constraints available to the DBMS, the physical data model can support some *integrity* business rules. For example, the above-mentioned CHECK constraint can enforce the requirement that a part-time employee cannot work more than twenty hours per week (see business rules for the EERD in the section 1.2.1). Minimal cardinality of some relationships (one-to-one and one-to-many) can be implemented in the physical model with the help of another constraint supported by the DBMS – the NOT NULL constraint.

Space requirements for data storage are supported by various physical parameters in table definitions.

Complicated structural and action business rules that cannot be implemented in the physical data model, e.g. minimum cardinality of many-to-many relationships, maximum cardinality of relationships, formulas for calculations of derived attributes, and others, are supported in the database with the help of other features of the DBMS, e.g. triggers.

1.4.3 Beyond the Data Model

Support of business rules involving *security*, *performance*, *reliability*, and *concurrent access* to data goes beyond the physical data model and is implemented in the database with the help of tools of the DBMS. These requirements are related not only to data and the database, but also to database applications. Requests to the database originate in an application, and the way these requests are organized defines how well user requirements will be supported. It is important that application designers and programmers understand how the database is designed and implemented, and what features of the DBMS are used for support of various user requirements. Designers and programmers must then use this understanding to build the database applications. Separately, neither a well-designed database nor an effective application guarantees the success of a database project. Success follows from: appropriate data design, implementation of a database that will allow an application to use data efficiently, and database applications that utilize the design of data, the database, and the tools of the DBMS appropriately. This symbiotic relationship between the database, DBMS, and application is shown in Figure 1-8.

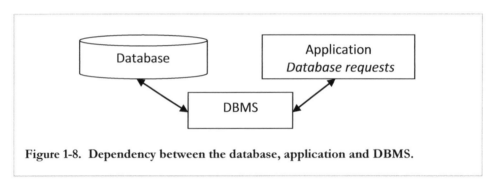

Figure 1-8. Dependency between the database, application and DBMS.

This book concentrates on the physical data design and the implementation of the database with respect to needs of database applications.

1.5. Structure of the Book

Chapter 2 describes the physical data design: the goals of this step and the features of the relational DBMSs used to achieve these goals.

Chapter 3 discusses a very special physical design solution – the distributed database. This chapter shows various approaches to distributed design; problems of data distribution and their resolution.

Chapter 4 explains how to use the DBMS tools for implementing database security measures.

Chapter 5 describes database query processing, DBMS tools for improving database performance, and how to combine data design with implementation of the database to achieve required database performance.

Chapter 6 demonstrates that concurrent access to data and system failures may cause database inconsistency. The concept of a transaction and how the DBMS performs transaction management to preserve data consistency under the conditions of concurrent access to data are explained.

Chapter 7 continues the discussion of the role of transactions in support of data consistency and in recovery of the database after failures.

Each chapter contains an example of implementation of a particular group of requirements that summarizes the discussion and can serve as a practical guide.

Appendix 1 provides five Case Studies that can be used to illustrate many of the features covered throughout the book including the physical design, use of a distributed database, and security requirements.

Appendix 2 covers selected operations of Relational Algebra that are used in the discussions in various chapters.

Appendix 3 covers the basics of Oracle Database Architecture.

Appendix 4 explains the newest addition to the Oracle security support – Oracle Database Vault.

Appendix 5 shows a fragment of an Oracle session and demonstrates the work of the optimizer.

Appendix 6 shows an example of Concurrent Transactions, with the scripts for the transactions, and the actual results of the Execution under Oracle.

Demonstrations of the concepts of the physical data design and implementation of a database are provided in the Oracle 11g DBMS.

Chapter 2. The Physical Data Model

A *physical data model* is a representation of a database design based on particular user requirements which will include the database artifacts required to achieve the goal of implementing a well-performing, reliable, and easy to use and manage database. Most structural and some action business rules are implemented in the relational data model through the structure of relations and integrity constraints. The physical data model specifies how the storage of data of this particular logical structure is organized and managed. This model largely defines the database performance, as well as the ease of use and maintenance.

The design of the physical model involves a particular DBMS and requires knowledge and understanding of how data are stored and managed by this DBMS. Furthermore, when performing physical modeling, it is necessary to know the specific business rules that define how the database will be used, such as: the expected size of the database, the types of requests to the database and the required performance of these requests, the expected number of users (including the number of users who may work concurrently), and other physical considerations. This chapter describes the basic principles of data storage organization and the benefits of different storage solutions, and demonstrates some approaches to physical design for various database usage scenarios.

2.1. Goals of Physical Modeling

The most general goals of physical modeling are to define the physical features of the data, the most important of which are: where data are stored, how storage is organized, what are the data types of the tables' columns, so that users are able to perform all the necessary data operations as quickly as needed. It is also important that the database is easy to use and maintain. For this, knowledge of how the DBMS manipulates data is crucial.

> **The physical model of data is tailored to user requirements with the help of features of the chosen DBMS.**

Often, some user requirements considered during physical design conflict with each other in terms of applying the features of the DBMS for implementing them. For example, data storage organization for the best performance of read queries may compromise the performance of modifying queries. That is why every physical design decision has to be analyzed for not only expected benefits, but also possible disadvantages or complications. In many cases, the final physical data model is the result of compromises – if all user requirements cannot be satisfied in the best possible way, then we choose a solution that is reasonably good for most of them.

2.1.1 Performance and Data Availability

The physical data model has significant impact on database performance. Query processing, performance, and database tuning are discussed in detail in Chapter 5. If described on a very general level, query processing involves locating requested data on disk, fetching the data from disk into memory, processing the data, and then writing the data, possibly modified, back to disk. Locating and fetching data are the most expensive steps in terms of consumption of computer resources and time. The physical model has to support such data storage so that locating and fetching data can be executed in the most efficient way.

2.1.2 Other Goals

It is important that a well performing database is easy to use and maintain, and appropriate physical design can significantly reduce the support and maintenance efforts and costs.

The most important integrity rules are implemented in the relational model (primary key, foreign key). The physical design can enhance the consistency and integrity of the data through specifying the data types of columns, providing additional constraints, and using special features of the DBMS. The more completely the required consistency and integrity are implemented, the easier it is to support and maintain the database.

2.2. Tables

The data in relational databases are stored in tables. Usually, tables are built for relations of the relational model. The definition of the table includes the data types of columns, the location of data, how the storage of data is organized, and how the DBMS should maintain the storage and access to data.

Discussions are provided on the Manufacturing Company case (see Appendix 1) with the following relational data model (primary keys of relations are underlined, and foreign keys are in italics):

```
Title (titleCode, titleDescription, salary)
Department (deptCode, deptName, location, deptType)
Employee (ID, emplName, emplType, deptCode, titleCode)
```

2.2.1 Data Types of Columns

The column data type defines the values that can be inserted into the column and the kind of operations that can be performed on these values. The SQL standard defines numeric, character, date, and timestamp[2] data types. In addition to these data types, different DBMSs support other data types, in particular, BLOB – Binary Large Object – for representing large amounts of binary data such as images, video, or other multimedia data, or CLOB – Character Large Object – for storing large amounts of character data.

The character and numeric Oracle data types are used to create the following table for the relation Title of the Manufacturing Company case:

```
CREATE TABLE Title (
    titleCode CHAR(2) PRIMARY KEY,
    titleDescription VARCHAR2(15),
    salary NUMBER (7));
```

---

[2] Added in the new SQL 2003 standard.

The column data type is chosen so that it can *represent all possible column values* and allow for *performing necessary operations* on the column. In the above example, the character data type is used for the attribute titleCode because title codes may include letters. Though numeric data from the column salary can be presented by either the character or numeric data types, the latter was used to allow different numeric operations on the column, e.g. calculating the average salary. Although the column type NUMBER(5) can accommodate all possible salaries (it is mentioned in the case description that salaries of employees are less than $100,000), it may be not enough to present the results of calculations on the column, e.g. SUM(salary), hence, the column type is NUMBER(7). Often, numeric columns have to be longer than is required by their possible values in order to enable various calculations on them.

Data types can enforce *data integrity*. For the table Title, title codes cannot be longer than two symbols, and the chosen data type guarantees it. However, if title codes were composed of digits only, then the numeric data type would be a better choice for the column because the character data type would not prevent inserting values with symbols other than digits. The choice of the numeric data type for the column salary ensures that values of this column will be only numbers.

One more consideration for choosing the data type is *economical space usage*. For example, for columns with variable length, like titleDescription, it is better to use the character data type with variable length – VARCHAR(15) – in which each value of the column in the database contains as many symbols as it actually has, e.g. the title description 'DBA' is stored as three symbols. In the case of the fixed length character data type – CHAR(15) – all values of the column, regardless of their actual length, will be padded with spaces and stored in the database as strings fifteen symbols long.

It is important to understand the details of data types supported in a particular DBMS. For example, Oracle supports two character data types with variable length: VARCHAR and VARCHAR2. Where appropriate, it is recommended to use VARCHAR2 as: 1) VARCHAR can store up to 2000 bytes and VARCHAR2 can store up to 4000 bytes; 2) NULL values of the column declared as VARCHAR will occupy space while NULL values of columns declared as VARCHAR2 will not.

Some DBMSs offer additional possibilities for column management. For instance, a very convenient feature is automatically generating and assigning of a value to a column when inserting data. Imagine a situation when a company wants each employee to have a unique ID, like in the table Employee of the Manufacturing Company case. In a company with thousands of employees, support of IDs can be rather complicated. Using special data types or special database objects that enforce automatic assignment of a new column value can be extremely beneficial. Examples of such features are the AUTONUMBER data type in MS Access and the IDENTITY column in MS SQL Server. If, for example, the column ID in the table Employee is declared as AUTONUMBER, then for every inserted new employee the system generates the next integer number and assigns it to the ID column: '1' for the first inserted employee, '2' for the second, and so on. In this case, the data type guarantees support (inserting values) and the uniqueness of values. In releases before Oracle 12 there was no feature equivalent to IDENTITY or AUTONUMBER; instead developers had to use the sequence object (is illustrated in the section 2.8). In Oracle 12 there is the IDENTITY feature on the numeric column. For example, we can use one of the options (GENERATED ALWAYS) provided by this feature in the definition of the ID column of the table Employee:

```
CREATE TABLE Employee (
   ID NUMBER GENERATED ALWAYS AS IDENTITY,
   emplName VARCHAR2(30),
   ...
);
```

Then, we will be simply inserting data about employees while the system will provide the values of ID for these inserts (note that an attempt to insert the ID directly will cause an error):

```
INSERT INTO Employee (emplName, ...) VALUES ('John', ...);
```

Another interesting feature of Oracle is *virtual columns*[3] – columns that are derived from other columns of the table but are not stored on disc. If for example employees of our case have a bonus that is calculated as a particular percent of the salary, then we can have the following table definition:

```
CREATE TABLE Title (
    titleCode CHAR(2) PRIMARY KEY,
    titleDescription VARCHAR2(15),
    salary NUMBER (7),
    bonus NUMBER GENERATED ALWAYS AS (ROUND(salary*0.3,2))
    VIRTUAL);
```

Note that data is not inserted in the virtual column; we can select from the virtual column as from a regular column:

```
INSERT INTO Title (titleCode, titleDescription, salary)
VALUES ('T1', 'DBA', 60000);

SELECT * FROM Title WHERE titleCode = 'T1';
```

TITLECODE	TITLEDESCRIPTION	SALARY	BONUS
T1	DBA	60000	18000

When choosing the data type, consider whether it allows for the support of all possible column values and operations, enforces the column's integrity, is economical, and makes support of the column easier.

---

[3] Compare this feature with creating a view on the table. Views are introduced in the section 2.5.1.

2.2.2 Constraints

DBMSs offer additional table and column constraints that are not included in the relational data model and that can improve data consistency and integrity. The most common constraints are:

- NOT NULL: Requires that the column on which the constraint is defined has a value for every row.
- CHECK: Defines a condition that is evaluated every time a row is inserted or the columns involved in the constraint are updated: each row has to satisfy the predicate.
- UNIQUE: Enforces uniqueness of a column or combination of columns in a table.

CHECK and UNIQUE constraints can include one column and be declared in line with this column as shown in the example below. When a constraint includes multiple columns, it has to be defined on the table as for example complex primary keys.

Consider, for example, business rules that require that each title has to have a description and salaries are in a specific range. While the relational model does not reflect these requirements, they can be enforced in the definition of the table Title:

```
CREATE TABLE Title (
    titleCode CHAR(2) PRIMARY KEY,
    titleDescription VARCHAR2(15) NOT NULL,
    salary NUMBER CHECK (Salary BETWEEN 30000 AND 90000));
```

More complicated integrity and consistency rules that cannot be declared through table constraints have to be implemented with the help of triggers – special database procedures (discussed in section 2.8).

2.2.3 Size and Location

When a table is created, the DBMS allocates disk space according to the size specifications. It is important to estimate accurately the expected size and growth rate of the table. The size of the table depends on the expected number of records, the length of one record (or an estimated average length if the record length varies), the amount of free space in data blocks, and some other parameters. Each DBMS offers a methodology of estimating the table size. The expected size and growth rate of the table are used to determine the storage space parameters.

2.3. Data Storage

Design of data storage requires an understanding of data storage organization in databases. See Appendix 3 for details of data storage in Oracle.

2.3.1 Storage Hierarchy

Physically, data are stored in data files. Each database has at least one data file. Data files are *logically* organized in storage spaces called *tablespaces*, and storage space for data objects, e.g. tables, is specified in tablespaces and not directly in data files. As a result, a database object can be stored in more than one data file, but always in one tablespace. For example, in Figure 2-1, the table Title is stored in the tablespace USER_DATA and has extents in two data files: df1.dbf and df2.dbf. Within a data file, each extent is a contiguous set of data blocks (or data pages). A data block is the smallest unit of operation and manipulation of the DBMS – if the system needs to access a particular row of a block, it reads the whole block. In some databases it is possible to have blocks of different sizes, e.g. in Oracle, different tablespaces can have different block sizes. In Oracle, the default size of the block is 8K.

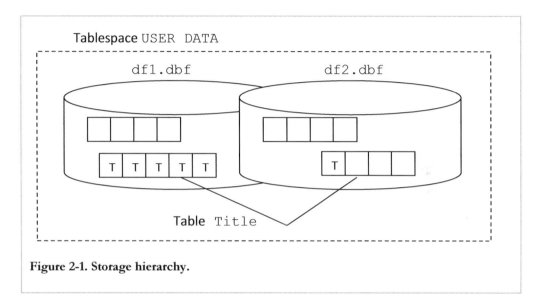

Figure 2-1. Storage hierarchy.

In summary, data storage consists of tablespaces. Each tablespace is a logical container for one or more data files. Data files contain extents of data blocks with data.

Here are some considerations of leveraging tablespaces to achieve the goals of the physical design:

- Improve performance
    - Storing different tablespaces' datafiles on separate disk drives reduces the contention of read/write operations on big objects, for example, on a big table.
    - Including several datafiles in a tablespace overcomes limitations of a single disk to accommodate a big object, e.g. a big table as it will be stored across several disks.
- Ease of management, availability
    - Storing data of different applications in different tablespaces prevents multiple applications from being affected if a tablespace must be taken offline.
    - Most DBMSs allow back up of individual tablespaces.

2.3.2 Data Blocks

At the finest level of granularity, a database stores data in data blocks (also called logical blocks or pages). One data block corresponds to a specific number of bytes of physical database space on disc. The rows of a table are physically stored in data blocks. When accessing the requested rows, the system reads the blocks in which these rows are stored. The fewer the number of blocks that are accessed during request processing, the better is the performance. This chapter discusses different approaches to storage organization that help in reducing the number of block accesses.

First, it is important to store rows of a table in the most effective way. Not all space in the data block is dedicated to data storage (Figure).

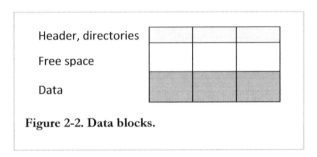

Figure 2-2. Data blocks.

Some space is occupied by the block header which contains information about the block that is used by the system, directories which contain information about the objects stored in the block and the addresses of the rows of the block. In addition, each block must contain free space to accommodate updates of existing rows that may cause the rows' expansion. Consider the situation in Figure 2-3 (block headers are not shown). The data block contains several rows and free space (Figure 2-3a). After the third row is updated, there is not enough free space in the block to fit the updated version of the row and the row has to be moved to another block. This moving of a row from one block to another is known as row migration as shown in Figure 2-3b. However, the system cannot change the initial address of the row when it was inserted (as it is already used in for example Indices). As a result, the information for the third row of our example is stored in two blocks – the row itself is now stored in the new block, and the address of this actual row (the 'forwarding address') is contained in the initial block used for the row (which will be accessed when the row is requested because the system remembers it as the storage block of the row). This situation is undesirable because in order to access the row, the system has to access two blocks instead of one. Numerous migrating rows may cause decreased performance.

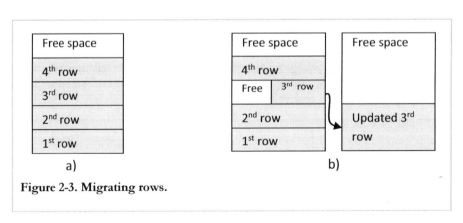

a)   b)

Figure 2-3. Migrating rows.

The DBMS allows specifying the percent of free space in the blocks of a table. Obviously, data blocks have to be as full as possible to store more rows, but, on the other hand, there must be enough space left for updates of the rows that are already in the block.

In addition to migrating rows we can have chained rows that are stored across several blocks. This situation can happen when for example the size of the row exceeds the size of the block. Chained rows are stored similarly to migrating rows: a block contains a part of the row with the forwarding address to the next block containing the continuation of the row.

Depending on the nature of the data and the database activities, database programmers have to find a compromise between partially full blocks and the risk of having migrating rows.

Appropriately chosen data types can improve data storage, e.g. choosing the VARCHAR data type for columns with variable length will result in more rows per block than when using the CHAR data type.

The size of the block also has an impact on performance and overall quality of data storage. Smaller block size is recommended for short rows but does not benefit long rows (as only few rows can be stored in a block with usually a high possibility of migrating rows). On the other hand, the overhead of the header is relatively high for small blocks. In Oracle, it is possible to have different block sizes for different tablespaces.

The table below summarizes some considerations when choosing the size of the block.

	Small blocks	**Large blocks**
Advantages	• Good for small rows with intensive random access as it reduces block contention (typical for Online Transaction Processing databases).	• Has lower overhead of the header; there is more room to store data. • Permits reading more rows into the buffer[4] with a single read/write (depending on row size and block size). • Good for very large rows.
Disadvantages	• Has relatively large space overhead due to the block header. • Not recommended for large rows. There might only be a few rows stored for each block; the change of migrating rows is significant.	• Wastes space in the buffer when accessing small rows. For example, with an 8 KB block size and 50 byte row size, 7,950 bytes loaded in the buffer are not used.

Smaller block sized (in Oracle, 2 KB or 4 KB) are usual for Online Transaction Processing

---

[4] Buffer and its role in data processing are explained in the chapter on query processing.

(OLTP), while larger block sizes (in Oracle, 8 KB, 16 KB, or 32 KB) are usual for data warehouses.

2.3.3 Heap Storage

Depending on the type of storage, data blocks are filled by the records of a table differently.

Heap storage adds new rows to the available free space in the blocks that already contain the table's data. If there is not enough space in these blocks, then the system goes to the next unused block of the table's extent and places the row there[5]. As a result, rows are stored without any particular order. Figure 2-4 shows the process of inserting data into the table Employee of the Manufacturing Company case that uses the heap storage organization:

a) Rows for the first three employees are inserted into the first block. Then, none of the next four rows can fit in the rest of the available space in the first block, and these rows are placed in the second block (Figure 2-4a).
b) One row (row 6) is deleted from the second block, and hence a free space becomes available there (Figure 2-4b).
c) For the next two new rows, the first, for the employee with ID = 10, is short enough to fit in the first block, and the second, for the employee with ID = 11, is placed in the second block (Figure 2-4c).

For tables using the heap storage method, the search for rows by a specific condition results in accessing multiple blocks across which the requested rows are scattered. Let us consider the query:

```
SELECT e.emplName, d.deptName
FROM Employee e INNER JOIN Department d
     ON e.deptCode = d.deptCode
WHERE deptCode = '002';
```

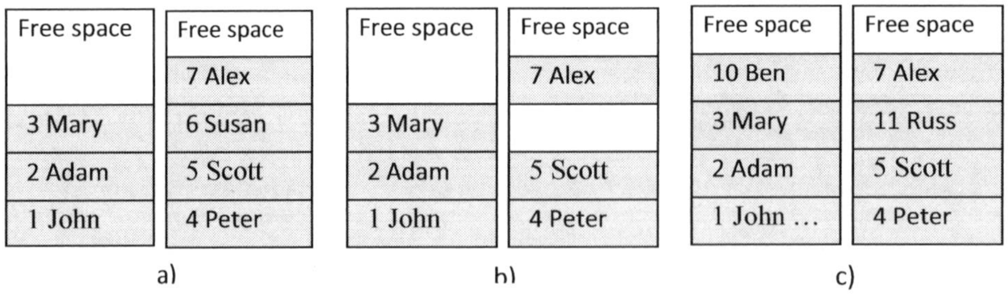

Free space	Free space	Free space	Free space	Free space	Free space
	7 Alex		7 Alex	10 Ben	7 Alex
3 Mary	6 Susan	3 Mary		3 Mary	11 Russ
2 Adam	5 Scott	2 Adam	5 Scott	2 Adam	5 Scott
1 John	4 Peter	1 John	4 Peter	1 John ...	4 Peter

        a)   h)   c)

Figure 2-4. Heap storage of data.

---

[5] If there are no blocks in the extent, the system allocates a new extent in correspondence with the table growth specifications.

For the Employee table using heap data storage as shown in Figure 2-5a, the search for the employees of the second department (deptCode = '002') requires the system to access all data blocks of the table Employee (two in this case) and one block of the table Department (the requested rows are shown in bold italics).

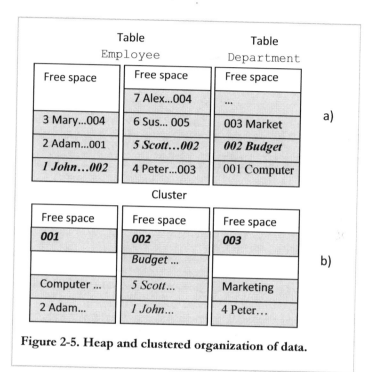

Figure 2-5. Heap and clustered organization of data.

2.3.4 Cluster Storage

If database applications frequently access data about employees of a particular department, then their performance can be improved by keeping the rows of employees of the same department together in the same block or blocks. In this case, as Figure 2-5 b shows, the system needs to access fewer blocks. For join queries, as the one we are discussing, performance can be further improved by storing the row of the respective department in the same group of blocks. Such an organization of storage in which rows that are similar by some criterion are stored in the same block is called *clustering*, and the group of blocks with similar rows is referred to as a cluster.

A column (or columns) that define how rows are clustered is called the *cluster key*. In our example, the cluster key is the column deptCode – rows of the tables Employee and Department that have the same deptCode value are stored together, and the value of the cluster key is stored only once.

Unlike heap storage, where the location of a row is random, the locations of rows in clustered storage are predefined. When a new row is inserted, it is not placed in the first block with available space, but in the block designated for storing rows with the same cluster key value as the inserted row[6]. Note that a table when stored as clustered usually occupies more blocks than when it is stored as heap. In our example, assume that all records of employees of the five departments are stored in three blocks of the heap, however, the clustered by `deptCode` storage will occupy five blocks according to the number of departments.

Access to data includes locating the data and reading the data into memory. Clustering can provide a more efficient means to read the requested data. But before continuing this discussion we need to introduce a new database object – index.

2.4. Indices

As we have just seen, rows in tables with heap storage organization are stored without any particular order and access to a specific portion of data in the table in many cases requires access to most of the table's data (this is called a full table scan). For example, to find the employee with ID = 1, the system has to perform the reading of all the data in the table Employee. Indices are special database objects that make access to data more efficient.

2.4.1 Role of Indices

The most common are B-tree (Binary-tree) indices. The description of their organization is beyond the goals of this book and can be found in [Connolly 2010], [Silberschatz]. The role of the index is similar to the role of the last and first names of the telephone directory in finding the address or telephone of a person. Telephone directory searches are simplified by ordered last and first names that allow one to apply some reasonable search strategies, e.g. if the last name starts with 'B', then we do not need to look in the end of the directory and can concentrate on its beginning. Indices are built for the columns of the table by which data are searched, like ID in the example above. Values of indexed columns are stored in an ordered way (similarly to the last and first names in the phone directory) in the index, and for each set of values the index contains pointers to the corresponding rows (blocks) of the table. For example, if users access data about employees by ID, it would make sense to create the index on this column:

```
CREATE INDEX i0 ON Employee(ID);
```

The index contains values of the column ID and pointers (addresses) to the corresponding rows of the table Employee. With the index, a request for data about a particular employee will result in:

1) Searching the index and finding the requested values of ID
2) Reading pointers to the corresponding rows of the table
3) Accessing the blocks containing these rows of the table Employee. Figure 2-6 schematically[7] shows such access.

---

[6] If the block is full, then the system adds a new block to the cluster and places the row in this block. The cluster becomes chained.

[7] B-tree indices are self-balanced trees.

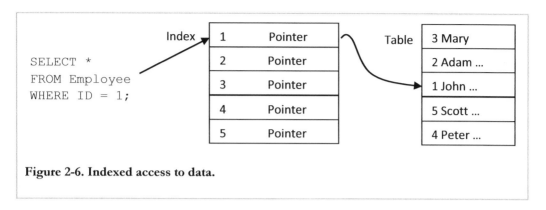

Figure 2-6. Indexed access to data.

The index on the column ID of the table Employee was created to demonstrate indexed access.

However in reality the index on the column ID would have been created automatically by the DBMS because the DBMS creates an index for the primary key of every table. Such an index is called the primary index. Indices on the non-key columns of the table are called secondary, and they are created to improve the performance of queries that access data based on conditions on these columns. For example, for queries that request data about employees given their name it is reasonable to consider the index on the column emplName. In many cases, indices can dramatically improve database performance.

The storage parameters for indices are defined similarly to the storage parameters of tables. It is recommended to store tables and their indices in different tablespaces with the files located on different disks. In this way, the performance is improved because the system can access a table and its index in parallel.

Some DBMSs support other types of indices, e.g. MS SQL Server offers hash indices and Oracle – bitmap and function-based indices (these indices are discussed in Chapter 5). The purpose of different types of indices is to improve the performance of read, delete and update queries (whereas insert queries are actually slowed by them). The discussion of indices and the conditions when they are beneficial is continued in Chapter 5.

2.4.2 Cluster Storage and the Use of Indices

The clustered storage organization that we illustrated above can be supported in two ways. The first type of clustering which is called *index clustering* requires a cluster index. Queries for clustered rows are accessed through the cluster index: first, the system reads the address of the table block for the requested cluster key value in the cluster index, and then it goes to the block with the rows. Cluster indices are smaller than table indices. The cluster index contains as many entries as there are values of the cluster key, while the table index contains as many entries as there are rows with values of the index column. For example, the index for the cluster built on the column deptCode of our discussed example has 200 entries – as many as there are departments, while the index on the column deptCode of the table Employee has 4000 entries

– as many as there are rows in the table.

Many DBMSs also support another type of cluster known as *hash cluster*. Rows in the hash cluster are stored based not on values of the cluster key itself, but based on the result of applying the hash function to the cluster key. The hash function applied to the cluster key defines the location of a new row when data is inserted, and the location of an existing row, when data is retrieved. Appropriately defined hash clusters perform the access to a row in a single disk read.

The hash and index clustering on the same cluster key result in similar storage. However, access to hash clusters is different from access to index clusters (see Figure 2-7). The hash cluster does not need an index to support it. When a row with a particular value of the cluster key is requested, the system applies the hash function to *calculate* the address of the row. In the index cluster, the address of the table row is *found* in the cluster index search.

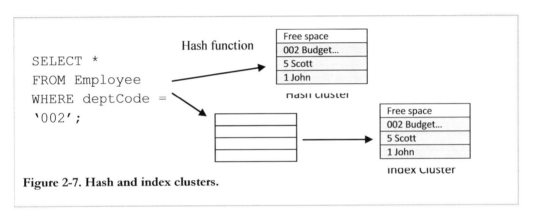

Figure 2-7. Hash and index clusters.

In addition to heap and cluster types of storage, most DBMSs offer other storage solutions, e.g. partitions and index-organized tables that are discussed later in this chapter. Each storage solution is aimed at reducing the number of disk accesses during query processing. Different solutions may be beneficial for different types of access to data. For example, the cluster solution works well for the select query discussed above, but it causes problems when the cluster key is frequently modified. Chapter 5 discusses database performance and gives recommendations about using different types of storage depending on types of data access.

DBMSs have other parameters that define how data are stored and processed, e.g. compression and encryption parameters. For each DBMS these parameters have to be considered for the physical data model because they have impact on database performance and ease of maintenance.

2.5. Transparency of the Physical Model

The physical data model is transparent to users – they do not know where the data are physically stored or how data storage is organized. Transparency is supported by the architecture of the DBMS.

2.5.1   3-level Database Architecture

Commercial DBMSs comply with the three-level architecture of the database suggested by the American National Standards Institute (ANSI) and Standards Planning and Requirements Committee (SPARC) in 1975. This architecture (Figure 2-8) defines three levels of abstraction of the data or three levels of data description in the database; it provides a separation of higher-level semantics of data from the physical implementation and makes the physical implementation transparent to users of the database.

The *external schema* defines how users see the data (users' views of data). For example, Scott and John are users of the discussed Manufacturing Company Case database: Scott works with ID, name, and salary of employees – this is his view of the database content; John works with employees' names, and codes and names of employees' departments – this is how he sees and understands data from the database. The external schema of the database consists of a number of views for different users. DBMSs have features that allow for implementing the external level. One of the database objects used for this purpose is a *view*. A view is a saved query. The following view for Scott represents Scott's needs in data:

```
CREATE VIEW vw_Scott AS
SELECT ID, name, salary
FROM Employee e, Title t
WHERE e.titleCode = t.titleCode;
```

When working with the database, Scott will be using the view, e.g.:

```
SELECT * FROM vw_Scott;
```

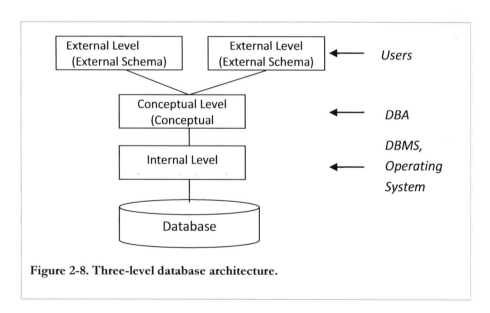

Figure 2-8. Three-level database architecture.

The view makes the database transparent to Scott – not only does Scott not know where the data are located and how data storage is organized, he does not even know what tables he is using.

35

The *internal schema* defines how the DBMS and operating system see the data of the database; it includes descriptions of data structures and file organizations, storage space allocations for objects of the database, rows placement, data compression and data encryption, and other physical parameters of data.

The *conceptual schema* serves as a link between the external and internal schemas; it provides a mapping from the internal schema to the external schema. This level supports the external level – each external view is based on definitions of objects in the conceptual level. The conceptual schema reflects the developer's vision of the database; it contains the definitions of tables, columns, and constraints.

The 3-tier architecture provides independence between the users' perception of the database and the physical implementation of the data. Such independence has the following benefits:

- Users see the data according to their need: If the users need changes, their view of data can be changed without rebuilding the database and without affecting the views of other users. For example, if Scott's needs changes and he wants to see ID, name, title, and salary, then anew view can be built without any changes to the database or to the existing view for John.
- Users see data the way they want to see it, completely unaware of the conceptual and physical aspects of the data: The user is unware of which tables the data comes from, where data are stored andin what data structures or formats, and what other structures were involved in processing the data (like indices or clusters). For example, Scott does not know that he is working with the tables Employee and Title and what structure the tables have, or that the DBMS uses the primary index on ID to retrieve data about a particular employee.
- Reorganizing data storage does not affect the conceptual model of the database and users' views: For example, the table Employee can be moved from one disk to another without the users knowing about the move, and data processing applications referencing this table will remain valid and unchanged.
- Redesigning the conceptual model does not necessarily affect the users' views: If the database programmer adds a column to the table Employee, none of the previous views based on this table need to be redefined or changed since they would not be using the new column. Some changes on the conceptual level may cause rebuilding user views, but the users still will be unaware of these changes. For example, if the table Title starts storing salaries in thousands of dollars (and not in dollars as before), then Scott's view will be changed:

```
CREATE VIEW vw_Scott AS
SELECT ID, name, salary * 1000 as salary
FROM Employee e, Title t
WHERE e.titleCode = t.titleCode;
```

Scott, however, will not notice the change. Of course, more "radical" changes of conceptual schema may cause users to change their perception of the data, like, for example, deleting a column from a table.

2.6. The Physical Data Model in Oracle

2.6.1   Heap Storage Organization

Table storage parameters are defined in the CREATE TABLE statement:

```
CREATE TABLE Title (
    titleCode CHAR(2) PRIMARY KEY,
    titleDescription VARCHAR2(15),
    salary NUMBER CHECK (Salary BETWEEN 30000 AND 90000))
PCTFREE 10
PCTUSED 40
TABLESPACE users
STORAGE (  INITIAL 50K
           NEXT 50K
           MAXEXTENTS 10
           PCTINCREASE 25 );
```

The *TABLESPACE* clause defines the tablespace where the table will be located (see the explanation of tablespaces above in this chapter and in Appendix 3). The *STORAGE* parameters specify the initial size and expansion of the table. In the above example, the initial size of the table is set to 50K. If expansion of the table is needed, the system allocates not more than 10 additional extents – the second extent will be equal to 50K, and every next extent will have the size of the previous extent increased by 25 percent. Such an approach for defining and capturing storage for a table is flexible and dynamic – the storage space for the table is allocated when needed.

The parameters *PCTFREE* and *PCTUSED* define how allocated data blocks are filled with data[8]. PCTFREE sets the percent of space in the block that has to remain free to accommodate future updates of the rows of the block. Once the block no longer has its free space percentage greater than or equal to PCTFREE, it is removed from the list of available blocks the DBMS keeps. For example, if PCTFREE is set to 20, it would mean that the block allows for row inserts until 80% is occupied, leaving 20% free for updates to existing rows in the block.

PCTUSED defines what percent of space in the block has to become free again (the percentage of the block used must be less than PCTUSED) for the system to return the block to the list of available blocks that can add new rows. For example, if PCTUSED is set to 40, it would mean that no new rows can be inserted until the amount of used space falls below 40%.

The appropriate use of these parameters can increase the performance of writing and reading operations on tables or indices, decrease the amount of unused space in the data blocks, and

---

[8] The new feature – Automatic Segment Space Management (ASS Management) – automates management of some aspects of the physical model and does not allow to specify PCTFREE, PCTUSED, and some other parameters that are used for manual storage management.

decrease the amount of migrating rows between data blocks. Chained rows – rows stored across several blocks – can occur not only when the length of the row exceeds the size of the block, but for the tables with more than 255 columns.

When the system has to insert a new row in a table, it looks into the list of available (free) blocks for this table, i.e. the list of blocks that allow adding a row, or in other words, the blocks for which the free storage percentage is above PCTFREE. After the block becomes full, it is deleted from the list of free blocks and can be returned to the list only after the percent of its used space drops below PCTUSED. A lower PCTUSED increases the unused space in the database, but reduces the processing cost of UPDATE and DELETE because the block will be moved out of the list of the free blocks less often. A higher PCTUSED improves space efficiency, but increases the cost of INSERT and UPDATE, because the block is eliminated from the list of free blocks and is returned back into the list frequently.

A lower PCTFREE leads to less unused space in the table blocks (more records in the block) and fewer blocks to accommodate the table. However, when this parameter is small, the possibility of migrated or chained rows is increased. A high PCTFREE setting, on the other hand, may result in sparse table storage but a lower possibility of chained rows.

The settings of PCTUSED and PCTFREE are dependent on the type of the activities expected on the table. For example, for a table that experiences frequent updates which may increase the size of the rows PCTFREE = 20 and PCTUSED = 40 is appropriate. On the other hand, for a very large table, for which storage efficiency is important and which experiences little insert, delete, and update activities, an appropriate setting is PCTFREE = 5 and PCTUSED = 90.

2.6.2 Clustered Storage Organization

The table Title in the previous section was stored as a heap. For some applications, it is beneficial to store a table in a cluster. Oracle supports two types of clusters: index and hash.

It is important to remember that clusters improve performance of some read queries, but intensive updating activity may result in the necessity to reorganize clusters and therefore can worsen performance.

To improve the performance of queries that are based on the join of the tables Employee and Department, we can consider storing these tables in an index cluster with the deptCode column as the cluster key. The cluster is created with the help of the following command:

```
CREATE CLUSTER Emp_dept (deptCode CHAR(3))
TABLESPACE USER_DATA
PCTUSED 80
PCTFREE 5
SIZE 40
STORAGE (…);
```

The command specifies the type of the cluster key, the tablespace in which the cluster is located, data packing parameters of the cluster blocks and the storage settings. The parameter

SIZE defines the expected length (in bytes) of one row in the cluster and, therefore, how many rows can be placed in one cluster block. If the parameter is too high, then fewer records are placed in one block and the cluster occupies more space than it actually needs. On the other hand, if the size is set too low, chaining of data may occur.

The cluster can be used for allocating the tables Employee and Department. Note that the cluster storage is already organized and you do not have to specify the tablespace and packing parameters for the tables – data are stored according to the corresponding parameters of the cluster:

```
CREATE TABLE Department (
      deptCode CHAR(3) PRIMARY KEY,
      deptName VARCHAR2(15),
      location NUMBER)
CLUSTER Emp_dept (deptCode);

CREATE TABLE Employee (
      ID NUMBER PRIMARY KEY,
      emplName VARCHAR2(20) NOT NULL,
      emplType VARCHAR2(10),
      deptCode CHAR(3) REFERENCES Department,
      titleCode CHAR(2) REFERENCES Title)
   CLUSTER Emp_dept (deptCode);
```

The index cluster needs a cluster index. The index has to be created before inserting the first record into any of the two cluster tables:

```
CREATE INDEX Emp_dept_index
    ON CLUSTER Emp_dept;
```

Hash clusters are created similarly to index clusters; however, they do not need the cluster index. The hash function, applied to the cluster key, defines the address of a row. This is really a "direct" and very efficient way to access data. DBMS documentation contains recommendations on using hash functions.

The following hash cluster with the hash function on the column deptCode is created for the table Employee:

```
CREATE CLUSTER Employee_cluster (
    deptCode CHAR(3))
    PCTUSED    80
    PCTFREE    5
    SIZE       40
    HASHKEYS   10
    STORAGE  (...);
```

The important parameters of the hash cluster are the expected number of values of the cluster key column (HASHKEYS) and the average row size (SIZE). The above values for these parameters are based on the company having 10 departments and an average row size of 40 bytes. These parameters are used by the DBMS to specify and limit the number of unique hash values that can be generated by the hash function used by the cluster and the number of rows per cluster block. The prepared cluster is used to store the table Employee:

```
CREATE TABLE Employee (
        ID NUMBER (5,0) PRIMARY KEY,
        emplName VARCHAR2(20) NOT NULL,
        emplType VARCHAR2(10),
        deptCode CHAR(3) REFERENCES Department,
        titleCode CHAR(2) REFERENCES Title)
    )
    CLUSTER Employee_cluster (deptCode);
```

In this example, the system hash function is used. It is possible to use user-defined hash functions as well. For every new row of the table Employee, the system calculates the hash value based on the deptCode (the value defines the address of the block for the row) and as a result, the rows with the same value of deptCode are stored together. For the retrieval of data about employees of a particular department, the same hash function is applied to the value of deptCode in queries with the condition:

```
...WHERE deptCode = x
```

The value of the hash function defines the block address of the rows of the query and enables the system to go directly to the blocks with requested data.

2.6.3 Index-Organized Tables

Oracle supports another organization of data storage – index-organized tables. In such tables, all table data, both the primary key and all non-key columns are stored in the index in key-sequenced order. In a heap organized table, the primary key index stores the primary key with the address of the corresponding row (in Oracle the address of the row is called the ROWID) in the table being indexed. For a key-based query, two accesses are required. First, the index must be accessed to find the address of the row (ROWID), and then a second access is made on the table. For index-organized tables only one access is needed, because the index contains the entire data in each row: primary key and non-key data.

The following statement creates the index-organized table Employee:

```
CREATE TABLE Employee (
        ID NUMBER (5,0) PRIMARY KEY,
        emplName VARCHAR2(20) NOT NULL,
        emplType VARCHAR2(10),
        deptCode CHAR(3) REFERENCES Department,
        titleCode CHAR(2) REFERENCES Title)
        ORGANIZATION INDEX;
```

Index-organized tables have several advantages:

- Fast access to data by queries with equality or range conditions on the primary key of the table (or any left-most part of the primary key): In the case of indexed access to a regular table, there are at least two block accesses: one to the index and another to the table, while for the index-organized table there is only one access to the table itself.
- Efficient storage: Because the indexed columns are not duplicated as in the "table plus index" case, and ROWID (address of the row) is not stored, the index-organized table occupies less space than the heap table plus its primary index.

Index-organized tables are ideal for those applications, which require fast primary key access.

If the index-organized table is accessed by queries with conditions on the non-key columns, it loses its performance advantage. Secondary indices on such storage organization are less efficient than they are on the heap table.

2.6.4 Partitions

Oracle 8 introduced a new storage feature – partitioning. Partitioning addresses key issues in supporting very large tables and indexes by letting you decompose them into smaller and more manageable pieces called *partitions*. Imagine that the database for the Manufacturing Company case is implemented as a centralized database. Local users of Boston have to perform access to the tables where the rows of Boston departments and employees are scattered across multiple blocks that contain data about the departments and employees of other locations as well (unless data is clustered by location). Accessing Boston data requires reading multiple blocks and the efficiency of such access is low.

Partitioning combines the benefits of the logical integrity of the centralized database and the physical independence of data in the distributed database (see discussion of distributed databases below in this chapter and in Chapter 3). Partitioning unambiguously assigns each row to assigned particular partition based on the partition key. The partition key is a set of one or more columns that determines the partition for each row. The following statement creates the table Department partitioned by location, which is the partition key:

```
CREATE TABLE Department (
   ...
   )
   PARTITION BY HASH(location)
   PARTITIONS 3;
```

This is an example of hash partitioning: for each of the three locations, the system hash function returns a particular value, and the rows with the same hash value are stored in the same physical partition. Figure 2-9 shows the difference in access to data for partitioned and non-partitioned tables.

Oracle also supports range and hybrid (combination of hash and range) partitioning. Range partitioning maps data to partitions based on ranges of partition key values that you establish for each partition as shown in the following example, which creates a table Title with two range partitions: one for the titles with low salary (less than 50000), and another for the titles with high salary (between 50000 and 100000). Note that partitions in this case have different physical characteristics (to accommodate differences in managing titles with low and high salaries) :

```
CREATE TABLE Title (
...
)
PARTITION BY RANGE(salary) (
PARTITION low_Salary VALUES LESS THAN (50000)
  TABLESPACE TS1
  STORAGE (INITIAL 5M, NEXT 1M, PCTUSED 75, PCTFREE 15)
PARTITION high_Salary VALUES LESS THAN (100000)
  TABLESPACE TS2
  STORAGE (INITIAL 2M, NEXT 20K, PCTUSED 80, PCTFREE 10));
```

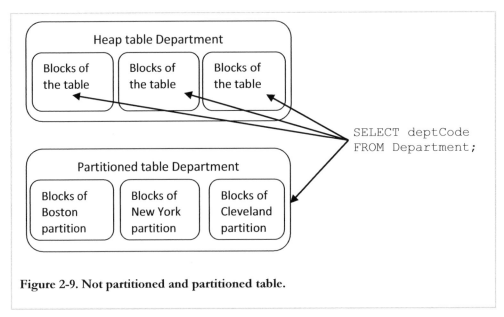

Figure 2-9. Not partitioned and partitioned table.

Storage parameters of each partition – location, size, and block packing – are specified similarly to the storage parameters of a separate table. Access to data on the partitioned table can be supported by global table indices. Additionally, a partition can have separate partition indices. For example, the partitioned by location table Department can have the global index on the deptType, and the Boston partition can have the index on the deptName.

Note the differences between clustering and partitioning:

- All blocks of a clustered table are organized in the same way according to the storage settings of the cluster. Blocks of different partitions can be organized differently because storage of each partition is defined separately.
- A table is clustered if for each value of the cluster key we expect not too many records that will be stored in one or several blocks. Partitions are beneficial for storing large numbers of records. The examples above were used for demonstration purpose only – obviously, partitioning the tables Department and Title does not seem appropriate. A better example

could be partitioning the table Employee by emplType if the table contains hundreds of thousands of records.

2.6.5 Changing the Physical Model

New user requirements and or changes in data usage can require changes of the physical model. Often the physical model needs to be changed when we discover that our assessment of some physical parameters was not correct, e.g. we have a table with many migrating rows, or our partitions cannot accommodate new data. Some changes require rebuilding the table, some other changes can be handled by the table alteration.

For example, we discovered that partitioning our table Department can be beneficial for our queries and hence we create a new table called Department_new with the new partitioning requirements:

```
CREATE TABLE Department_new (
     ...
     )
     PARTITION BY HASH(location)
     PARTITIONS 3
     AS SELECT * FROM Department;


INSERT INTO Department_new
(SELECT * FROM Department);
```

After the new table is created, we can drop the original table and rename this new table to the original table name

The following example illustrates alteration of the table when we need to create a new partition either on the high end of the partitioning range

```
ALTER TABLE Title
ADD PARTITION very_high_Salary VALUES LESS THAN 150000;
```

or in the middle of it

```
ALTER TABLE Title
SPLIT PARTITION high_Salary AT (75000)
INTO (PARTITION modest_Salary,
      PARTITION high_Salary);
```

2.6.6 Transparency of the Database

Various physical aspects of the data in Oracle databases, such as the actual organization of the data (heap, cluster, index, index-organized or partitioned storage of data), the percent of free space in data blocks, the existence of indices are transparent to database users and in many cases to database programmers.

Database programmers work with the conceptual schema of a table, which is available from the data dictionary. For example, the following command shows the structure of the table Employee:

```
SQL> DESCRIBE Employee;

 Name              Null?              Type
 --------          ---------------    ----------------------
 ID                NOT NULL           NUMBER
 EMPLNAME          NOT NULL           VARCHAR2(30)
 EMPLTYPE          NOT NULL           VARCHAR2(10)
 . . .
```

When inserting a new row into the table Employee, the programmer uses this information without knowing the details of how the row is physically written into the database:

```
INSERT INTO Employee(ID, emplName, emplType, …)
VALUES (1234, 'John', 'Full-time', …);
```

If physical parameters of the table are changed or the table is moved to another tablespace, this query will remain unchanged because it is independent of the physical schema of the table Employee.

The Oracle DBMS, on the other hand, uses the internal schema to process data from the Employee table. When inserting a row, the DBMS must find the block for the row placement (according to parameters PCTFREE and PCTUSED, and the type of storage), check whether the tablespace has to be extended if all allocated data blocks are full, represent the data changes in all indices on the table, and perform some other actions. All this processing is hidden from the users and programmers.

2.7. Distributed Data Storage

A *distributed database system* allows applications to access data from local and remote databases. The distributed implementation of a database can significantly improve its *performance*, *reliability* and *availability*. In a distributed database, data are physically stored in several databases. This allows for better performance of some database applications and makes data accessed easier by local sites. Replicating data on different sites of the distributed database improves the reliability of the whole database and improves accessibility of data by local users.

The discussion of distributed databases is limited to the solution supported by most commercial DBMSs. A collection of multiple *logically interrelated* and *physically independent* databases is considered a distributed database if there exists at least one application that uses data from these different databases; such an application is called *global*.

According to this definition, the distributed database is composed of separate autonomous databases that are supported independently. In case all databases in the distributed database are implemented in the same DBMS, such a database is called homogenous. Discussion of other distributed solutions with databases physically dependent on each other (tightly integrated or semi-autonomous) or implemented in different DBMSs (heterogeneous) is beyond the scope of this book and can be found in [Özsu].

There are several instances where distributed databases are beneficial:

- Localizing access to specific portions of data
- Improving reliability and availability of data
- Improving performance: data are localized for the greatest demand, and access to multiple database systems is parallelized.

Distributed solutions are justified for large databases because of their complexity and cost.

A distributed DBMS is a software system that enables management of a distributed database.

2.7.1 Promises of Distributed Databases

The possible advantages of distributed databases are discussed using the example of the Manufacturing Company case. Because the offices in the three different cities deal with local data – data about local departments and employees working in these departments – it may be reasonable to distribute the data so that a database used by a particular office stored only the local data. Such a solution can have several benefits.

2.7.1.1 Improved Performance

The mentioned distribution of data means that each database contains parts of the tables Department and Employee with data about local departments and employees working in these departments. Parts of tables residing in different databases are called fragments, and the process of splitting a table is called fragmentation.

Such data localization can improve the performance of local applications in the cities (Figure 2-10) because:

- Each local application handles smaller amounts of data
- If data are brought closer to local users, access to the data is faster
- The management of a smaller database is easier.

The performance of some global applications may be improved as well. For example, if a global application requests data about all the employees of the company with a particular title code, then the global request is distributed to three databases, and data processing is performed in parallel (such execution is called intra-query parallelism). The parallel processing of smaller amounts of data is faster than the processing of the whole amount of data. Suppose there are 3000 employees evenly distributed across the databases of the three cities (1000 employee rows in each local database). Then the retrieval of data about employees of a particular title is performed as a search on 1000 rows in each of the three databases in parallel, and data could be retrieved faster than using a search on 3000 rows in the centralized database. However, the performance of distributed queries also depends on data transfer between databases; the cost of data transfer may be significant and can compromise the performance of some distributed queries.

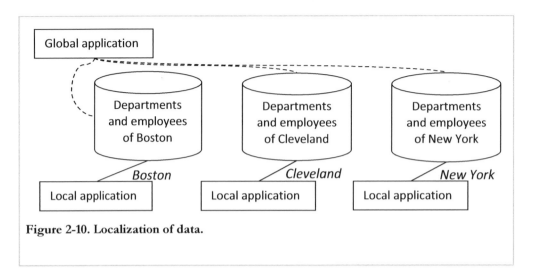

Figure 2-10. Localization of data.

In addition to intra-query parallelism, the distributed database can provide greater inter-query parallelism, when more queries can be executed in parallel increasing the throughput of the database – three databases in our case can process more requests simultaneously than the centralized database.

The distribution and localization of data may also improve the performance of other applications in the company because the load on the company's network will be reduced.

2.7.1.2   Scalability

In a distributed solution, an expansion of a database or an increase in the number of database users is easier to handle than in a centralized one – new servers can be added to the distributed database without affecting the performance of existing databases. In the centralized solution, on the other hand, to accommodate growth of the database or an increase in database load, it is necessary to upgrade hardware and software, which may make the database temporarily unavailable and require modification of the database or database applications[9].

2.7.1.3   Increased Reliability and Availability

Using several databases allows for replicating data and increasing data reliability. Figure 1-1 shows that if the Boston database goes down or even is destroyed, the application can switch to the Cleveland database that keeps a synchronized copy of the Boston data (replica).

Distribution also improves data availability. Imagine that the database administrator has to perform some reorganization of the Cleveland data. In a centralized database, this activity may result in the temporary unavailability of the tables Department and Employee. If data are localized (data for Boston's departments and employees are kept in the Boston database), then the availability of this data to local applications is not dependent on the condition and availability of data and database servers in other locations.

---

[9] In some cases, a cluster of database servers and a DBMS supporting the cluster architecture can be another approach.

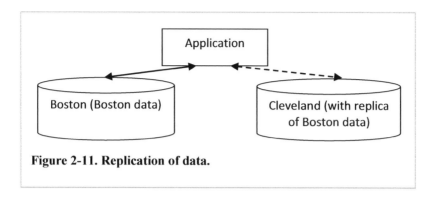

Figure 2-11. Replication of data.

2.7.2 Complicating Factors

A distributed solution, though it might bring significant improvements in the performance and reliability of the database, is more complicated and costly. The following are the complexities of the distributed approach:

- Lack of standards and methodology:
  - ✓ As with physical design in general, there is no straightforward methodology of data distribution design, often it is a 'trial and error' approach.
  - ✓ There are no standards or methodology on converting a centralized database into a distributed one.
- Complex design of data distribution. Decisions on splitting tables into fragments, allocating and, possibly, replicating fragments and unfragmented tables are often difficult to make.
- Complex implementation, including implementation of integrity constraints and transparency of data distribution.

2.7.2.1 Complexity of Design

Decisions on the distribution of data often are difficult to make because of conflicting needs in data. For instance, in our case, in addition to the mentioned requirements about offices in three cities that use data about local departments and employees, we learned about users in Boston who process data about full-time employees, users in New York who perform similar processing of data about part-time employees, and users in Cleveland who work with data about consultants. In each city, the application, which supports data about the employees of a particular type, will have to access three different databases on the fragmentation shown in Figure 2-10. The availability of data for this application will be compromised because it will depend on the availability of three databases. The performance of this application may become worse because it will have to access two remote sites to perform its tasks (Figure 2-12).

Localizing data by employee type for the new application, on the other hand, will make the existing local applications more complicated and, most probably, slower. The decision about the distribution of data about departments and employees depends on the importance of the local needs for data. Usually, a decision on the importance of an application is based on how frequently it accesses the data. If, for example, the application that supports the data about local departments and employees is executed more frequently than the new application, then the initial distributed solution will improve the performance of the more important application and be beneficial, even though it may make the performance of the other application worse.

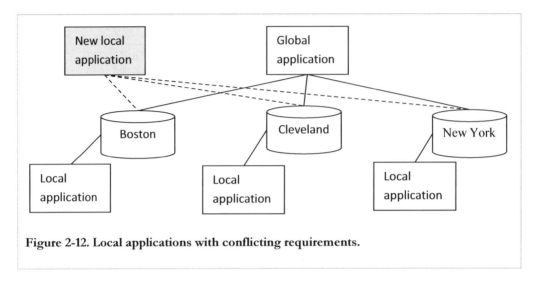

Figure 2-12. Local applications with conflicting requirements.

The decision on the allocation and replication of fragments and tables often involves balancing between intentions to increase reliability and availability of data on the one hand, and the necessity to improve performance and lower the cost of data support on the other.

2.7.2.2   Complexity of Implementation

For distributed solutions, the implementation of some aspects of relational databases requires additional efforts:

- Most DBMSs do not provide transparency of distribution and replication of data. These transparencies, therefore, must be implemented by the database programmer (see 2.7.4).
- Most distributed DBMSs do not support distributed integrity constraints. Usually, these constraints have to be implemented through database triggers or in applications.
- Resolving performance problems and tuning the distributed database are more complicated than working with a centralized database; they involve considering such additional issues as the distribution of data, communication costs, and obtaining sufficient locally available performance information.
- Additional performance problems may be caused by data replication.
- There are certain issues in implementing security in distributed and replicated databases; these issues are discussed in Chapter 4.

Some other problems, like distributed concurrency control and consistency of replicated data, recovery of replicas, switching from failed databases to functioning ones, distributed deadlock management are usually resolved by the DBMS.

2.7.3   The Distributed Database in Oracle

Oracle provides support of distributed databases. Consider a distributed solution for the Manufacturing Company case. Figure 2-13 shows part of this distributed database – the New

York and Boston databases with localized data about the company's departments (the table Department in New York contains the rows of New York departments and the table Department in Boston – the rows of Boston departments). The case description mentions that the application that is executed from the New York office requires data about all departments. The application should be able to access the Boston's portion of the data about the departments. Obviously, the databases have to be connected physically via the network. Oracle makes a database "visible" to another database through a database link. A database link defines a one-way communication path from one Oracle database to another; it is a logical connection between the databases (made possible by the physical network connection between them) that specifies the name and location of the remote database.

In this case, the New York database has to "see" the Boston database and, therefore, has to contain the following database link (as in the Figure 2-13):

```
CREATE PUBLIC DATABASE LINK boston USING
boston.ourcompany.us.com;
```

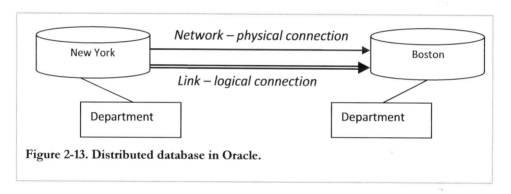

Figure 2-13. Distributed database in Oracle.

Users of the New York database can access the Boston table Department by explicitly specifying the database where the table is located:

```
SELECT * FROM Department@boston;
```

Note that the Boston database does not "see" the New York database through this link.

2.7.4   Transparency of Distribution

The physical distributed design of the database is not transparent to the users as the users must not only know that the database is distributed but also know the locations of the tables needed. If the table Department is relocated from Boston to another database (e.g. Cleveland), the way users access data will be affected and some applications will have to be rewritten, e.g. the last query of the previous section.

The goal of transparency of distribution is to make the distributed database appear as though it is a single Oracle database. The Oracle distributed database has features that hide (or allow hiding) the physical location of database objects from applications and users. Location transparency allows users to address objects such as tables in a unified way regardless of the database where the objects are located.

Location transparency has several benefits, including:

- Access to remote data is simple because database users do not need to know the physical location of the remote database object.
- Administrators can move database objects with no impact on users' requests or existing database applications.

An object's location can be made transparent with the help of *synonyms*. Synonyms are additional names for a database object. For example, we will create the synonym for the remote table Department of the Boston database in the New York database:

```
CREATE PUBLIC SYNONYM Department_Boston FOR
Department@boston;
```

Now users of the New York database can access the remote table Department with the help of a simpler query that does not depend on the location of this table:

```
SELECT * FROM Department_Boston;
```

The users' view of the distributed database is simpler now (as shown in Figure 2-14) and they see it as the centralized database.

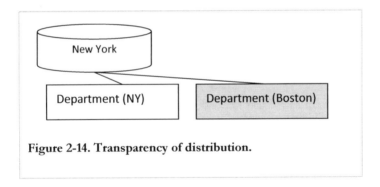

Figure 2-14. Transparency of distribution.

However, the database is still not transparent to users (or applications) that need to access data about all departments because they need to know that data about departments are fragmented and correspondingly build their requests:

```
SELECT * FROM Department
UNION
SELECT * FROM Department_Boston;
```

The fragmentation of data can be made transparent with the help of *views*. For example, for the global New York application we will build the following view:

```
CREATE VIEW Department_all AS
SELECT * FROM Department
```

```
UNION
SELECT * FROM Department_Boston;
```

Now data about all departments can be accessed through the view:

```
SELECT * FROM Department_all;
```

In many database applications, different transparencies are implemented with the help of *stored procedures*. The stored procedure is a database object implemented in the procedural extension of SQL (PL/SQL in Oracle). Users execute the procedure without knowing the details of how data are processed by the commands within the procedure. For example, the following procedure created in the New York database performs the inserting of a new row in the table Department of the Boston database:

```
CREATE PROCEDURE insert_Department
            (par_Code CHAR, par_Name VARCHAR2, par_Location
            VARCHAR2, par_Type VARCHAR2) AS
BEGIN
      INSERT INTO Department@boston
      VALUES (par_Code, par_Name, par_Location, par_Type);
END;
```

Adding a new Boston department can be performed by executing the procedure with the appropriate parameters' values:

```
EXEC insert_Department ('999', 'Accounts Payable',
'Cleveland', 'Business');
```

Stored procedures implement the transparency of data and data processing. Consider the case where we need to create a new department that requires some checking operations, and adding a row into the auditing table that keeps track of who created the new department and when they did it. In such a case, if these actions are implemented within a procedure, users are unawre of them and are relieved from executing these actions themselves for every insert operation.

Such objects as synonyms, views and procedures can be used for implementing the transparency of distributed databases. Note that every object is created by a particular database user and belongs to this user's schema. Other users need special permissions to be able to use these objects. Schemas and security issues are discussed in detail in Chapter 4.

2.8. Example: Building the Physical Model of Data

Let us discuss the physical design of the table Employee – a part of the physical data model for the Manufacturing Company case. This discussion is provided for the centralized database solution; the distributed design for this case is shown in Chapter 3.

Building the physical model of data includes making decisions about data types for the columns, additional integrity constraints, the initial size and growth of the table, the type of storage, and storage parameters.

Decisions about a column data type are based on user requirements for a column's possible values and the expected data manipulations on the column. The following data types are chosen for the columns of the table Employee:

- *ID.* This column is the primary key of the table and its values are assigned within the company. Integer numbers are a good choice for this column for a couple of reasons. First, this makes the column short and simple – necessary properties for the primary key column. In addition, it allows for using the IDENTITY feature mentioned above or a special Oracle object – sequence – to automatically generate new unique values of this column for the new rows.
- *emplName.* VARCHAR2(30)The names of persons include letters and are of variable length. Columns of such type usually have the VARCHAR2 data type. The length of the column is limited to 30 symbols.
- *emplType.* VARCHAR2(10)allows storing the three possible values('Full-time', 'Part-time', 'Consultant')of the column. However, a better solution might be to store shorter values, e.g., the first letter, which will not only reduce resources usage but will also reduce the possibility of error when entering the value – we suggest CHAR (length 1 is the default).
- *deptCode and titleCode.* These columns are the foreign keys to other tables of the database and we will use the same data types as these columns have in their parent tables Department and Title, respectively. Assume that both of these columns have the CHAR data type as both may contain digits and letters. Both columns are fixed length: three symbols for *deptCode* and two symbols for *titleCode*.

The NOT NULL constraint on the column emplName enforces the requirement that each employee in the database has a name. The CHECK constraint on the column emplType ensures that values of the column are limited to 'F', 'P', and 'C'.

The table is stored as a heap. The table blocks do not need much free space because columns ID, deptCode, and emplType are fixed-length, and columns emplName and emplType are unlikely to change often. Therefore, PCTFREE can be low. Users do not expect many staff changes, which means there will not be too many deleting and inserting operations, and, therefore, PCTUSED can be high. Given these requirements, PCTFREE can be set to 5, and PCTUSED to 90.

Users expect to support about 4000 employees, and we can roughly estimate the initial size of the table using the average row length and the percent of free space. The average row length depends on the average length of the emplName column, which we estimate as 20. Then the average row length is 30 bytes: 4 bytes for ID, 20 bytes for emplName, 1 byte for emplType, and 5 bytes for deptCode and titleCode.

The initial size of the table is estimated as 126000 bytes: 30 bytes multiplied by 4000 rows and increased by 5% of free space. The estimation is rough and does not consider some other storage factors, e.g. space in the data blocks occupied by block headers and directories; the initial size is rounded to 130K.

The table is not expected to grow fast; and we will specify five possible extensions of 50K each.

Here is the resulting physical model of the table:

```
CREATE TABLE Employee (
    ID INTEGER PRIMARY KEY,
    emplName VARCHAR2(30) NOT NULL,
    emplType CHAR
        CHECK (emplType IN ('F', 'P',C')),
    deptCode CHAR(3) REFERENCES Department,
    titleCode CHAR(2) REFERENCES Title)
    PCTFREE 5
    PCTUSED 90
    TABLESPACE users
    STORAGE (  INITIAL 130K
            NEXT 50K
            MAXEXTENTS 5
            PCTINCREASE 0 );
```

It is important to utilize specific features of the DBMS to make the support of data easier. In this example, we want to show how to use a special feature of Oracle – sequence – for generating unique values. We will create a simple sequence that starts with the value 1 and generates the next value with an increment of 1:

```
CREATE SEQUENCE seq_Employee;
```

To use the sequence object for generating unique ID numbers for the table Employee, we need to create a special type of procedure – a trigger on the table. The trigger that we need here will be automatically invoked for every insert statement on the table, generate the next value of the sequence, and assign this value to the ID column of the new row.

```
CREATE TRIGGER tr_ins_Employee      -- creating the trigger
BEFORE INSERT ON Employee           --the  trigger is invoked
                                    before every insert
FOR EACH ROW                        --the trigger action takes
                                    place for every inserted row
DECLARE
    vNext NUMBER;
BEGIN
    vNext:=                         -- request the sequence to
    seq_Employee.NEXTVALUE;         generate the next value
    :NEW.ID := vNext;               -- assign the new sequence
                                    value to ID of the new row
END;
```

Every insert statement

```
INSERT    INTO    Employee    (emplName,    emplType,    deptCode,
titleCode)
VALUES (...);
```

invokes the trigger and generates a new value for the ID column. Generating the new value and assigning it to ID is transparent to users.

2.9. Summary

The physical data model specifies where the data are stored and how data storage is organized. Building the physical model requires knowledge of the conditions under which the database will be used and user requirements for the expected sizes of tables, performance of various requests, availability of data, number of users concurrently working with data, and other considerations. In addition, developers have to understand the features of the DBMS and utilize these features properly to build the physical model.

The main goals of a good physical data model are providing the required performance and availability of data, economical space usage, and easy database maintenance. This chapter discusses the basic features of DBMSs for achieving these goals. Each DBMS has additional specific tools and features, and developers need to understand them and use them to full advantage.

The important steps in building the physical model are:

- *Choosing the data types for the columns of tables.* A data type has to: 1) represent all possible values of a column and 2) allow for all needed operations on the column's values. A data type also 3) imposes constraints on the column's values and it can be used to enhance the column's integrity. Additional considerations for choosing a data type include 4) performance (e.g. VARCHAR2 vs. CHAR) and 5) the economical use of storage space. Some DBMSs offer specific data types that can substantially reduce the cost of data maintenance (e.g. IDENTITY).
- *Applying additional integrity constraints.* DBMSs support additional integrity constraints not included in the relational model, such as NOT NULL, CHECK, and UNIQUE. These constraints implement user requirements that are not presented in the relational data model and improve data integrity. More complicated user requirements are implemented with the help of special database procedures – triggers.While some requirements can be supported by the database application, we strongly advocate making the database responsible for data quality – such quality support measures cannot be bypassed and will be implemented only once to be leveraged by any application.
- *Defining storage type.* The type of storage organization is dependent upon how the data will be used. Developers have to choose between heap (or random) and organized storage. The most common type of storage organization is clustering, when rows that have the same value of a column (index cluster) or the same value of a special function applied to a column (hash cluster) are stored in the same blocks. When a request for data is constrained by conditions on the column used for clustering, because the requested rows are stored together, the system can access all needed data in a few block reads. DBMSs support other types of organized data storage, e.g. index-organized tables and partitions. In some cases, achieving the necessary performance requires the distribution and localization of data. A special case of data distribution – a replicated database – is the ultimate resolution of the problem of data reliability and availability.
- *Specifying storage parameters.* Storage parameters of a table define where (in which tablespace) the table is stored, its initial size and growth, the packing of data in data blocks, and other physical properties.

Review Questions

1. What are the main goals of physical data design?
2. What DBMS features are used for performing physical design?
3. How does storage organization affect performance on the database?
4. What types of organized storage do you know?
5. When is it recommended to use clusters?
6. In what situations is it beneficial to distribute data?
7. What are the benefits of the 3-tier architecture of a database?
8. How does the DBMS read data from a table and process the data?
9. What table storage parameters do you know? What is the role of each of them?
10. What types of organized data storage in Oracle do you know?
11. How would you implement transparency for a distributed database?

Practical Assignments

1. Describe the database storage hierarchy. Explain how a table's data is stored in a database.

2. Explain how parameters PCTFREE and PCTUSED control the packing of data in data blocks.

3. Choose the data types for the table Student (ID, name, dateOfBirth) and explain your decisions.

4. Choose data types for the columns of the table T (A, B, C, D) and specify column constraints for the following conditions:
    *   Values of the column B are alphanumeric strings five symbols long, and for each row of the table, the column B must always have a value and this value has to be unique.
    *   The column C is designed to store numeric values not greater than 50000; users often request totals of the column C.
    *   The column D stores dates of the year 2005.

5. Estimate PCTFREE and PCTUSED for the following tables and situations:
    a. CREATE TABLE T1 (field1 NUMBER, field2 CHAR(3), field3 DATE). Intensive updating, inserting and deleting activities are expected.
    b. CREATE TABLE T2 (field1 NUMBER, field2 VARCHAR(250)). Intensive inserting and deleting activities are expected.
    c. CREATE TABLE T3 (field1 VARCHAR2(50), VARCHAR2(300)). Intensive updating activities are expected.
    d. CREATE TABLE T1 (field1 NUMBER, field2 CHAR(3), field3 DATE). Intensive retrieving activities are expected.
    e. CREATE TABLE T3 (field1 VARCHAR2(50), field2 VARCHAR2(300)). Intensive retrieving activities are expected.

6. A database contains two tables T1 (A, B, C) and T2 (C, D, E). The column C of T1 is the foreign key to T2. Explain in which of the following situations it is reasonable to use clusters, and create clusters and clustered tables.
    a. The data in the tables are often modified.

    b.   The performance of select queries with conditions ... `WHERE C = x` on the table T1 is important.

    c.   The performance of queries with conditions ... `WHERE C <> x` on the table T1 is important.

    d.   The performance of queries with conditions ... `WHERE C > x` on the table T1 is important.

    e.   The performance of the queries on the join of the tables is important.

7. Explain when it is beneficial to store the table T `(A, B, C)` as index-organized.

8. Define the difference in conditions for your decisions to store the table `Employee` as clustered or partitioned by the attribute `emplType`.

9. Define the difference in conditions for your decisions to store the table `Employee` as distributed or partitioned by the attribute `emplType`.

10. What would be your choice of the storage organization of the table `Employee` if the following querying patterns were the most important ones:

    a.   ... `WHERE ID = x;`

    b.   ... `WHERE emplName = x;`

    c.   ... `WHERE deptCode <> x;`

    d.   ... `WHERE titleCode BETWEEN x and y;`

    e.   ... `WHERE titleCode =x;`

11. Describe distributed data design for one of the case studies from Appendix 1.

12. Build the physical data model for one of the case studies from Appendix 1.

Chapter 3.   Distributed Database Design

Today's amazing growth of databases is caused by the needs of business and is possible because of continuous technological advances. Under these circumstances, good performance and scalability of growing databases become very important, as well as reliability and constant availability of data. Distributed database design can significantly improve these database features.

> **The distributed database is a collection of physically independent and logically related databases. Each database of the distributed database is capable of processing data independently; however, some applications process data from multiple databases.**

We will discuss possible distributed solutions for the Manufacturing Company case described in Appendix 1. The relational model of the database includes three relations: Department, Title, and Employee. The diagram in Figure 3-1 shows the dependencies between the relations: Employee references Department and Title, or in other words, Employee is the child relation, and Department and Title are the parent relations.

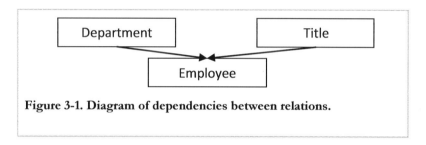

Figure 3-1. Diagram of dependencies between relations.

Making decisions about data distribution requires an understanding of how the different database applications work with the data. For the Manufacturing Company case, departments are located in three cities: Boston, New York, and Cleveland. Each of the company's employees is assigned to one department. An application in each city is responsible for the support and maintenance of data about the local departments and the employees assigned to these departments. The New York office, in addition to supporting local data, is in charge of some reports for all departments and employees of the company.

Each office has a database server; the servers are connected via the network as shown in Figure 3-2.

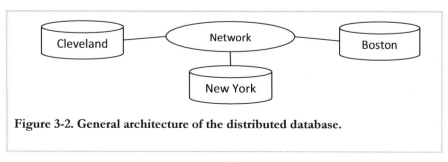

Figure 3-2. General architecture of the distributed database.

For our future discussions and analyses, we will use the following sample data of the relations:

Title

titleCode	titleDescription	salary
T1	Accountant	10000
T2	Analyst	20000
T3	Programmer	30000
T4	DBA	40000
T5	Manager	50000

Department

deptCode	deptName	location	deptType
001	Computer Center	Boston	IT
002	Budget	New York	Business
003	Marketing	Boston	Marketing
004	Database Support	Cleveland	IT
005	Purchasing	New York	Business

Employee

ID	empName	emplType	deptCode	titleCode
1	John	Full-time	002	T1
2	Adam	Consultant	001	T3
3	Mary	Part-time	004	T4
4	Peter	Full-time	003	T2
5	Scott	Consultant	002	T1
6	Susan	Full-time	005	T5
7	Alex	Part-time	004	T2

The distributed solution, which is more expensive and more complex than the centralized one, is justified by the following expectations:

- Improving performance of local applications in each city and the global New York application
- Achieving better reliability and availability of the data
- Ensuring that the database is scalable and will be able to function with an increased number of users and larger amounts of data.

3.1. Prerequisites of the Distributed Design

Distribution of data is one of the considerations in performing the physical design of the database. Decisions related to physical design are based on the logical data model and user requirements that specify:

- The structure of the company and the architecture of the company's network
- How data will be used by database applications, including what data is needed by each application, the amounts of processed data, and the frequencies of applications' execution.

This chapter discusses how to use these requirements for designing appropriate distributions of data.

When performing the design and implementation of the distributed database, it is important to understand that the physical data model has to correspond to the logical model and preserve all semantics of the latter.

3.2. Review of Basic Features of the Distributed Database

The basic features of distributed databases which were discussed in Chapter 2 are as follows:

- The distributed database is a collection of logically interrelated shared data stored across several physically independent databases.
- Participating databases are linked by a network.
- Each participating database is controlled by a DBMS autonomously.
- Relations of the logical data model can be split into fragments.
- Fragments and unfragmented relations are implemented as tables in participating databases.
- Fragments and relations can be replicated in several participating databases.
- Each participating database is involved in at least one global application, i.e. application processing data from several participating databases.
- The distributed database has to appear like a centralized database to the users.

The distribution and replication of data have to provide better database performance, improve reliability and availability of data, and make the database more scalable. These are achieved by localizing the data through fragmentation and replication, and providing users with easy access to needed data.

3.3. General Approaches to Distribution

3.3.1 Types of Fragmentation

Implementing entire relations in different databases of a distributed database is not a typical distribution scenario. It is important to remember that the main goals of distributed databases are to improve performance, availability, and reliability through the localization of data. If, for example, the table Department is stored in the Boston database and the table Employee is stored in the New York database, then this distribution does not localize data for the applications of the Manufacturing Company case. First, each of the local applications needs to access remote databases to get necessary data about local departments and employees, and second, to get this local data, the local application has to process data about departments and employees from other locations as well. This design neither improves reliability nor availability, as if one of the databases goes down, most of the users will have to wait to do their processing.

Usually, distributed design involves fragmenting relations of the logical model and allocating the fragments in the database at the locations where users most often need data from the fragments.

Relations can be fragmented *horizontally*, where *rows* of a relation are stored in different databases, and *vertically*, where *columns* of a relation are stored in different databases. Horizontal and vertical fragmentations of the relation Department are shown schematically in Figure 3-3 and Figure 3-4, respectively.

Horizontal and vertical fragmentations can also be combined in a hybrid fragmentation.

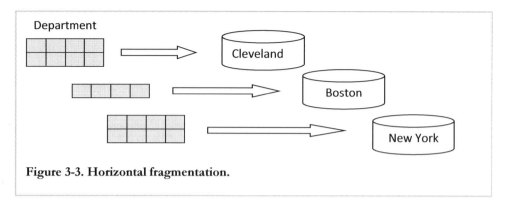

Figure 3-3. Horizontal fragmentation.

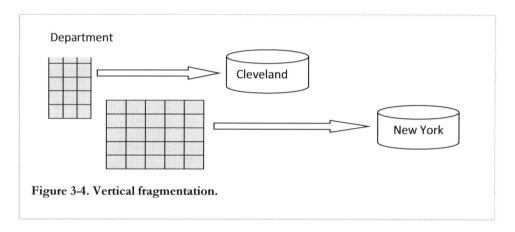

Figure 3-4. Vertical fragmentation.

The results of data processing should not depend on whether the database is implemented as centralized or distributed. Fragmentation must abide by the following simple rules:

1. *Completeness.* Data should not be lost in the process of fragmentation. Each data item must be included in at least one fragment.
2. *Disjointness.* Data should not be duplicated in the process of fragmentation to avoid inconsistency and incorrect results of queries. Each data item must be included in not more than one fragment.

These two rules of correctness of fragmentation mean that:

Each data item must be included in one and only one fragment.

In addition to these formal rules we want fragmentation to result in an even distribution of data across fragments, e.g., we do not want one of the fragments to contain 90% of records of the table and another one to contain 10% as such fragmentation will undermine the goals of distribution.

If necessary, all data from a correctly fragmented relation have to be made available, and to accomplish this there is an operation for each type of fragmentation that allows restoring all the data from the fragments. The discussion of fragmentation and restoring data from fragments is provided with the help of the relational operations that are described in Appendix 2.

3.4. Horizontal fragmentation

3.4.1 Information Requirements

Case 3.1.

> *In the Manufacturing Company case, users of each city work with data about local departments (the departments located in the city).*

This situation makes us consider horizontal fragmentation of the relation Department in three fragments: the first will contain all the rows of the relation with location 'Boston', the second – the rows with location 'New York', and the third – the rows with location 'Cleveland'. Data is localized because users in each city have the data they need in their local databases (i.e., the databases they directly work with), and each local application deals with needed data only and is not burdened with support of other data.

Case 3.2.

> *In addition to the requirements for Case 3.1, there is another application in Boston that processes data about all IT departments, and there is a similar application in Cleveland which works with data about the Business and Marketing departments.*

The previous distributed solution does not provide data localization for these applications – to get the needed data about the departments of a particular type, users have to access remote databases (i.e., the databases to which the users are not connected directly). Most probably, the performance of the applications of this case, as well as the availability of data, will be worse than in the centralized database. The fragmentation suggested for the Case 3.1 does not offer data localization for the new applications. However, if we decide to reconsider the fragmentation and localize the data for the new applications from Boston and Cleveland by allocating all rows of the IT departments in the Boston database and the rows of all other departments in the Cleveland database, the distribution is not localized for the applications dealing with data about local departments.

Here we encounter one of the mentioned problems of distributed design (and physical design in general) – often we have to make our decisions for conflicting user requirements. To resolve this conflict, we have to find out which group of users' needs are more important. Usually the "importance" of an application is judged by how often it accesses data and how crucial its performance is. If, for example, the users of the applications mentioned in Case 3.1 access data about local departments several thousand times per day for each city, while the users of the additional applications mentioned in Case 3.2 access data for a particular department type several times a month, then performance of the first group of applications seems more important and we will try to localize the data for this group of applications.

There exists an empirical 80/20 rule: 80% percent of data processing in a company is performed by 20% of the applications. The needs of the applications that fall into these 20% should be considered first.

These two simple cases show that horizontal fragmentation is beneficial only if it localizes data for the most frequently used applications.

> **Horizontal fragmentation of a relation is performed based on information about what rows of the relation are accessed, how frequently and from which sites.**

3.4.2   Primary Horizontal Fragmentation

When fragmentation is performed by applying user requirements about what rows of the relation are accessed, from which sites and how frequently, it is called *primary* horizontal fragmentation.

A general rule for correctness of horizontal fragmentation is that each row of the relation must be included in one and only one fragment.

> **Each row of a relation must be included in one and only one horizontal fragment.**

After the most important applications are defined, the designer must concentrate on the relations involved in these applications and analyze the conditions by which rows of these relations are accessed from different sites. These conditions define the local needs in data. For requests in SQL, these are the WHERE clauses of queries executed from different applications.

Let us consider the fragmentation of the relation Department for Case 3.1. Applications access data about local departments with the help of the following query, where '?' stands for one of the three locations of the company.

```
SELECT * FROM Department WHERE location = ?,
```

The conditions (also called predicates), which define rows used by each site, are:

P_1 : location = 'Boston'

P_2 : location = 'New York'

P_3 : location = 'Cleveland'

Horizontal fragmentation is defined with the help of the relational operation *Selection* (see Appendix 2). For the relation $R(A_1, A_2, ..., A_m)$ and predicates p_i, i from 1 to N, N fragments of R are defined with the help of the selection operation on R by conditions of p_i:

$$R_i = \sigma_{pi} (R), 1 \leq i \leq N$$

For our case, the three local needs for data expressed by predicates on the attribute location of the relation Department produce three fragments of the table:

$$\text{Department}_1 = \sigma_{\text{location = 'Boston'}} (\text{Department})$$

$$Department_2 = \sigma_{location = \text{'New York'}} (Department)$$

$$Department_3 = \sigma_{location = \text{'Cleveland'}} (Department)$$

The fragmentation is correct because it is complete and disjoint.

Boston:

deptCode	deptName	location	deptType
001	Computer Center	Boston	IT
003	Marketing	Boston	Production

New York:

deptCode	deptName	location	deptType
002	Budget	New York	Business
005	Purchasing	New York	Business

Cleveland:

deptCode	deptName	location	deptType
004	Database Support	Cleveland	IT

The initial relation is restored from its horizontal fragments with the help of the relational operation *Union*:

$$Department = Department_1 \cup Department_2 \cup Department_3$$

The initial relation is restored correctly if the fragmentation is correct.

Case 3.3.

> *The users in Boston and New York work with data about local departments; users in Cleveland work with data about local and New York departments.*

The predicates, which define rows of the relation Department used on each site, are:

P_1 : location = 'Boston'

P_2 : location = 'New York'

P_3 : location = 'Cleveland' OR location = 'New York'

The fragmentation of Department by these predicates is the following:

Boston:

deptCode	deptName	location	deptType
001	Computer Center	Boston	IT
003	Purchasing	Boston	Production

deptCode	deptName	location	deptType
002	Budget	New York	Business
005	Purchasing	New York	Business

New York:

Cleveland:

deptCode	deptName	location	deptType
002	Budget	New York	Business
004	Database Support	Cleveland	IT
005	Purchasing	New York	Business

This fragmentation is obviously incorrect – it is not disjoint, since the rows for the departments of New York are included in two fragments: in New York and Cleveland. If someone who was unaware of this special fragmentation decides to count departments of the company, the result will not correspond to the actual number of departments. The duplication of data about the New York departments in the Cleveland database makes data inconsistency possible (remember that the databases are supported independently).

Duplication caused by violation of the disjointness rule should not be confused with replication. Replicas are synchronized copies of objects of one database in another database and they are declared as such when created. For a distributed database, we can replicate whole fragments or tables. The support of replicas (keeping the copies of data in sync) is provided by the DBMS.

To produce the correct fragmentation, we need to analyze the frequencies of access of data about the New York departments from the New York and Cleveland sites. If the local New York application needs this data more often than the application in Cleveland, then we can use the fragmentation used for the Case 3.1. If, on the other hand, Cleveland applications are more important, then we will have the following fragmentation:

P_1 : location = 'Boston'

P_2 : location = 'Cleveland' OR location = 'New York'

Case 3.4.

> *The Boston users need data about the IT departments; Cleveland users need the data about all other departments. The New York users do not work with data about departments.*

The predicates for this case are:

P_1 : deptType = 'IT'

P_2 : deptType = 'Business' OR deptType = 'Marketing'

Fragmentation by these predicates gives two fragments:

$$\text{Department}_1 = \sigma_{\text{deptType = 'IT'}} (\text{Department})$$

$$\text{Department}_2 = \sigma_{\text{deptType = 'Business' OR deptType = 'Marketing'}} (\text{Department})$$

If a new department of the type 'Advertising' is added to the company, the fragmentation becomes incorrect – it will be incomplete because the new department will be not placed in any fragment.

A different set of predicates gives a better fragmentation solution for this case:

P_1 : deptType = 'IT'

P_2 : deptType ≠ 'IT'

The discussed cases show that the correctness of fragmentation is defined by correctness of the set of predicates. When building the set of predicates we cannot simply map the conditions of data access from each site. For the fragmentation to be complete and disjoint, the set of predicates must satisfy the conditions of completeness and disjointness:

- *Disjointness.*: For each two predicates p_i and p_j, where i ≠ j, for each row of the relation: p_i AND p_j = FALSE.
- *Completeness.* For all N predicates, for each row of the relation: p_1 OR p_2 OR … p_N = TRUE.

The correct primary horizontal fragmentation is defined by correct predicates. The set of predicates for fragmentation must be complete and disjoint.

In all previous cases the predicates were simple and defined on one attribute. Consider a more complicated situation.

Case 3.5.

> *Each city of the company has two offices: the first office is working with data about local IT departments, and the second office is working with data about all other local departments.*

For this case, local access to data is defined by composite conditions on two attributes:

P_1 : location = 'Boston' AND deptType = 'IT'

P_2 : location = 'Boston' AND deptType ≠ 'IT'

P_3 : location = 'New York' AND deptType = 'IT'

P_4 : location = 'New York' AND deptType ≠ 'IT'

P_5 : location = 'Cleveland' AND deptType = 'IT'

P_6 : location = 'Cleveland' AND deptType ≠ 'IT'

It is easy to check that the fragmentation by these predicates is correct (note that for our example some of the fragments are empty). However, this fragmentation does not make sense because there are more fragments than databases, and we will not be able to allocate all fragments. It is important to remember that fragmentation has to be performed with understanding of the architecture of the company's network and availability of database servers.

For this case, we could use the fragmentation of the Case 3.1 based on the 'location' attribute or the fragmentation of the Case 3.4. based on the 'deptType' attribute; the latter fragmentation, however, results in a poorer localization of data. Distribution of data can be combined with local measures for performance improvement. For example, if data usage patterns call for it, for the fragmentation by the 'location' attribute we may consider the partitioning of each fragment by deptType.

The set of predicates must not only be correct, but also *relevant*. In this case it means that there must be at least one application that accesses the resulting fragments differently from the others. If, for example, for the Case 3.1 we choose the set of predicates:

P_1 : deptType = 'IT'

P_2 : deptType ≠ 'IT'

then applications on each site will always access both fragments. This fragmentation does not fulfill the goals of the distributed database – data localization – because it is irrelevant (though it is correct).

The distributed design of a database must result in a *minimal* fragmentation, which is *correct* and *relevant*.

3.4.3   Derived Horizontal Fragmentation

In the Manufacturing Company case, users access data about local departments and employees assigned to these departments. We performed fragmentation of the relation Department in the previous section. Let us consider localization of data about employees. If we start with locating the whole table Employee in the Boston database, then users in Boston will be able to access data about employees working in the Boston departments with the help of the query:

```
SELECT e.*
FROM Department₁ d, Employee e
WHERE d.deptCode = e.deptCode;
```

As we can see, the above join query always accesses only those rows of the table Employee that are joined to rows of the fragment table Department₁. Therefore, it does not make sense to keep the whole table Employee in the Boston database – rows of employees that do not work in the Boston departments are never accessed by Boston users. Similarly, the New York and Cleveland users are dealing only with rows of the Employee table that can be joined to the New

York and Cleveland fragments, respectively, and they do not need the whole table Employee on their sites.

When two relations, one of which is a parent and another one is a child of the relationship, are used in the same application (this is a very common situation), and the parent relation is fragmented, then it is reasonable to consider fragmenting the child relation by joining it to the corresponding fragment of the parent relation (Figure 3-5).

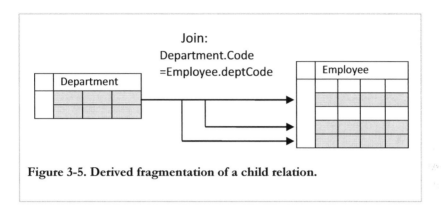

Figure 3-5. Derived fragmentation of a child relation.

This is called *derived* fragmentation, and each child fragment is defined by the *Semi-join* operation:

$$\text{Child Fragment}_i = \text{Child Relation} \blacktriangleright \text{Parent Fragment}_i.$$

The number of derived fragments is equal to the number of primary fragments.

For our case, the derived fragmentation of the relation Employee is defined by the following formulas:

$$\text{Employee}_1 = \text{Employee} \blacktriangleright_{\text{deptCode}} \text{Department}_1$$

$$\text{Employee}_2 = \text{Employee} \blacktriangleright_{\text{deptCode}} \text{Department}_2$$

$$\text{Employee}_3 = \text{Employee} \blacktriangleright_{\text{deptCode}} \text{Department}_3$$

Employee$_1$ (Boston):

ID	empName	emplType	deptCode	titleCode
2	Adam	Consultant	001	T3
4	Peter	Full-time	003	T2

Employee$_2$ (New York):

ID	empName	emplType	deptCode	titleCode
1	John	Full-time	002	T1
5	Scott	Consultant	002	T1
6	Susan	Full-time	005	T5

Employee$_3$ (Cleveland):

ID	empName	emplType	deptCode	titleCode
3	Mary	Part-time	004	T4
7	Alex	Part-time	004	T2

The diagram of the derived fragmentation is shown in Figure 3-6. Each of the databases has a primary fragment of the relation Department and the corresponding derived fragment of the relation Employee. Each derived fragment is the child of the corresponding primary fragment.

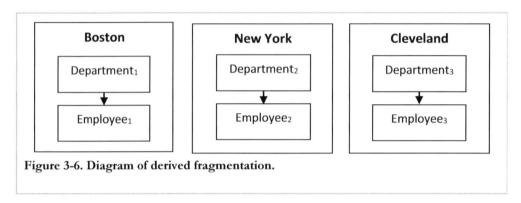

Figure 3-6. Diagram of derived fragmentation.

Sometimes a relation has more than one fragmented parent relation. Consider the situation, when in addition to fragmentation of the relation Department, the relation Title is fragmented by conditions on the attribute salary (e.g., the Boston site is interested in titles and employees with high salary, while the New York site is working with titles and employees with low salaries):

P_1 : salary > 30000

P_2 : salary ≤ 30000

The relation Employee is the child of two fragmented relations: Department and Title. From which primary fragmentation should we derive the fragmentation of Employee? Once again, we have to analyze user requirements. How will data from the table Employee be used more frequently – in a join with the table Title or in a join with the table Department? If the queries with the join of Employee and Department are more frequent, then we will decide to derive the fragmentation of the relation Employee from the fragmentation of Department. Figure 3-7 shows the diagram of this fragmentation. Access to the data about local departments and employees is localized: for example, the retrieval of data about the Boston departments and employees uses the Boston fragments Department$_1$ and Employee$_1$. However, access to the data about titles and employees is distributed, e.g. the query about employees with high salaries involves the fragment Title$_1$ and all three fragments of the relation Employee.

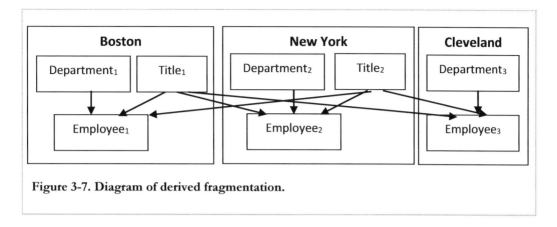

Figure 3-7. Diagram of derived fragmentation.

An additional consideration is the amount of data transferred between databases – fragmentation that requires minimal data transfers is preferable. If it is difficult to make a decision about a derived fragmentation based on access frequencies and amounts of transferred data, it is recommended to choose the fragmentation with a simpler join condition.

The correctness of the derived fragmentation follows from the correct primary fragmentation and referential integrity constraint.

Reconstruction of the derived fragmentation is performed by the *Union* operation:

$$\text{Employee} = \text{Employee}_1 \cup \text{Employee}_2 \cup \text{Employee}_3$$

Derived fragmentation is often beneficial because it localizes logically related data, which is used together. Derived fragmentation is illustrated by a simpler diagram of fragmentation, which in turn illustrate intra- and inter- query parallelism. For example, for the derived fragmentation in Figure 3-7, the global application that needs the data about all departments and all employees of the company can distribute a global query to the sites and execute parts of the query in parallel (the parts of the query do not depend on each other). For the same derived fragmentation, the local applications can be executed in parallel and independently because each of them uses data only from the local site.

3.5. Vertical Fragmentation

3.5.1 Information Requirements

The goal of vertical fragmentation is to keep close attributes – attributes that are accessed together in applications – in the same fragment. It is difficult to define the closeness of attributes formally; often neither designers nor users can specify it. The closeness of attributes for vertical fragmentation (called affinity) is calculated based on the following information requirements:

- Usage of attributes in applications.
- Frequency of execution of applications on different sites.

3.5.2 The Correctness of Vertical Fragmentation

Vertical fragmentation is defined by the relational operation *Projection*:

$$R_i = \Pi_{X_i} (R), \text{ where } X_i \text{ is a subset of attributes of R.}$$

The rules of correctness for the vertical fragmentation are:

1. *Completeness.* Each attribute must be included in at least one fragment.
2. *Disjointness.* Each non-key attributes must be included in only one fragment; the primary key attributes are included in each vertical fragment.

The initial relation is restored from vertical fragments with the help of the relational operation *Join*.

Case 3.6.

> *The New York users need data about the names of all employees and codes of the departments to which employees are assigned. The Cleveland users are working with data about the types and title codes of all employees.*

The following vertical fragmentation will localize data for this case:

$$Employee_1 = \Pi_{ID, empName, deptCode} (Employee)$$

$$Employee_2 = \Pi_{ID, empType, titleCode} (Employee)$$

Employee₁ (New York):

ID	empName	deptCode
1	John	001
2	Adam	002
3	Mary	003
4	Peter	001
5	Scott	002
6	Susan	005
7	Alex	004

Employee₂ (Cleveland):

ID	emplType	titleCode
1	Full-time	T1
2	Consultant	T3
3	Part-time	T4
4	Full-time	T2
5	Consultant	T1
6	Full-time	T5
7	Part-time	T2

The initial relation is restored by joining the fragments:

$$Employee = Employee_1 \blacktriangleright\!\blacktriangleleft_{ID} Employee_2$$

3.6. Hybrid Fragmentation

Applying fragmentations of different types to the same relation is called hybrid (also mixed or nested) fragmentation.

Case 3.7.

Users in each city process data about the local departments and the names of local employees. In Cleveland, they have an additional office that works with data about the types and title codes of all employees, and this office has its own database server.

Local users of each city do not need all the data about local employees, only the ID and name. They also need the department code to associate an employee with the local department to which the employee is assigned. We can start with the vertical fragmentation of the relation Employee to separate the data about employees that is needed by all local users from data needed by the additional application in Cleveland, and then perform horizontal fragmentation to localize data about departments and employees.

Step1: vertical fragmentation of Employee is similar to the fragmentation of the Case 3.6.

$$Employee_1 = \Pi_{ID, empName, deptCode} (Employee)$$

$$Employee_2 = \Pi_{ID, empType, titleCode} (Employee)$$

Step 2: primary horizontal fragmentation of Department.

$$Department_1 = \sigma_{location = 'Boston'} (Department)$$

$$Department_2 = \sigma_{location = 'New York'} (Department)$$

$$Department_3 = \sigma_{location = 'Cleveland'} (Department)$$

Step 3: derived horizontal fragmentation of the vertical fragment Employee$_1$.

$$Employee_{11} = Employee_1 \ltimes_{deptCode} Department_1$$

$$Employee_{12} = Employee_1 \ltimes_{deptCode} Department_2$$

$$Employee_{13} = Employee_1 \ltimes_{deptCode} Department_3$$

The relation Employee can be restored from the fragments with the help of the union and join operations:

$$Employee = (Employee_{11} \cup Employee_{12} \cup Employee_{13}) \bowtie_{ID} Employee_2$$

Data is distributed in the following way.

Boston database:

Department₁

deptCode	deptName	location	deptType
001	Computer Center	Boston	IT
003	Marketing	Boston	Production

Employee₁₁

ID	empName	deptCode
2	Adam	001
4	Peter	003

New York database:

Department₂

deptCode	deptName	location	deptType
002	Budget	New York	Business
005	Purchasing	New York	Business

Employee₁₂

ID	empName	deptCode
1	John	002
5	Scott	002
6	Susan	005

Cleveland database in the second office:

Cleveland database in the first office:

Department₃

deptCode	deptName	location	deptType
004	Database Support	Cleveland	IT

Employee₁₃

ID	empName	deptCode
3	Mary	004
7	Alex	004

Employee₂

ID	emplType	titleCode
1	Full-time	T1
2	Consultant	T3
3	Part-time	T4
4	Full-time	T2
5	Consultant	T1
6	Full-time	T5
7	Part-time	T2

The relation Title was not fragmented because there were no user requirements that would make the distribution of this relation relevant. Let us discuss the allocation of the table Title. The relation Title is a parent to the relation Employee; for this fragmentation it is a parent to the fragment Employee₂ because the attribute titleCode, which is the foreign key to Title, is included in the fragment Employee₂. Because the table Title is used together with the table Employee₂, it has to be located in the same database – the first office in Cleveland.

Diagram for this hybrid fragmentation is shown in Figure 3-8.

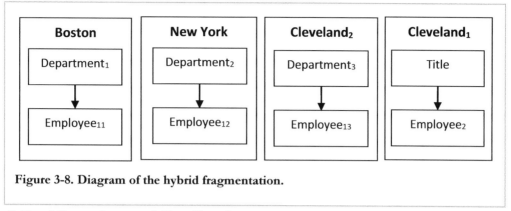

Figure 3-8. Diagram of the hybrid fragmentation.

3.7. *Allocation and Replication*

3.7.1 Allocation

Distributed design includes the allocation of fragments and relations in individual databases comprising the distributed database. Some fragments and relations can be replicated in several databases. Decisions about the allocation and replication of data are determined by the primary goals of distributed databases: improving performance and increasing data availability through data localization.

The allocation of *fragments* is defined by the fragmentation itself – we fragment in order to localize data. Therefore, each fragment goes to the database where the conditions of data define access for users directly working with it. For example, because users of Boston request data about local departments with the help of queries constrained by ... WHERE location = 'Boston', we defined the predicate p_1: location = 'Boston', and therefore, the fragment Department$_1$ obtained by this predicate will be allocated in the Boston database. Derived fragments are allocated in the same database as their corresponding primary fragments.

The goal of allocation of *unfragmented relations* is the same as the general goal of distributed design – to localize data and minimize data transfer costs. For example, in the case of the hybrid fragmentation, the unfragmented relation Title is allocated in the database of the first Cleveland office because it is used together with Employee$_2$, which is located there.

For the case of derived fragmentation shown in Figure 3-6 we did not discuss the allocation of the unfragmented relation Title. This relation can be used locally together with each fragment of the relation Employee. Because we do not expect the table Title to be large and updated often, it will not be expensive to replicate it on each site, giving local access to it for each application. In this case, replication enforces the localization of data – see Figure 3-9 with replicas of Title at New York and Cleveland databases.

When making decisions about allocation and replication, the following factors are taken into consideration:

- *Sites where relations and fragments are used.* A fragment is allocated on the site, where data from it is used, and unfragmented relation is allocated on the site where it is most frequently used.
- *Size of relations and fragments and amounts of requested data.* In order to localize data it is often beneficial to replicate a relation of a modest size. A fragment or a relation is allocated to minimize the amount of data transferred between databases.
- *Expected frequency of data modifications.* It is not recommended to replicate a relation that is often modified – modifications of several copies of data located in different databases may worsen the performance of modifying queries.

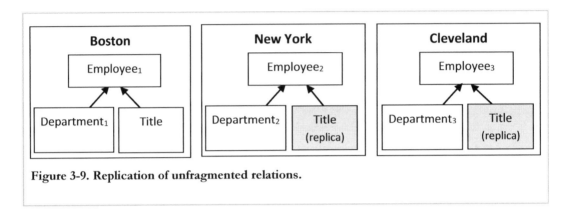

Figure 3-9. Replication of unfragmented relations.

3.7.2 Replication

The main purposes of replication are improving data availability and reliability, and localizing data. If we want data to be available as the business requires it (often it is 24/7), we will want to have data in a separate database and be synchronized with the data in the store we are working on. Further in this chapter we will show that in some cases of distribution it is beneficial to replicate some data to fully localize data access.

The most important support problem of replicated data is the synchronization of replicas. In some cases, replicated data has to be updated immediately after the modification of the source data; such replication is called *synchronous*[10]. An alternative to synchronous replication is *asynchronous* replication, where the update of replicated data is delayed (the delay may be from seconds to hours or days). Asynchronous replication is used when the immediate modification of replicas is not beneficial to the performance of the distributed database or when immediate modification is not possible (e.g., the remote site is not available).

In the replicated database it is important to define the sites from which replicated data can be modified; such sites are called *master sites*. Sites on which data is available only for reading are called *slave* or *snapshot*. Figure 3-10 shows the scheme of access to data in the replicated database with two master and one slave sites. When data is modified on one of the master sites, modifications are replicated on the two other sites of the database: the master and the slave.

---

[10] Note that synchronous replication can be supported with the help of triggers where for each operation in one database a similar operation is performed in other databases.

The data can be read from all three sites.

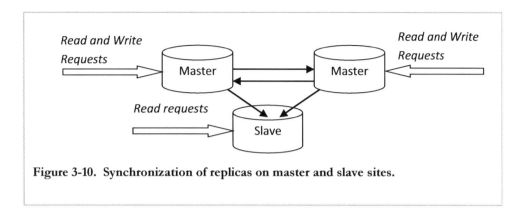

Figure 3-10. Synchronization of replicas on master and slave sites.

3.7.3 Replication in Oracle

Oracle supports multi-master and snapshot replication. Replicas are defined and supported by special database tools.

Additionally, snapshot replication of separate tables can be implemented with the help of the Oracle *materialized view* object (the materialized view is the advanced snapshot, which can be refreshed when the source table is modified).

An interesting feature of Oracle replication is *procedural replication*. When transactions change large amounts of replicated data, the network is overloaded by transfers of changed rows to synchronize replicas. In order to avoid this, data modifications are implemented in stored procedures. Then, such stored procedures are replicated on different sites. When the modification procedure is started on one site, the replicated copies of this procedure are started on other sites and modify the data in the same way as the data are modified on the initiation site. Therefore, only calls to procedures are passed across the network

3.8. Preserving Semantics of the Relational Model

3.8.1 Integrity Control

The semantics of the database should not be affected by the way data are stored. One of the mentioned problems of the distributed database is the necessity of additional support of relational semantics. The semantics of the relational model are expressed by the structure of the relations and two integrity constraints: the primary and foreign keys. Correct fragmentation preserves the structure of the relations. However, integrity constraints, as we will show, are not preserved in the fragmented database and require special attention.

3.8.2 The Primary Key

In Case 3.1, the relation Department was fragmented into three fragments by conditions on the column location. For each fragment of Department, the attribute deptCode is defined as the primary key to support the constraint locally:

Department₁ (deptCode, deptName, location, deptType)

Department₂ (deptCode, deptName, location, deptType)

Department₃ (deptCode, deptName, location, deptType)

However, local constraints do not prevent duplicating values of deptCode in the distributed database. For example, though we have the department with deptCode '001' in the Boston database, it is possible to add another department with deptCode '001' to the New York fragment:

Boston:

deptCode	deptName	location	deptType
001	Computer Center	Boston	IT
003	Marketing	Boston	Production

New York:

deptCode	deptName	location	deptType
002	Budget	New York	Business
005	Purchasing	New York	Business
001	...	...	...

Most distributed DBMSs do not support global integrity constraints, and to preserve the semantics of the relational model we need to implement its support. Usually, in addition to integrity constraints, data integrity is supported by special procedural database objects called *Triggers*. Triggers are special procedures that are defined on particular events of a table and they start every time these events happen. A global primary key of the relation Department can be implemented with the help of a trigger for the insert event on each fragment of the relation. For every inserted row, the trigger will check the other fragments for duplication of the deptCode of the newly inserted row and if it finds a duplicate, then the insertion will be rejected (see the Section 3.9 of this chapter for examples of triggers for integrity support).

Let us discuss a different situation with fragmentation of the relation Department: users in Boston work with data about departments with codes below '003', users in New York work with data of all other departments, and users in Cleveland do not work with departments' data. This leads us to the following fragmentation of Department:

$$\text{Department}_1 = \sigma_{\text{deptCode} < \text{'003'}} (\text{Department})$$
$$\text{Department}_2 = \sigma_{\text{deptCode} >= \text{'003'}} (\text{Department})$$

Each fragment inherits the primary key of the initial relation to support uniqueness locally. Do we need to support a global primary key in this case? Obviously not – any record added to the second fragment cannot have a duplicate in the first fragment, and any record added to the first fragment cannot have a duplicate in the second fragment. Disjointness of predicates, and in this case predicates that are defined on the attribute of the primary key, guarantee this.

> **If predicates, by which a relation is fragmented, include an attribute of the primary key, then global integrity is enforced by the disjointeness of the predicates. When fragmentation is performed by conditions based on the non-key attributes, then additional measures are required to support global integrity.**

If the primary key of a derived fragment includes the foreign key by which the derived fragmentation is performed, then the primary key of the derived fragment is enforced globally by the fragmentation. Otherwise, like in the case of the derived fragmentation of the relation Employee of the Manufacturing Company case, additional global support of the primary key of the derived fragment is required.

Support of global integrity with the help of triggers compromises the localization of data. When performing local data processing, an application has to access remote databases, and, therefore, becomes dependent on their availability. The local performance of modifying operations becomes worse. To avoid these complications, it is recommended to apply other measures. For example, for fragmentation of the relation Department based on the location attribute, we can agree that each database uses its own pool of values for the attribute deptCode. This agreement will be enforced by the CHECK constraint on each fragment of the relation Department, e.g. if in the New York office codes of departments cannot exceed '333', then the New York fragment will be created as follows:

```
CREATE TABLE Department (
    deptCode CHAR(3) PRIMARY KEY CHECK (deptCode <='333'),
    . . . );
```

In some cases, the uniqueness of a primary key is supported outside the particular business. For example, if instead of IDs of employees, the Manufacturing Company used their social security numbers, the uniqueness of which is supported globally across the country, there will be no need to support the uniqueness of IDs across the company. However, in the case of the distributed solution, the uniqueness of social security numbers does not guarantee that the same employee is not assigned to several departments in different cities, and we will have to use triggers on the independent databases comprising our distributed database.

3.8.3   The Foreign Key

The relation Employee has two foreign keys: deptCode and titleCode. In the case of the derived fragmentation considered in section 3.4.3, the fragmentation of the relation Employee was derived from the fragmentation of the relation Department and each fragment of Employee contains employees assigned to the departments of the primary fragment of Department located on the same site. Each fragment of Employee has the local fragment of Department as a parent. This is clearly seen in the diagram of the fragmentation in Figure 3-7.

The foreign key constraint on a field that participates in derived fragmentation has to be defined as a foreign key on each derived fragment to the corresponding primary fragment.

The situation with the second foreign key – titleCode – is different and depends on several design decisions. First, we need to know where the parent relation Title is located.

If we decide to replicate the unfragmented relation Title on each site, then this parent relation will be fully available to each child fragment of the relation Employee. Such a distributed approach will enable us to declare the attribute titleCode of each fragment as the foreign key to the corresponding (located on the same site) replica of the relation Title (see Figure 3-9).

Figure 3-11 shows the diagram of fragmentation for a different distributed solution, when the relation Title is located on the Cleveland site only and the New York and Boston fragments of Employee have no local parent table for the foreign key titleCode. The foreign key cannot be declared to a remote parent table and, therefore, in the New York and Boston databases this constraint has to be implemented with the help of a trigger on each fragment of the relation Employee (see section 3.9 of this chapter for examples of triggers for integrity support). For every insert of an employee, the trigger will check the Cleveland table Title for the existence of the title code of the inserted row; if the title code is not found, then the insertion will be rejected. In the Cleveland database, the fragment of Employee can reference the local relation Title.

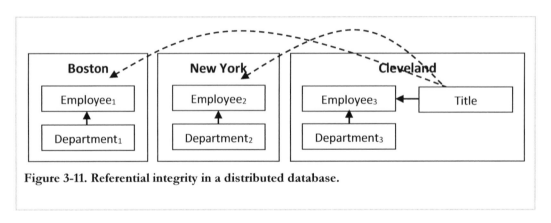

Figure 3-11. Referential integrity in a distributed database.

The support of a foreign key that is not involved in a derived fragmentation depends not only on the location of the parent relation, but also on whether it is fragmented or not. Consider a situation when the relation Title is fragmented by conditions on the salary attribute:

$$Title_1 = \sigma_{Salary < 20000} (Title)$$

$$Title_2 = \sigma_{Salary >= 20000} (Title)$$

The fragments are located in the New York and Cleveland databases, and the diagram of fragmentation is shown in Figure 3-12.

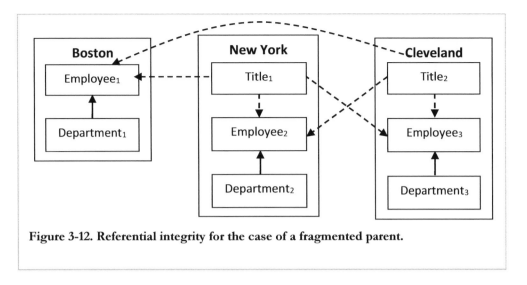

Figure 3-12. Referential integrity for the case of a fragmented parent.

The diagram of fragmentation in this case is even more complicated than in the previous example: each fragment of Employee is related to two fragments of Title. Referential integrity for titleCode has to be supported with the help of triggers. In the Boston database, the trigger will have to check two remote databases – the New York and Cleveland – for existence of the title code of a newly inserted row. Triggers in New York and Cleveland will have to check the local and remote fragments of Title. If the value of the title code is not found, the insertion of the new row is rejected. Note that for this situation, for fragments of Employee in the New York and Cleveland databases, the foreign keys to the local fragments of the relation Title cannot be defined because they would limit the title codes of employees to the codes of their local fragment.

> **The implementation of the foreign key constraint on a column that does not participate in derived fragmentation depends on where the parent relation is located and whether it is fragmented or not. The foreign key constraint cannot be established to the parent relation on another site or to a fragment of the parent relation.**

3.8.4 The Integrity of Vertical Fragmentation

The main problem in a vertically fragmented relation is the synchronization of insert and delete operations on the fragments. For example, for the Case 3.6 we have to ensure that if a row is inserted in one fragment of the relation Employee, then the row for the same employee is added to the second fragment. Similarly, if data about a particular employee are being deleted from the database, the data must be deleted from both vertical fragments of the relation Employee. We can implement this with the help of special procedures for inserting and deleting data[11]; each of the procedures will perform a corresponding action on the fragments in both

---

[11] Direct INSERT and DELETE operations on the tables have to be forbidden, and users only will have permission to execute the procedures. See Chapter 4 on security that explains how to accomplish this.

databases. Deletes can also be implemented via triggers.

Similar measures can be discussed for updates of the key attributes that are included in all vertical fragments. However we must remember that it is recommended to choose the key attributes of a relation so that they do not change their value during the lifetime of a row.

3.8.5 Other Constraints

Most DBMSs support the NOT NULL and CHECK constraints. These are single-row constraints – they are separately evaluated on each row of a relation (as opposed to the primary and foreign key constraints, the evaluation of which involves other rows of the relation itself or the parent relation).

The NOT NULL constraint does not require any special support; it is applied on each fragment of a relation.

The CHECK constraint may change if a relation is fragmented by conditions on the column with the constraint. Assume that there is the CHECK constraint on the column salary of the relation Title:

> ...CHECK Salary BETWEEN 10000 AND 50000.

For fragments of Title:

$$Title_1 = \sigma_{Salary < 20000} (Title)$$

$$Title_2 = \sigma_{Salary >= 20000} (Title)$$

the CHECK constraint will be simplified:

> $Title_1$: CHECK Salary >= 10000

> $Title_2$: CHECK Salary <= 50000.

3.8.6 Transparency of Distribution

It is important to make the distributed database appear to users as a centralized database, or, in other words, to make the distribution transparent to users. In Chapter 2 we discussed the ways of achieving transparency of physical and logical details of the database with the help of synonyms, views, and procedures.

Transparency of distribution is needed for users who work with data from different databases; we call such users global. For these users, we need to reconstruct data from fragments and hide the allocation of fragments and relations. The simplest way to achieve this transparency is to use views with the reconstruction of all data: the union of fragments for horizontal fragmentation and the join of fragments for vertical fragmentation. Such views have to be created in the database where the users perform global access to the data. For the Manufacturing Company case, transparency of distribution has to be implemented in the New

York database, where the users access data about all departments and employees of the company.

3.9. Examples: Implementing a Distributed Database in Oracle

Let us follow the steps of distributed design for the Manufacturing Company case. Analysis of company's applications and local needs in data led us to the following distributed design.

Primary fragmentation of the relation Department:

$$Department_1 = \sigma_{location = \text{'Boston'}} (Department)$$

$$Department_2 = \sigma_{location = \text{'New York'}} (Department)$$

$$Department_3 = \sigma_{location = \text{'Cleveland'}} (Department)$$

Derived fragmentation of the relation Employee:

$$Employee_1 = Employee \blacktriangleright Department_1$$

$$Employee_2 = Employee \blacktriangleright Department_2$$

$$Employee_3 = Employee \blacktriangleright Department_3$$

The relation Title is left unfragmented.

Considering the needs in data, we decide on the allocation of fragments and relations that is shown in Figure 3-13:

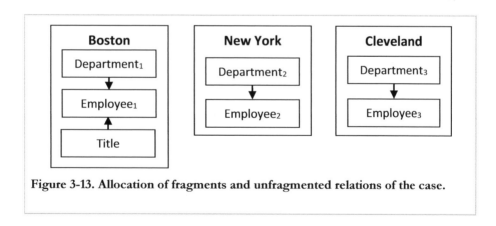

Figure 3-13. Allocation of fragments and unfragmented relations of the case.

Because the data from the table Title may be used by every site and the table is not large and it does not change often, it makes sense to replicate it on each site. However, for the demonstration of support of global referential integrity with the help of triggers we will allocate Title in the Boston database.

Because the New York and Cleveland databases are similar, we will continue our discussion for the Boston and New York sites only. Assume that in the New York database there is a database link to the Boston database. This link is needed for global users and implementation of the global integrity:

```
CREATE PUBLIC DATABASE LINK boston USING
boston.ourcompany.us.com;
```

To implement global integrity in the Boston database, we will need the database link to the New York database:

```
CREATE PUBLIC DATABASE LINK ny USING
ny.ourcompany.us.com;
```

Implementation of the distributed database will include the following steps:

1. Create tables for fragments and unfragmented relations in each database according to the design. The fragmentation of Department is enforced by the CHECK constraint on the attribute location. The correctness of the fragments of Employee is supported by referential integrity on deptCode of each fragment.
2. Create a trigger[12] on each fragment of Department to support the global integrity of deptCode (because primary fragmentation of Department is based on the non-key attribute location).
3. Create a trigger on each fragment of Employee to support the global integrity of ID (because Employee is fragmented by the non-key attribute deptCode).
4. Implement the referential integrity of deptCode for Employee (fragments of Employee are derived from fragments of Department, and we can define deptCode of each Employee fragment as the foreign key to the corresponding fragment of Department).
5. Implement the referential integrity of titleCode. It is supported differently on two sites: the fragment of Employee in the Boston database can reference Title because it is located on the same site, while for the fragment of Employee in the New York database we will simulate referential integrity by the use of a trigger.
6. Implement local transparency.
7. Implement transparency of distribution in the New York database.

	Boston	New York

1.	`CREATE TABLE Department (`
	`    deptCode CHAR(3) PRIMARY KEY,`
	`    deptName VARCHAR2(20) NOT`
	`    NULL,`
	`    location VARCHAR2(25) CHECK`
	`    (location = 'Boston'),`
	`    deptType VARCHAR2(15));`
	
	`CREATE TABLE Employee (`
	`    ID NUMBER PRIMARY KEY,`
	`    empName VARCHAR2(30) NOT`
	`    NULL,`
		`CREATE TABLE Department (`
		`    deptCode CHAR(3) PRIMARY KEY,`
		`    deptName VARCHAR2(20) NOT`
		`    NULL,`
		`    location VARCHAR2(25) CHECK`
		`    (location = 'New York'),`
		`    deptType VARCHAR2(15));`
		
		`CREATE TABLE Employee (`
		`    ID NUMBER PRIMARY KEY,`
		`    empName VARCHAR2(30) NOT`
		`    NULL,`

---

[12] We apply this type of global integrity support to demonstrate triggers. As mentioned before, it is better to constraint values of deptCode in each database with the help of the CHECK constraint.

	`empType VARCHAR2(10),`
	`deptCode CHAR(3),`
	`titleCode CHAR(2));`
	
	`CREATE TABLE Title (`
	`        titleCode CHAR(2) PRIMARY`
	`        KEY,`
	`        titleDescription`
	`        VARCHAR2(25),`
	`        salary NUMBER);`
		`empType VARCHAR2(10),`
		`deptCode CHAR(3),`
		`titleCode CHAR(2));`

2.	*Create a trigger for support of the global primary key of Department.*	*Create a trigger for support of the global primary key of Department.*
3.	*Create a trigger for support of the global primary key of Employee.*	*Create a trigger for support of the global primary key of Employee.*

4.	`ALTER TABLE Employee`
	`ADD CONSTRAINT`
	`fk_employee_department FOREIGN KEY`
	`(deptCode) REFERENCES Department;`
		`ALTER TABLE Employee`
		`ADD CONSTRAINT`
		`fk_employee_department FOREIGN KEY`
		`(deptCode) REFERENCES Department;`

5.	`ALTER TABLE Employee`
	`ADD CONSTRAINT fk_employee_title`
	`FOREIGN KEY (titleCode) REFERENCES`
	`Title;`
		Create a trigger for support of the foreign key to Title in the Boston database.

6.	`CREATE VIEW vw_Employee AS` `SELECT * FROM Employee;`	`CREATE VIEW vw_Employee AS` `SELECT * FROM Employee;`

7.		`CREATE VIEW vw_allEmployees AS`
		`SELECT * FROM Employee`
		`    UNION`
		`SELECT * FROM Employee@Boston;`

The trigger in the Boston database for support of the global primary key of Department can be implemented in the following way:

```
CREATE OR REPLACE TRIGGER tr_department_code
BEFORE INSERT OR UPDATE OF deptCode ON Department
FOR EACH ROW
DECLARE
    sDeptCode VARCHAR2(3);
BEGIN
    SELECT deptCode INTO sDeptCode
    FROM Department@ny WHERE deptCode = :NEW.deptCode;
    -- looking for deptCode of the inserted record in the
table Department
    -- on another site. If we are here, then the select was
successful.
    -- If we have a duplicate, the insert must be rejected.
```

```
    RAISE_APPLICATION_ERROR (-20999, ' Duplication of
deptCode');
EXCEPTION
   WHEN NO_DATA_FOUND THEN

   -- If we are here, then select did not return any data.
   -- No action is needed.
 NULL;
END;
```

The trigger in the New York database for support of the global foreign key titleCode of Employee could be implemented in the following way:

```
CREATE OR REPLACE TRIGGER tr_employee_title
BEFORE INSERT OR UPDATE OF titleCode ON Employee
FOR EACH ROW
DECLARE
   sTitleCode VARCHAR2(2);
BEGIN
   SELECT titleCOde INTO sTitleCode
   FROM Title@Boston WHERE titleCode = :NEW.titleCode;
   -- looking for titleCode of the inserted record in the
table Title.
   -- If we are here, then the select was successful.
   -- The record can be inserted.
EXCEPTION
   WHEN NO_DATA_FOUND THEN
   -- If we are here, select did not return any data.
   -- Integrity is violated. Insert must be rejected.
 RAISE_APPLICATION_ERROR (-20999, ' Non-existing titleCode');
END;
```

If we chose another approach and decided to replicate the table Title on each site, then we could implement replication with the help of materialized views. Assume that the Boston site is in charge of supporting data about titles and it is the master site for this data. As in the previous design, the table Title will be created in the Boston database. The New York and Cleveland databases will have replicas of this table implemented as materialized views:

```
CREATE MATERIALIZED VIEW Title
   PARALLEL
   BUILD IMMEDIATE
   REFRESH FAST ON COMMIT
   AS SELECT * FROM Title@Boston;
```

Additionally, we will need to create a view log on the master tables – the table Title in the Boston database as shown below:

```
   CREATE MATERIALIZED VIEW LOG ON Title;
```

The option REFRESH ON COMMIT causes the view to be refreshed every time the table Title in the Boston database is modified. Applications on the New York and Cleveland sites will be able to use data from Title without remote accesses to the Boston database.

Starting with Oracle 9i, the materialized view has a primary key and technically can be referenced by a table. Therefore, the titleCode attribute of fragments of Employee in the New York and Cleveland databases can be implemented as the foreign key to the corresponding materialized view. Each site will be fully localized and independent from others.

3.10. Summary

Distributing data across several database servers is one of the options used in performing the physical design of a database. The distributed database can be beneficial for a company that runs applications that need only specific portions of the data. By localizing the data and bringing the required portions of data directly to the users of the applications, the distributed database can significantly improve the performance of such applications. The distributed design can improve data reliability and availability by replicating data in several of the databases that are part of the distributed database; it can provide a better scalability of the database and database applications.

The decision on the distribution of data requires a thorough analysis of the company's structure, the different needs of users in data, and the organization of the company's network.

The design of a distributed database includes fragmentation of relations of the logical model, allocation of fragments and unfragmented relations, and replication. Fragmentation, allocation and replication are performed to achieve the main goals of the distributed database – localization of data and improvement of performance of the most important applications, and increased reliability and availability of data.

Relations can be fragmented horizontally and vertically. Each fragmentation must be complete and disjoint. If a parent relation is fragmented horizontally, it is often reasonable to consider derived horizontal fragmentation of a child relation. A global relation is restored by the union of horizontal fragments and by the join of vertical fragments.

The distributed database must be transparent to users – they should see it as a centralized database. The transparency of distribution must be implemented by database programmers.

Distributed DBMSs do not support global relational constraints. Preserving the semantics of the relational model is one of the problems of implementation of the distributed database. Relational semantics is implemented with the help of special procedures – triggers, or by applying organizational measures and limiting possible values of the key attributes in different databases.

Though it was mentioned that one of the problems of distributed databases is the absence of a straightforward methodology of design, the following sequence of steps can serve as the design guidance:

- *Analyzing the structure of a company.* Research the topology of a company and its network. Define the locations of the databases.
- *Defining the needs in data.* Examine applications of the company, define the most important and frequently used ones. Understand the applications' needs in data.
- *Designing fragmentation.* Consider horizontal and/or vertical fragmentation of relations that could improve the performance of the company's important applications.
- *Performing derived fragmentation.* When performing horizontal fragmentation of several relations with relationships between them, first consider primary fragmentation of the owner of a relationship, and then proceed with derived fragmentation of the members of the relationship. Remember that derived fragmentation has several benefits: 1) it gives a simple diagram of fragmentation with no or few relationships between fragments and relations located in different databases; 2) it enhances the parallel execution of global queries; 3) it does not require special support of referential integrity. In summary, derived fragmentation results in a good and "clean" localization of data.
- *Allocating and replicating fragments and relations.* Allocate fragments according to distributed design and allocate unfragmented relations to enhance data localization. Consider replicating unfragmented relations that are used on different sites, are not too large, and are not modified too often. Replicate important data that are crucial for the functioning of the system.
- *Supporting relational semantics.* Implement global support of integrity constraints of the database.
- *Making distribution transparent.* Implement transparency of distribution, make the distributed database appear like a centralized database to the users.

Review Questions

- What are the promises and problems of distributed databases?
- How can distribution increase the reliability of the database?
- How can distribution improve the performance on the database?
- What is localization of data? How can localization be achieved?
- What are the information requirements for horizontal and vertical fragmentations?
- How do you define correctness for horizontal and vertical fragmentation?
- How many vertical fragments can you have for the relation R($\underline{A, B}$, C)?
- When is derived fragmentation possible? What are the benefits of derived fragmentation?
- How you restore a relation from its fragments?
- What are the benefits and disadvantages of replication?
- What transparencies must be implemented in the distributed database?
- How do you implement transparency of allocation and fragmentation in the distributed database?
- Does distribution change the semantics of the database?
- Which distributed situations require special support of global relational semantics?

Practical Assignments

1. It is know that the Manufacturing Company discussed in this chapter is planning to expand and will be opening several new offices in different cities. These offices will not have database servers and data for them will be processed on the New York server. For this

situation, redefine the predicates of horizontal fragmentation of the relation Department from the case 3.1.

2. For the Car Rental Company case explain why the following fragmentations are either incorrect or irrelevant:

a) p_1 : city = 'X' AND type = 'truck'
p_2 : city = 'X' AND type <> 'truck'
p_3 : city = 'Y' AND type = 'truck'
p_4 : city = 'Y' AND type <> 'truck'
p_5 : city = 'Z' AND type = 'truck'
p_6 : city = 'Z' AND type <> 'truck'

b) p_1 : city = 'X' AND type = 'truck'
p_2 : city = 'Y' AND type <> 'truck'
p_3 : city = 'Z' AND type = 'truck'

c) p_1 : year = '2005'
p_2 : year = '2004'
p_3 : year <= '2003'

3. The relation Title was fragmented by predicates:

P_1 : Salary > 30000
P_2 : Salary < 30000

What rules of fragmentation are violated? How you will define the correct fragmentation for this case? Explain your answer.

4. What rules of fragmentation are violated in the following vertical fragmentations of the relation R (A, B, C, D):

a) $R_1 = \Pi_{A, B, C} (R)$
$R_2 = \Pi_{A, B, D} (R)$

b) $R_1 = \Pi_{A, B, C} (R)$
$R_2 = \Pi_{A, D} (R)$

5. What rules of fragmentation are violated in the following horizontal fragmentations of the relation R (A, B, C) where the attribute C can be any integer number:

a) p_1 : 10 <= C AND C < 100
p_2 : C >= 100

b) p_1 : 10 <= C AND C < 100
p_2 : C >= 100
p_3 : C < 10

  c) $p_1 : 10 <= C$ AND $C <= 100$
     $p_2 : C >= 100$

6. For cases from the Appendix 1.
  a) Design the distribution of data.
  b) Suggest an appropriate allocation and replication of data approach.
  c) Build the physical model of the distributed database in Oracle.
  d) Implement transparency of the distributed database.
  e) Implement integrity constraints for your distributed solutions.

7. In Chapter 2 we discussed that organizing storage, e.g. by clustering, in some cases makes data management more complex or expensive. If for example the table Employee is clustered by deptCode, and an employee is transferred to another department, then the system needs to do more work than in the case of the heap storage of the table. In case of a distributed database the burden of data management in such situations will be on the developer. For a case from the assignment 6 think how you will manage situations when due to changes of the value of the attribute by which you fragmented a table a record has to be moved from one fragment to another. Issues to consider: 1) your global support of the primary key of the table; 2) the foreign key of the child table(s); 3) the need to maintain the history of the business (we usually cannot simply delete records).

Chapter 4.   Security

Data are valuable resources which must be protected from unauthorized access, either intentional or accidental. The terms of access to data are specified in the security portion of the business rules. Security business rules are supposed to define:

- Who (which users or applications) can access data in the database?
- What portion of data each entitled user can access?
- What operations each entitled user can perform on this data?

Security measures of the database and database applications must correspond to these requirements. In this chapter, we discuss the features of DBMSs that are used for implementing *database* security.

Database security measures are only a part of the complex technological security support in today's information systems (IS). In addition to technological measures, security is supported by various administrative approaches and routines. This chapter concentrates on securing the data within the database.

4.1. Database Security

The security of data is supported at several different levels, including network, application, and database (Figure 4-1).

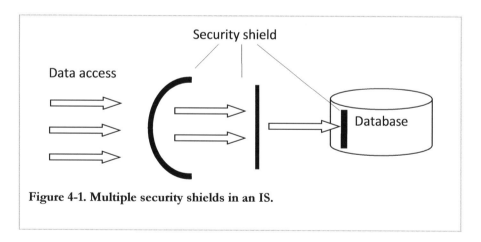

Figure 4-1. Multiple security shields in an IS.

This chapter focuses on security measures implemented in the database. Although security implemented outside the database plays an important role, it is crucial to understand that this outer security shield is not sufficient to protect the data and cannot substitute for the in-database security. The main shortcoming of the outer security shield is that it can be bypassed.

For example, let's say for the sake of argument that the user John is not allowed to access the database and the user Scott can access some portions of the data in the database. The application through which users work with the database implements the required security rules: (a) John cannot log into the application at all, (b) Scott can use the application, but his access to data is restricted by this application. However, there are no special security measures implemented in the database to prevent John or Scott from accessing data that they are not supposed to access. Therefore, if John or Scott decide to use another application, e.g. SQL*Plus in Oracle, they may be able to access the restricted data. As Figure 4-2 shows, relying on outer security measures (like security implemented in the application) and not enforcing the in-database security can lead to security breaches.

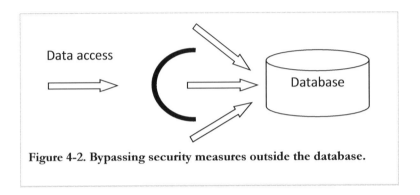

Figure 4-2. Bypassing security measures outside the database.

In-database security measures (Figure 4-3) cannot be bypassed and hence make the overall data protection more reliable.

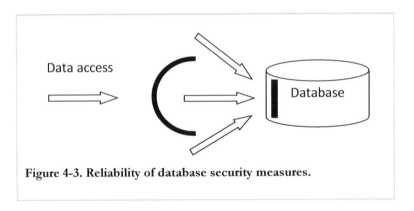

Figure 4-3. Reliability of database security measures.

Another advantage of implementing security in the database is that security policies are applied once, instead of being implemented repeatedly in different applications on the database.

Data security must be supported within the database.

To satisfy user requirements on data security, security measures must specify which users can perform which operations and on what data.

Database security is about ensuring that only authorized users can perform allowed operations on the data.

Security measures define certain relationships between *users, operations,* and *data.* The required security can be ensured by checking whether the triplet of access (user, operation, data object) is valid. For example, if the user John requests data about the age of employees from the table Employee, the system checks whether *John* has the permission to *select* from the attribute *Age* of the table Employee.

This chapter discusses security and protection from security threats such as theft and fraud, loss of confidentiality, and loss of privacy; all of which are violations of valid relationships between a user and operations the user can perform on particular data.

In some text books the discussion of security includes such issues as integrity and availability of data. We want to emphasize the difference between the concepts of security, and integrity and availability.

The integrity of data is the correspondence of data to specific structural or action-oriented business rules. It must be supported by the appropriate implementation of integrity constraints[13], and it cannot be enforced by security measures. For example, if according to a business rule which states that the values of the attribute Age in the table Employee has to be between 18 and 65, then the CHECK constraint on the attribute Age will guarantee the integrity of this attribute. However, the CHECK constraint does not implement any security control. If the security of data requires that only the user John can modify the attribute Age, then security measures have to prevent any other user from changing values of this attribute. On the other hand, security measures are not related to integrity – even with a successful implementation of security, but without the corresponding integrity constraint, the user John can make a mistake while entering data into the Age attribute and violate the correctness of data.

Security measures shield data from unauthorized access, while integrity measures protect data from any authorized changes that can violate the correctness of the data (Figure 4-4). However, in some cases integrity can be additionally enforced with the help of security tools. For example, in Chapter 3 we discussed integrity in the distributed database. For vertical fragmentation, inserting and deleting data has to be performed on all fragments, and it is recommended that the direct insert and delete operations on fragments should not be allowed. Instead, users should execute special procedures that implement the inserting and deleting of data into all fragments. Although these special procedures are implementing secure access, they also ensure the integrity of the data.

The availability of data is discussed in detail in Chapter 7. The database and other components of the IS have to be reliable to provide the availability of the data. If the database is unavailable, security measures cannot change the situation and make data available to those who are authorized to use it. On the other hand, when data is available via a properly functioning IS, it is important to secure the data and ensure that unauthorized users cannot access it (Figure 4-5).

---

[13] Either by the declarative integrity constraints in a table definition, such as PRIMARY KEY, FOREIGN KEY, CHECK, or with the help of triggers.

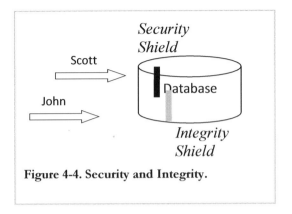

Figure 4-4. Security and Integrity.

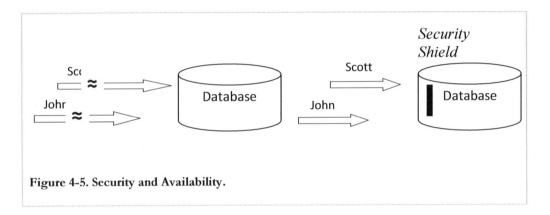

Figure 4-5. Security and Availability.

Security measures provided by DBMSs include:

- *Authentication of users*. Authentication measures define users who are entitled to work with a database and their credentials which the DBMS uses to authenticate users trying to get access to a database.
- *Authorization of access to data*. For users who are authenticated by the database, authorization measures define the kind of actions that these users can perform on that database.

Most DBMSs support a special method of protecting data – encryption. Encryption is the encoding of data by special procedures. Interpretation of encrypted data without the corresponding decryption key is difficult. Even if users can access the data, they will not be able to interpret and use the data.

In this chapter we will limit our discussions to the authentication and authorization tools of DBMSs.

4.2. The Basic Tools for Implementing Security

4.2.1   Users and Schemas

The first part in the security triplet of access is the *user*. When a user is trying to access a database resource, first the database must recognize or authenticate the user. The user name and password are the primary authentication tools. User authentication can be enhanced by additional measures, such as limiting the number of attempts to log into the database with incorrect user names/passwords, locking access to the database for a user after the submission of a certain number of incorrect passwords, or specifying an expiration date of the user's identification, and other means.

Users are objects of the database (not included in any schema). As with every other database object, a new user has to be created in the database, and then the user's identification information must be specified. This involves security issues such as who can create new database users? Can any registered database user create new users? Let us assume that there is a user, e.g. the database administrator, who can create users. Later in the chapter, we will discuss the special privileges needed for managing other users. The administrator creates the user Scott and assigns him the password 'tiger':

```
Admin>   CREATE USER Scott IDENTIFIED BY tiger;
```

After a user is created, establishing relationships between the *user*, database *objects* and *operations* has to be provided.

The fact that a user is registered in the database does not mean that he can perform any operation – for every action, which is possible in the database, the user must be given explicit permission or *privilege*. Privileges for operations are *granted* to users, e.g. granting a connection to a database in Oracle is performed as:

```
Admin>   GRANT CREATE SESSION TO Scott;
```

As security involves users, actions, and data objects, a user may be granted the privilege to perform an action on all objects of a particular type, e.g. the following statement allows the user Scott to create tables:

```
Admin>   GRANT CREATE TABLE TO Scott;
```

Creation of any other object of the database: view, snapshot, index, trigger, etc. must be explicitly granted, if allowed.

Privileges, once given, can be taken away:

```
Admin>   REVOKE CREATE TABLE FROM Scott;
```

All objects created by a particular user[14], belong to this user, or, in other words, the user is the owner of these objects. These objects compose the user's schema (Figure 4-6). The name of the schema is the same as the name of the user. Note that not all users of the database have schemas – only those who have objects. If a user is allowed to create objects, e.g. tables, this implies that the user can perform all other legal operations on the created objects, e.g. DROP,

---

[14] Or on the user's behalf by a user who has such special privileges.

ALTER, SELECT, INSERT, DELETE, and UPDATE on the tables.

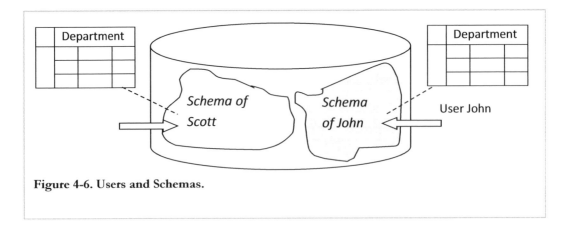

Figure 4-6. Users and Schemas.

A user does not need privileges to manipulate objects from his schema.

Having been given the database account, the create session and create table privileges, Scott can now get access to the database, create his tables and manipulate them. Scott does not see and cannot access any object from schemas of other users of the database, e.g. objects of John, without getting special privileges for access.

When accessing an object from another schema, the user has to specify the full object name, which is composed of the schema name and the object name. For example, if Scott wants to access the table Department in John's schema, the following request will not be successful:

```
Scott>   SELECT * FROM Department;
```

Instead of accessing John's table, Scott will see data of his own table Department because if the name of an object is not prefixed by the schema name, the system looks for the object in the schema of the user who issues the request. Scott will be able to see data from John's table Department with the help of the following statement:

```
Scott>   SELECT * FROM John.Department;
```

Whether this request is successful depends on the privileges granted to Scott on John's table Department.

Schemas are an efficient database security tool; they restrict users' access to objects that do not belong to them.

A user must be explicitly granted privileges for a particular type of access to an object of another user. The owner of the object (or users with special privileges that are discussed later) can grant such privileges. With the following statement, John can grant Scott the privilege to select from the table Department from his schema (note that here John refers to his table and does not need to prefix the table name by the name of the schema).

```
John>    GRANT SELECT ON Department TO Scott;
```

With only this privilege granted, Scott cannot modify data in John's table Department as for each new action on John's table, Scott needs a corresponding privilege.

Users need privileges for every operation on every data object owned by another user.

When being granted a particular privilege, a user may be authorized to pass this privilege to other users with the help of the WITH GRANT option. By the following command, John not only grants Scott the privilege to select from his table, but also gives him the right to grant this privilege to other users:

```
John>    GRANT SELECT ON Department TO Scott WITH GRANT
         OPTION;
```

Now Scott can grant the privilege to select from the table Department from John's schema to other users:

```
Scott>   GRANT SELECT ON John.Department TO Adam;
```

The WITH GRANT option has to be used with caution because it can lead to uncontrollable spreading of privileges and possible violations of security requirements.

Often users need access privileges for only some columns of a table. For example, John reconsiders the privileges of Scott and wants to limit Scott to seeing only the attributes deptCode and deptName from his table Department. This can be performed by first revoking Scott's current privilege and then granting privileges on only the specific columns needed as shown below:

```
John>    REVOKE SELECT ON Department FROM Scott;

John>    GRANT SELECT deptCode,deptName ON Department TO
         Scott;
```

4.2.2 Roles

Often numerous users of the database require similar privileges, e.g. accountants of the financial office of a company usually need similar access to data. It is difficult and time consuming to repeat the same granting actions for every user. For simplification of handling security issues, most DBMSs include a separate object *role* (or *user group*). Role is a set of privileges. After a role is created and some privileges are granted to the role, then the role (as the set of privileges) can be granted to users or other roles (Figure 4-7). For example, accountants of the financial office need several privileges on John's table Department. After creating the role for this group of users and granting to this role all required privileges, a new user-accountant can receive the needed privileges through one granting statement, like Scott in the example below:

```
Admin>   CREATE ROLE Accountant;
John>    GRANT SELECT, INSERT ON Department TO Accountant;
Admin>   GRANT Accountant TO Scott;
```

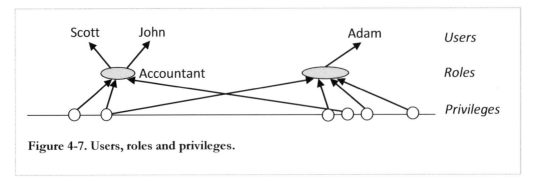

Figure 4-7. Users, roles and privileges.

Through the role Accountant, Scott was granted two privileges: SELECT and INSERT on John's table Department. This is equivalent to executing two direct corresponding GRANT commands.

Not only is it easier to pass privileges to numerous users through roles, but roles also make privilege management easier. If security requirements for a group of users change, these changes applied to the corresponding roles will be automatically reflected in privileges of the users who have been granted the roles. For example, if a new privilege is added to the role Accountant, then the privilege is automatically passed to user Scott and all other users through the role Accountant:

```
John>    GRANT UPDATE ON Department TO Accountant;

Scott>   UPDATE John.Department SET …;
```

In other words, at any given moment, a user who has been granted a particular role has the privileges associated with that role at that moment.

Compare this to the situation when SELECT and INSERT ON Department are granted to Scott and many other users-accountants directly:

```
John>     GRANT SELECT, INSERT ON Department TO Scott;
```

If one of these two privileges needs to be revoked from this group of users, multiple revoke operations – for each user in the group – needs to take place.

4.2.3   Object and System Privileges

In the previous sections, a data object from the triplet (*user, action, data object*) was a particular object of a specific schema. Privileges on particular objects are called *object* privileges, e.g. the following statement grants Scott the privilege to select from the Department table:

```
Admin>   GRANT SELECT ON Department TO Scott;
```

It is also possible to give a privilege on all data objects of a particular class in one statement, e.g. the following statement grants Scott the privilege to select from all tables:

```
Admin>   GRANT SELECT ON ANY TABLE TO Scott;
```

Such privileges are called *system* privileges. Without any additional permission, Scott will be able to select data from all tables of other users. System privileges also include such privileges as CREATE USER, CREATE ROLE, CREATE TABLE, and other privileges for special operations. System privileges have to be granted with caution.

Now we can answer the question raised at the beginning of the chapter – which users can create other users or roles? Users with the system privileges CREATE USER and CREATE ROLE can perform these operations. But who grants these users the system privileges?

The process of installation of a database usually includes the creation of a number of users with special privileges and roles, and with predefined passwords[15]. In Oracle, for example, one such user is SYS who has all privileges, including privileges to create other users and grant these users privileges. Usually, SYS creates a number of user accounts for database administrators and grants them system privileges. Then, these users can manage the other users of the database. We can think of the security system as a pyramid: from fewer users with many privileges to a larger number of users with fewer privileges – see Figure 4-8. Please note that on different levels we have different kinds of privileges: mostly system privileges on higher levels and mostly object privileges on lower levels.

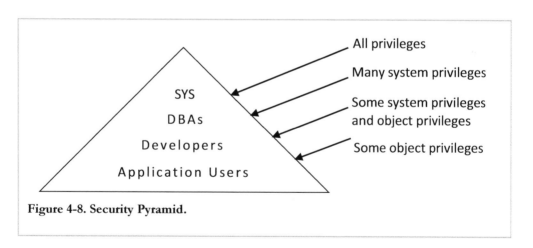

Figure 4-8. Security Pyramid.

The following scenario illustrates creation of the security pyramid:

SYS> CREATE USER DBA1 IDENTIFIED BY lion; SYS> GRANT CREATE USER TO DBA1;	SYS creates a user account that will perform administrative task, e.g.

---

[15] The passwords have to be changed upon installation.

...	creating user accounts.

`DBA1> CREATE USER scott IDENTIFIED BY tiger;`
`DBA1> GRANT CONNECT TO scott;`
`DBA1> GRANT CREATE TABLE TO scott;`
...
	DBA1 creates an account for a database developer who will need to create different database objects.

`DBA1> CREATE USER john IDENTIFIED BY panther;` `DBA1> GRANT CONNECT TO john;`	DBA1 creates an account for a database user who will be using objects created by developers.

`Scott> CREATE TABLE foo (...);`
`Scott> GRANT SELECT ON foo TO john;`
...
	Scott creates a table and grants some privileges on this table to John.

We discussed how object privileges are passed from one user to another – the owner of an object can grant privileges on operations on the object to other users with the grant option. System privileges can be passed to other users when they are granted with the ADMIN OPTION, e.g. the administrator grants Scott the privilege to create users and to grant this privilege to other users:

```
Admin>  GRANT CREATE USER TO Scott WITH ADMIN OPTION;
```

Now Scott can grant (revoke) the privilege to create users to (from) other users. It is not recommended to give privileges with the admin option to regular (non-administrative) users of the database.

4.3. Database Objects and Security

Usually, security requirements are more complicated than the requirements mentioned in the previous section, and the basic security tools are not sufficient to implement all the requirements. Other database objects, such as views and procedures, are often used for enhancing security.

4.3.1 Views

With the security measures discussed before, the finest grain of security that can be achieved is a column of a table. However, in many cases, users are required to access only particular rows of a table. For example, for the table Department in the Manufacturing Company database, users from Cleveland can access only the rows of the departments located in Cleveland.

Such security requirements can be implemented with the help of views. In Chapter 2 we showed how views are used to implement the transparency of the data in the centralized database and the transparency of the fragmentation in the distributed database. Views are also an important tool for implementing security.

In the case where a user is supposed to access only certain data in a table, the user should not be granted access to the table (or might have privileges revoked on the table in case the user was previously granted the privileges). Instead, the user can be granted access to a view defined on the table. If a view is defined on particular columns and rows of the table, the user would be able to access only these columns and rows through the view (Figure 4-9).

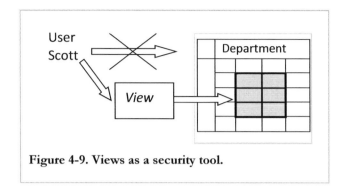

Figure 4-9. Views as a security tool.

View processing includes transforming the query on the view into the query on the view definition. For example, the user John creates a view and grants reading privileges on the view to Scott (while revoking the reading privileges on the whole table):

```
John>    CREATE VIEW vw_Department AS
         SELECT deptCode, DeptName
         FROM Department WHERE location = 'Cleveland';

John>    REVOKE SELECT ON Department FROM Scott;

John>    GRANT SELECT ON vw_Department TO Scott;
```

Now Scott can select only from the view:

```
Scott>   SELECT * FROM John.vw_Department;
```

In Scott's request, the name of the view is substituted by the view definition and the request is transformed into the following query:

```
SELECT * FROM
(SELECT deptCode, DeptName
FROM John.Department WHERE location = 'Cleveland');
```

With such a security solution, Scott cannot see data beyond the view definition.

Views can be used for data modification as well. If in addition to the select privilege, Scott is granted the update privilege on the view, he can update data in the table Department through the view:

```
John>    GRANT UPDATE ON vw_Department TO Scott;

Scott>   UPDATE John.vw_Department SET deptName = 'New name'
         WHERE deptCode = '004';
```

Views can prevent passing data inconsistent with the view definition into the view's table. This is accomplished with the help of CHECK OPTION. Let us redefine the view vw_Department:

```
John>    CREATE VIEW vw_Department AS
         SELECT deptCode, DeptName
         FROM Department WHERE location = 'Cleveland'
         WITH CHECK OPTION CONSTRAINT Department_Cleveland;
```

Now the check option constraint will control the data inserted into the table through the view corresponding to the view's conditions. For example, after Scott is granted the insert privilege on the view, his first insert into the table Department will be successful, while the second will fail because the inserted value 'Boston' for the attribute location is inconsistent with the view's constraint location = 'Cleveland':

```
John>    GRANT INSERT ON vw_Department TO Scott;

Scott>   INSERT INTO John.vw_Department VALUES
         ('999', 'Accounts Payable', 'Cleveland'); (succeeds)

Scott>   INSERT INTO John.vw_Department VALUES
         ('888', 'Accounts Receivable', 'Boston'); (fails)
```

Definitions of views may be more complicated, e.g. can include joins or aggregates. Each DBMS has specific limitations on the possibilities of modifying data through complex views.

4.3.2 Stored Procedures

In Chapter 2 we discussed how stored procedures are used for implementing transparency of allocation and distribution. Stored procedures are also used for support of data security. Like views, procedures provide indirect access to specific portions of a table's data when full access to the table is not allowed.

Consider the security requirements that were supported with the help of the view in the previous section — Scott can access only data about the Cleveland departments from John's table Department. To implement these requirements using stored procedures, we create two procedures — for updates and inserts on the table:

```
John> CREATE PROCEDURE update_Cleveland
         (par_deptCode CHAR, par_deptName VARCHAR2) AS
         BEGIN
            UPDATE Department SET deptName = par_deptName
               WHERE deptCode = par_deptcode AND location =
               'Cleveland';
         END;


John> CREATE PROCEDURE insert_Cleveland
         (par_deptCode CHAR, par_deptName VARCHAR2) AS
         BEGIN
            INSERT INTO Department
```

```
                    VALUES (par_deptCode, par_deptName, 'Cleveland');
            END;
```

The user Scott is denied the privileges of performing direct operations on the table Department and is granted the privileges to execute these procedures. Note that the procedure for updates – update_Cleveland – ensures that the updated department is located in Cleveland (if the department is located in another city or does not exist, no rows are updated). The second procedure for inserts – insert_Cleveland – assigns Cleveland as the location for the new department.

```
John>    GRANT EXECUTE update_Cleveland, insert_Cleveland
            TO Scott;

Scott>   EXEC John.insert_Cleveland ('999', 'Accounts
            Payable');
```

Parameters of this procedure call are passed to the INSERT statement of the procedure and the following insert takes place:

```
INSERT INTO John.Department
VALUES ('999', 'Accounts Payable', 'Cleveland');
```

Procedures enable the implementation of complicated security requirements that cannot be supported by the basic security measures or views.

4.3.3 Synonyms

In the previous sections we showed that the objects used for implementing transparency – views and procedures – can be effective security tools because through them, users can get access to specific portions of data of the table without getting access to the whole table. Another transparency object – synonym – is not used for implementing security because it is just an additional name for a database object and users can access the synonym only if they have the corresponding access privileges on the object itself. For example, if John creates a public synonym for his table Department, other users will need privileges on the table in order to access the synonym. Below, Scott succeeds in accessing the synonym, while Adam who does not have access privileges on the table, fails:

```
John>    CREATE PUBLIC SYNONYM syn_Department FOR
            Department;

John>    GRANT SELECT ON Department TO Scott;
```

Because we used the option PUBLIC in the definition of the synonym, all users will be able to see and use it without referring to the schema of Scott (most of the other objects do not have this option).

```
Scott>   SELECT * FROM syn_Department; (succeeds)

Adam>    SELECT * FROM syn_Department; (fails)
```

Synonyms cannot enhance security – synonyms of an object have the same security measures as the object.

4.3.4 Security and Transparency

Views and procedures – objects that are used for implementing security of the database – are also used for the support of data transparency. Though technically transparency and security are different features of the database, there is a logical connection between them. If users are not allowed to access a particular database resource, this resource has to be transparent to them. By sustaining security we can achieve transparency, and we can use transparency for implementing security. However, while transparency is a highly desirable feature of the database, security is a required one.

Let us again discuss views and see how they can not only enforce security, but can also make security measures less dependent on database changes. If we define security measures on views, and not on tables, we enforce the transparency of the data for these security measures. For example, the table Department is in John's schema, and Scott is running an application that accesses this table. If for some reason the table is moved to another schema or is renamed, then the application has to be changed, as well as the security measures – see Figure 4-10a).

If there is a tier of views (see discussion of transparency in Chapter 2), and security measures are defined on those views, then changes to the table will only cause a redefinition of the views and can be transparent to the security measures and applications see Figure 4-10b).

4.3.5 Additional Security Measures

In many DBMSs security is enhanced by additional measures:

- *Limiting resources:* Often administrators establish limits on users' resources consumption, such as CPU time, memory, storage and other resources, to prevent the excessive use of resources.
- *User accounts management:* It is recommended to manage users' accounts by setting expiration

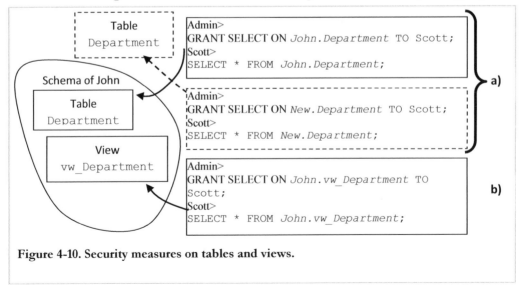

Figure 4-10. Security measures on tables and views.

dates and requiring regular modifications of passwords, control of passwords' complexity, etc.

- *Auditing:* Often various database activities are audited – information about users' actions is recorded in the database. Audit information can help in discovering security breaches.

4.4. Security in the Distributed Database

In a distributed database, each component database should have the required security measures for access of local users. If the database is accessed remotely (from another database), the database has to authenticate the access and check whether it is authorized. Therefore, when users need to access data from several databases, in addition to the local authentication of users and authorization of local access, developers have to implement distributed security, which includes remote user authentication and distributed authorization of access throughout all component databases.

4.4.1   Remote User Authentication

We will call the site from which a user is working, the local site, and the site which the user tries to access, the remote site. If a user who is working on the local site is accessing data in the remote database, the local database sends identification information to the remote database. Here, the local database is perceived by the remote database as a user requesting access. The local site can identify itself in several different ways:

1. *As a specific user of the remote database.* For example, the Boston database is always authenticated in the New York database as the user John. Any user of the Boston database who tries to access the New York database is authenticated there as John. This approach requires the user John to be created in the New York database (Figure 4-11).

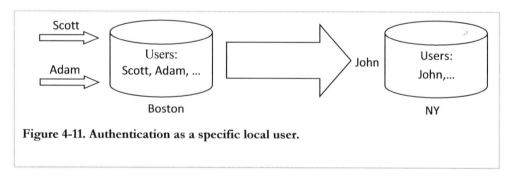

Figure 4-11. Authentication as a specific local user.

2. *As a local user who is requesting remote access.* For example, for Scott's request, the Boston database is authenticated by the New York database as Scott, and for John's – as John. In this case, local users who need remote access must be replicated in the New York database (Figure 4-12).

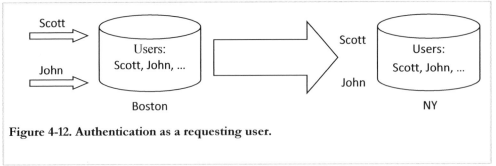

Figure 4-12. Authentication as a requesting user.

3. *As one or more of the local users.* Identification information depends on the local user requesting remote access and the type of access. For example, in some situations, Scott's request to the New York database results in authentication of the Boston database as Scott and in others – as John. Depending on how Scott is accessing the remote database, users Scott or John must be replicated in the New York database (Figure 4-13).

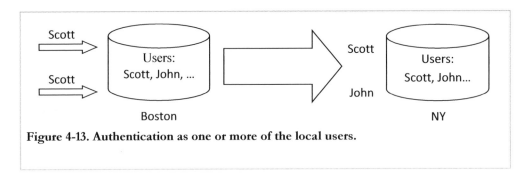

Figure 4-13. Authentication as one or more of the local users.

4.4.2   Distributed Authorization of Access

If a user is authenticated by a remote database, the user's access to the remote data will be defined by authorization rules.

Authorization for remote access cannot be established from the local database – each database manages authorization autonomously. Combining authentication methods and replication of users with authorization rules on the remote site can produce multiple security scenarios.

Consider the situation when the local database identifies itself as a local user and requests a remote resource as in Figure 4-12. The local user Scott who is replicated in the remote database requests data from his table Employee in the New York database:

```
Scott>   SELECT * FROM Employee@ny;
```

The New York database receives this as a request from Scott and authenticates it. After that, Scott is allowed to access the remote table Employee from his schema.

The scenario is different for the situation when the local database identifies itself as a specific local user as in Figure 4-11. The request that originates from Scott reaches the New York database as a request from John. Because the table name in the request is not prefixed by a schema name, the remote database will look into John's schema and hence the request will be unsuccessful.

For the request to be successful, the following two considerations have to be made:

- Scott has to rewrite the request as:

```
Scott> SELECT * FROM Scott.Employee@ny;
```

- The user John has to be granted a corresponding privilege on Scott's table Employee in the remote database (by Scott or another authorized user):

```
GRANT SELECT ON Scott.Employee TO John;
```

Authorization of access in the remote database depends on how the local database authenticates itself. On the other hand, the way the remote database permits access for local users determines the solution for authentication of the local database. Analysis of several different distributed security solutions in Oracle are discussed later in this chapter.

4.4.3   Distribution and Security

The support of security for distributed and centralized database solutions is different. Recall how we discussed restricting Scott's access to particular rows of the table Department with the help of a view or procedure in the centralized database. If we consider the distributed solution from Chapter 3 (when each site has a fragment of the table Department with local departments), then security measures will be different. We will not need views or procedures to limit access to specific rows; instead, Scott will be a local user of the Cleveland database and will have privileges to access the Cleveland fragment of the table Department. We should also ensure that Scott does not have access to the New York and Boston databases.

4.5. Security Measures in Oracle

4.5.1   Basic Features

Basic security in Oracle is supported by users, schemas, and granting (revoking) privileges. The following example demonstrates some basic security features.

Admin:	CREATE USER Scott IDENTIFIED BY tiger; GRANT CREATE SESSION TO Scott;	Administrator creates the user Scott and grants him the privilege to log into the database.

Scott:	CREATE TABLE Emp
	    (ID NUMBER,
	    name VARCHAR2(30));
	
	Insufficient privileges
		Scott successfully logs into the database. After that, he tries to create a table and fails because he does not have the corresponding privilege.

Admin:	`GRANT CREATE TABLE TO Scott;`	Administrator grants Scott the privilege to create tables.

Scott:	`CREATE TABLE Employee`
	`      (ID NUMBER PRIMARY KEY,`
	`      name VARCHAR2(30));`
		Scott creates a table.

Admin:	`CREATE USER Adam IDENTIFIED BY`
	`lion;`
	`GRANT CREATE SESSION TO Adam;`
		Administrator creates the user Adam and grants him the privilege to log into the database.

Adam:	`SELECT * FROM Scott.Emp;` 　　　　*`Table or view does`* 　　　　　　*`not exist`*	Adam tries to select from the table Employee in Scott's schema, but without the required privilege he does not see the table.
Scott:	`GRANT SELECT ON Employee TO` `Adam;`	Scott grants Adam the privilege to select from his table.
Adam:	`SELECT * FROM Scott.Employee;` 　　　　*`0 rows selected`*	Adam successfully accesses the table (the table is empty).
Scott:	`SELECT * FROM Employee;` 　　　　*`0 rows selected`*	Scott selects from his table with the same result as Adam.
Scott:	`REVOKE SELECT ON Employee FROM` `Adam;`	Scott revokes from Adam the privilege to select from the table.

Adam:	`CREATE TABLE Proj`
	`      (pno NUMBER PRIMARY KEY,`
	`      ID NUMBER REFERENCES`
	`      Scott.Employee)`
	　　　　`Insufficient`
	　　　　`privileges`
		Adam wants to create a table and fails because he does not have sufficient privileges.

Scott:	`GRANT CREATE TABLE TO Adam;` 　　　　*`Insufficient`* 　　　　*`privileges`*	Scott wants to grant Adam the privilege to create tables and fails because he does not have the privileges to grant the create table privilege to other users (he was granted the create table privilege without admin option).

Admin:	GRANT CREATE TABLE TO Adam;	Administrator grants the privilege for creating tables to Adam.
Adam:	CREATE TABLE Proj (pno NUMBER PRIMARY KEY, ID NUMBER REFERENCES Scott.Employee); *Table or view does* *not exist*	Adam's second attempt to create a table fails because he references the table from another schema without having the required privileges.
Scott:	GRANT REFERENCES ON Scott.Employee TO Adam;	Scott allows Adam to reference his table Employee.
Adam:	SELECT * FROM Scott.Employee; *Table or view does* *not exist*	Adam tries to select from Scott's table and fails because this privilege has been revoked.
Adam:	CREATE TABLE proj (pno NUMBER PRIMARY KEY, ID NUMBER REFERENCES Scott.Employee);	Adam succeeds in creating a table with the reference to the table of Scott.

Previous demonstrations of using views and procedures for implementing security were provided in Oracle in Sections 4.3.1 and 4.3.2.

4.5.2 Roles and PUBLIC Pseudo-User

In addition to the basic functionality, roles in Oracle have some special properties:

- Roles granted to a particular user can be dynamically enabled or disabled, which enables control of the user's privileges depending on the situation. For example, if the user Scott opens a session and starts an application, all roles granted to him may be disabled by the statement SET ROLE NONE. All previously granted roles can be enabled by SET ROLE ALL. A particular role can be enabled by SET ROLE *role*.
- Roles can be protected by passwords. When enabling a role, a user must specify the password assigned to the role:

      CREATE ROLE Accountant IDENTIFIED BY tiger;

- Special secure application roles can be enabled only by authorized PL/SQL packages. This mechanism restricts the enabling of such roles to the invoking application.

Oracle has three predefined roles with different sets of system privileges: CONNECT,

RESOURCE, and DBA. These roles can be granted to users, e.g. the following statement grants the user Adam the role CONNECT and with it such privileges as ALTER SESSION, CREATE CLUSTER, CREATE DATABASE LINK, CREATE SEQUENCE, CREATE SESSION, CREATE SYNONYM, CREATE TABLE, CREATE VIEW:

```
GRANT CONNECT TO Adam;
```

In Oracle, there is a pseudo-user named PUBLIC who is not a regular user as it cannot have a schema. A privilege or role granted to PUBLIC will be given to every user – past, present, and future. Therefore, privileges should be granted to PUBLIC with caution.

4.5.3 Authentication

The database authenticates a user by *name* and *password*:

```
CREATE USER Scott IDENTIFIED BY tiger;
```

Additionally, users can be authenticated by the *operating system*. Oracle relies on the operating system authentication and does not require the user to authenticate himself if they are created as:

```
CREATE USER John IDENTIFIED EXTERNALLY;
```

Another way to authenticate a user is the *proxy* authentication. A proxy user is a user who is allowed to connect to the database on behalf of another user. If a user needs a proxy connection, this user is given few privileges such as the privilege to connect to the database. After the user connects to the database, the database opens a second--a proxy--session on this user's behalf. In the commands below we create the user Adam and grant him the privilege to connect to the database. After that we make the user Scott a proxy user for Adam. Now, if Adam connects to the database, the database will create a session as the user Scott on behalf of Adam. This Scott session that was created on behalf of Adam is subject to all of the rules and privileges of the user Scott – it can only do what Scott is allowed to do.

```
CREATE USER Adam IDENTIFIED BY lion;

GRANT CREATE SESSION TO Adam;

ALTER USER Scott GRANT CONNECT THROUGH Adam;
```

The proxy user authentication introduced in Oracle 10g provides help in resolving the security problems that exist in some enterprise multi-tier applications. Often a user logs into a client application and then relies on the application to login on his behalf in the database. Applications often use pre-spawned Oracle connections that are created by a single Oracle user ID with the generic name, e.g. the user Sap for the SAP application rather than using thousands of different user ids. Unfortunately, when the end-users connect anonymously through a proxy application, there is no end-user level auditing and security through traditional security tools like granting privileges or using roles.

With Oracle proxy users, though the application connects to the database using the generic user name, the end-user's authentication information is also carried to the database with the help of the enhanced SQL command that allows proxy:

```
CONNECT Sap[Scott]/tiger
```

The application generic database user is created as before. However, we do not grant this user any privileges except the privilege to connect to the database. For example, for the SAP application:

```
CREATE USER Sap IDENTIFIED BY lion;

GRANT CREATE SESSION TO Sap;
```

Additionally, we create end-user database accounts with all required privileges and define these accounts as proxy accounts for the application account:

```
ALTER USER Scott_ny GRANT CONNECT THROUGH Sap;
```

When the user Scott connects to the application, the application logs into the database (as Sap in our example) and then the database connects Scott into the database. This way the database preserves control over all actions of Scott and can provide an audit trail on Scott's actions. This is schematically shown in Figure 4-14.

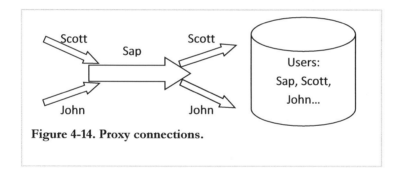

Figure 4-14. Proxy connections.

4.5.4 INSTEAD OF Triggers

In 4.3.1, when discussing views, we mentioned that not all views allow for modifications thus limiting their usage for implementing security and transparency. For example, the views that contain set operators, DISTINCT operator, aggregate or analytic functions, GROUP BY, ORDER BY, most joins, and some other constructs cannot be modified directly.

To overcome this limitation, Oracle introduced INSTEAD OF trigger.

For example, to limit access to data about employees of Boston we have the view that is based on the join of two tables:

```
CREATE OR REPLACE VIEW vw_Empl_Boston AS
SELECT e.emplID, e.emplName, d.deptCode, d.deptName
```

```
FROM Employee e INNER JOIN Department d
     ON e.deptCode = e.deptCode
WHERE location = 'Boston';
```

Because we want to be able to update data about employees through this view, we need to create the INSTEAD OF trigger as shown below (the example illustrates updates of the employees' names; for updates of other attributes the trigger needs to be expanded):

```
CREATE OR REPLACE TRIGGER trig_vw_Empl_Boston
INSTEAD OF INSERT OR UPDATE ON vw_Empl_Boston
FOR EACH ROW
BEGIN
    UPDATE employee
    SET emplName = :NEW.emplName
    WHERE emplID = OLD:emplID;
END;
```

With this trigger, when a user tries to update the view

```
UPDATE empl_view SET emplName = 'John' WHERE emplID = 123;
```

the system starts the trigger that will perform

```
UPDATE employee SET emplName = 'John' WHERE emplID = 123;
```

4.5.5 Fine-Grained Access Control

In many cases, the discussed security tools are not enough to implement the required security support. Imagine a bank application through which users, who are bank customers, access their bank accounts. Obviously, none of them can get access to the whole table (or tables) with data about accounts. If we try to apply the views solution and create a view for each user, the database will contain thousands of views, if not more, and maintenance of such a database will be extremely expensive.

We may think of using procedures, e.g. a procedure for depositing or withdrawing money on an account. Assume that there is the table Account (<u>accountNumb</u>, balance) with data about balances on customers' accounts. Here is a simple example of such a procedure:

```
DBA> CREATE PROCEDURE test
          (par_account NUMBER, par_sum NUMBER) AS

     BEGIN
          UPDATE Account
          SET balance = balance + par_sum
        WHERE accountNumb = par_account;
     END;
```

The procedure has two parameters: the first defines the account number of the customer, the second – the amount of the deposit. The bank application passes the account number and the amount of deposit to the procedure which then executes the UPDATE statement.

For example, if a customer with account 12345 wants to deposit $100, the application will perform the following procedure call:

```
EXEC dba.test(12345, 100);
```

This call will pass the parameters into the procedure and the following UPDATE statement will be executed:

```
UPDATE dba.Account SET balance = balance + 100
WHERE accountNumb = 12345;
```

With the help of this procedure we can limit customers to accessing the data of their accounts only. Each customer will be granted the privilege to execute the procedure (either individually as below or through a role):

```
GRANT EXEC ON test TO Scott;
```

Though the solution looks elegant, there is a problem caused by the fact that a user's authentication is not performed in the database, but in the application. The application defines the account of a user and passes this information to the procedure. Suppose that the account 12345 belongs to Scott. Now imagine the situation when user John with the account number 67890 (who also can execute the procedure) connects to the database through another application, e.g. SQL*PLUS, and then issues the following two statements, the first of which, resulting in withdrawing $1000 from Scott's account, violates security requirements:

```
John> EXEC dba.test(12345, -1000);

     EXEC dba.test(67890, 1000);
```

This is a good demonstration of what we warned about in the beginning of the chapter – security implemented in the application can be bypassed.

Oracle has special tools for implementing fine-grained access control when using views is impractical and procedures do not guarantee the needed protection. Security requirements are implemented through special functions called security policies. Security policies are attached to tables or views and every time a user issues a DML statement on the secured table or view, Oracle attaches the policy to the statement. Attachment of the policy is performed transparently to the user. Fine-grained access control allows for context-dependent and row-based security control (see Figure 4-15).

Fine-grained access is implemented with the help of the supplied package DBMS_RLS. Packages are objects of the database, which are composed of procedures, functions, and definitions of types and variables. Oracle has a number of supplied packages, which support additional functionality of the database. Procedures of the DBMS_RLS package allow specifying the table or the view to which the policy is added, the name of the policy, the function which implements the policy, the type of statement to which the policy applies (SELECT, INSERT, UPDATE, or DELETE), and some additional information.

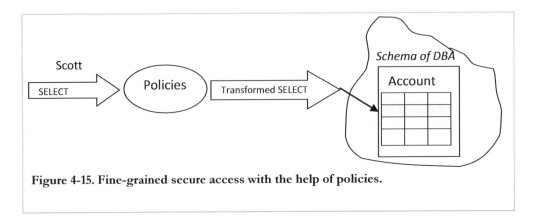

Figure 4-15. Fine-grained secure access with the help of policies.

The following example explains how Oracle security policies work for the example of the bank application. Assume that in addition to the table Account there is the table Customer(name, accountNumb, ...)with information about customers.

1. Define what predicate has to be added to each statement. In our case, we need a predicate that ensures that a customer accesses data from his account only. If a customer has logged into the database using his name, then the following predicate will return the customer's account number, which can later be used to restrict access to data (the system variable USER contains the name of the current user):

```
accountNumb = (SELECT accountNumb
         FROM Customer
         WHERE name = USER);
```

2. Create a function that returns this predicate. With the help of the package DBMD_RLS we attach the function to the table Account as a security policy for any DML statement, so that this function adds the predicate to every DML statement on the table Account (for details see Oracle documentation).
3. Because of the attached security policy, for every statement on the table Account, Oracle calls the function that implements the policy and modifies the statement by attaching the predicate to it. For example, a simple select by Scott on the table Account will be transformed in the following way:

```
SELECT * FROM Account
WHERE accountNumb =
(SELECT accountNumb FROM Customer WHERE name = SCOTT);
```

4. Oracle executes the dynamically modified statement, and because of the added predicate, the user can access only the account associated with his name.

Fine-grained access control is based on database authentication of users and is more reliable than the procedural solutions discussed before. This tool supports what is called a Virtual Private Database in which each user sees his own private portion of the database.

4.5.6 Label Security

The Oracle Label Security feature is built upon the fine-grained control features; it is useful in situations similar to the following. Imagine a table with a company's documents of different security levels – from documents that can be accessed by all users to documents which have strongly restricted access. For example, the table Document below contains two types of rows: rows that can be accessed by all users and rows that can be accessed by employees of the company only.

docID	docName	docLabel
1	Company profile	Public
2	Company payroll	Internal
3	Company partners	Public
...		

We use labels in the following way:

- Define how to label the rows according to their security type, e.g. 'Public' and 'Internal', and keep the labels in a new column docLabel.
- Define security levels for all labels by assigning numbers; higher numbers mean more restrictions. In our case, the value 'Internal' implies more restrictions than the value 'Public', and we assign 10000 to 'Public' and 20000 to 'Internal'.
- Define security policies on the column docLabel and its values, and attach them to the table Document.
- Associate security labels with users.

A user's request to data is transformed by adding the respective security predicate defined on the labels of the column docLabel. For example:

- User Scott is associated with the label 'Public'.
- His request to the table Document is transformed by adding a conditional clause that allows him to access rows that have security levels lower than or equal to level 10000 of the 'Public' value. He can access only the records labeled 'Public'.
- User John is associated with the label 'Internal', and he is able to access rows with the security levels lower than or equal to 20000 or, in our case, all rows of the table.

Figure 4-16 shows associations between users, labels, and security levels.

Note that if there are only few security levels, then we can apply the views solution – create a view for each security level using the column docLabel and grant users the privileges on corresponding views.

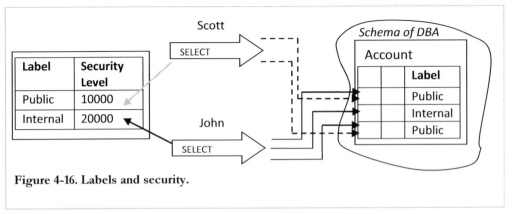

Figure 4-16. Labels and security.

4.5.7 Additional Measures

4.5.7.1 Profiles and Limiting Resources

The management of security measures in Oracle can be enhanced by user profiles. A profile defines additional password constraints and computer resources limitations. In the following profile, the password constraints the maximum number of attempts to log in as 3, the account lock time after 3 unsuccessful attempts as 1 day, and the number of days the same password can be used for authentication as 30 days. The resources part of the profile defines that a user can have an unlimited number of concurrent sessions, not more than 30 seconds on each CPU call, and be connected to a database for not longer than 45 minutes:

```
CREATE PROFILE clerk LIMIT
      FAILED_LOGIN_ATTEMPTS    3
      PASSWORD_LOCK_TIME       1
      PASSWORD_LIFE_TIME       30
      SESSIONS_PER_USER        UNLIMITED
      CPU_PER_CALL       3000
      CONNECT_TIME       45;
```

The administrator can create different profiles for different groups of users. After a profile is assigned to a user, the user's password will be managed according to the password parameters of the profile, and while working with the database the user will be subject to the profile resources limitations:

```
ALTER USER Scott PROFILE clerk;
```

4.5.7.2 Auditing

Auditing activities on the database can help to recognize unauthorized access. In addition to customized auditing usually implemented in triggers, Oracle supports standard auditing with the help of the SQL command AUDIT. In the first of the following examples, auditing is assigned for select operations on any table, and in the second – for any select and update operation performed by users Scott and John:

```
AUDIT SELECT TABLE;
```

```
AUDIT SELECT TABLE, UPDATE TABLE BY Scott, John;
```

Audit records include such information as the operation that was audited, the user performing the operation, and the date and time of the operation. For further analysis, audit records are stored in the data dictionary table called DBA_AUDIT_TRAIL, or in operating system files.

To audit occurrences of a SQL statement, you must have AUDIT SYSTEM system privilege. To audit operations on a schema object, the object you choose for auditing must be in your own schema or you must have AUDIT ANY system privilege.

4.5.8   Privileges and the Data Dictionary

The data dictionary contains information about security measures implemented in the database, such as the users and the objects they have privileges to access, the allowed type of access, the owners of these objects, who granted the privileges, and other similar information.   For example the user Scott can see his object privilege to select from Adam's table Test that was granted to Scott by user SYS without the grant option from the dictionary view USER_TAB_PRIVS:

```
Scott>   SELECT * FROM user_tab_privs;
```

GRANTEE	OWNER	TABLE_NAME	GRANTOR	PRIVILEGE	GRANTABLE
SCOTT	ADAM	TEST	SYS	SELECT	NO

The view USER_ROLE_PRIVS shows information about a user's roles. The following example shows that Scott was granted two system roles CONNECT and RESOURCE, both without the admin option:

```
Scott>   SELECT * FROM user_role_privs;
```

USERNAME	GRANTED_ROLE	ADMIN_OPTION	DEFAULT	OS_
SCOTT	CONNECT	NO	YES	NO
SCOTT	RESOURCE	NO	YES	NO

Administrators can see users' object privileges in the view DBA_TAB_PRIVS, system privileges in the view DBA_SYS_PRIVS, and roles in the view DBA_ROLE_PRIVS.

4.5.9   Oracle Database Vault

Oracle Database Vault enhances the database security features by offering the ability to restrict the access of users with system privileges.   Additionally, it permits controlling actions depending on the context of access, such as the time, the computer where the request originates, etc. The features of the Vault are described in the Appendix 4.

4.6. *Security in the Distributed Oracle Database*

In the distributed Oracle database separate databases can "see" other databases through database links. Oracle provides several types of links. The type of a database link in the distributed database depends on security requirements.

Information about the links available to a user is contained in the view ALL_DB_LINKS.

4.6.1   Types of Database Links

The database link defines the logical connection or the communication path from one database to another. When a user tries to access a remote database via the link, Oracle opens a database session in the remote database on behalf of the request of the local user. There are two types of database links: private and public. The type of a link defines which local users can get to the remote database with the help of the link (Figure 4-17).

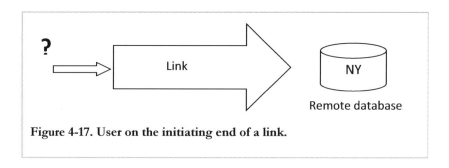

Figure 4-17. User on the initiating end of a link.

4.6.1.1   Private Links

Private database links can be created in a particular schema. Only the owner of the private link can use it to connect to the remote database directly (Figure 4-18).

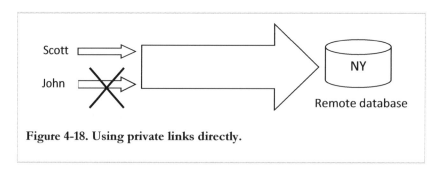

Figure 4-18. Using private links directly.

In the following example, Scott creates a private link to the New York database and tries to delete a row from the remote table Employee. Note that because the name of the table is not prefixed with the name of the schema, it means that Scott is trying to delete records from his table Employee in the New York database through his private link[16]. Scott can use his private

---

[16] Scott must be replicated in the New York database.

link to access objects from other schemas in the New York database if he has corresponding privileges. User John cannot use the private link of Scott.

Scott:	CREATE DATABASE LINK ny USING ny.ourcompany.us.com;	Scott creates a private database link.
Scott:	DELETE FROM Employee@ny WHERE ID = 12345; *1 rows processed*	Scott uses the link to access his table in the remote database.
Scott:	SELECT * FROM Adam.Employee@ny; *Table or view* *doesn't exist*	Scott uses the link to access data from the Employee table in Adam's schema in the remote database and fails because he does not have the required privilege.
John:	DELETE FROM Employee@ny WHERE ID = 67890; *Not enough* *privileges to use* *the link*	John tries to use the private link of Scott and fails.

Only the owner of the private link can use the link directly in remote requests.

The advantage of the private link is its security. Only the user who is the owner of the link can get to the remote database through this link directly. In 4.5.9.3 we will show how under certain conditions a private link can enable other users of the local database to get connected to the remote database.

4.6.1.2   Public Links

Public database links make a remote database visible to any user of the local database.

In the next example, John, using the public link created by Scott, succeeds in reaching the remote database where he is authenticated as John. His first request fails because he does not have the table Employee in his schema. His second request to Scott's table Employee succeeds. Note that for this example Scott and John must be replicated in the New York database, and John must be granted the privilege to select from Scott's table Employee.

Scott:	CREATE PUBLIC DATABASE LINK ny USING ny.ourcompany.us.com;	Scott creates a public database link.

John:	DELETE FROM Employee@ny
	WHERE ID = 12345;
	       Table or view doesn't
	       exist
		John uses the link to access the remote table Employee and fails because he does not have such table in his schema.

John:	DELETE FROM Scott.Employee@ny WHERE ID = 12345; *1 rows processed*	John succeeds in using the link to access the remote table Employee in Scott's schema.

Any local user can use the public link for remote requests.

Public links are less secure than the private links, but with the help of one public link the administrator can enable all local users to access the remote database. Note that the required security still can be managed by appropriate authorizations in the remote database.

4.6.2 Security Options for Database Links

The type of the link – private or public – defines who in the local database can use the link and get access to the remote database. Another property of the link – the security option – specifies how the local database identifies itself to the remote database, or, in other words, who is the user associated with at the destination end of the link (Figure 4-19).

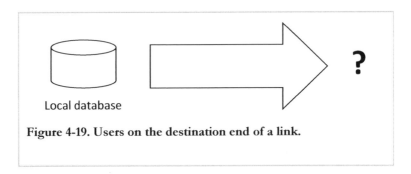

Local database

Figure 4-19. Users on the destination end of a link.

4.6.2.1 Fixed User Database Links

The fixed user database link specifies the credentials of a user who will be connected to the remote database. If the fixed user database link is used:

- Users of the local database connect to the remote site as the fixed user.
- They establish a connection to the fixed user's schema in the remote database (Figure 4-20).

Users of the fixed user link should not be replicated in the remote database.

In the following example, every user of the local database who tries to connect to the remote database is authenticated in the remote database as Scott/tiger. Note that Adam accesses

Scott's table Employee in the remote database without specifying Scott's schema because he is authenticated by the remote database as Scott.

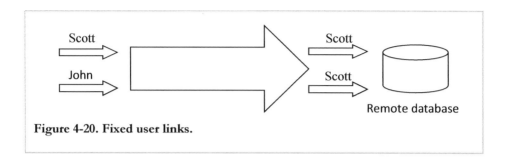

Figure 4-20. Fixed user links.

John:	CREATE PUBLIC DATABASE LINK ny USING ny.ourcompany.us.com CONNECT TO Scott IDENTIFIED BY tiger;	John creates a public database link with the fixed user security option.
Adam:	DELETE FROM Employee@ny WHERE ID = 12345; *0 rows processed*	Adam uses the public link and accesses Scott's table Employee in the remote database as Scott.

The disadvantages of the fixed links are: 1) all users of the local database can access the remote objects for which the fixed user has authorizations, and 2) the local user is authenticated as the fixed user on the remote site, and the fixed user's privileges rather than the actual user's privileges on the remote site are in effect. This can compromise the security of the distributed database.

4.6.2.2 Connected User Database Links

The connected user database link does not include any user credentials in the definition of the link. The remote database uses the local credentials of the connected user. For example, if Scott connects to the remote database, he is always authenticated there as Scott (Figure 4-21).

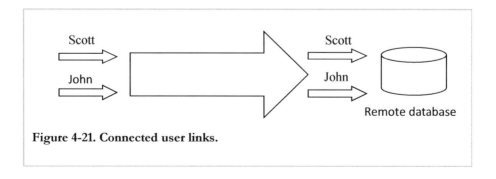

Figure 4-21. Connected user links.

Users of the connected user link – their names and passwords – must be replicated in the remote database.

To create a connected user database link, you simply omit the CONNECT TO clause. The following example creates a connected user database link:

```
CREATE PUBLIC DATABASE LINK ny USING ny.ourcompany.us.com;
```

Among other considerations, the connected user link is used when users need to perform specific operations in both databases, e.g., create tables.

4.6.2.3 Current User Database Links

Oracle supports an interesting security option – current user – that connects to the remote database as one of local users, but not necessarily as the user who requests remote access. The current user database link is specified by the CURRENT_USER option:

```
CREATE DATABASE LINK ny USING ny.ourcompany.us.com;

CONNECT TO CURRENT_USER;
```

When a local user is requesting a remote resource directly, the current user link acts like the connected user link. That means the local database sends the credentials of the local user to the remote database. The local user in this case has to be replicated in the remote database. If, on the other hand, a local user tries to access the remote resource indirectly – through a local procedure that contains the remote request – then the local database presents itself to the remote database as the owner of the procedure. For example, in the local database Scott has the stored procedure test which contains a remote request, and he has granted the privilege to execute this procedure to John. When John executes the procedure, the link within the procedure sees Scott (not John) as the current user of the database. Figure 4-22 shows how users from the local site are authenticated on the remote site through the current user link.

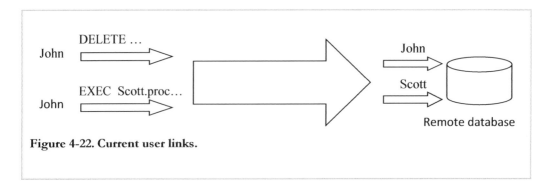

Figure 4-22. Current user links.

The current user security option can make private links available to users who execute procedures belonging to the same schema as the private link. In the following example, user John fails to use the private link of Scott directly, but succeeds in using it indirectly through

Scott's procedure. John does not have to be replicated on the remote site because the remote database authenticates the owner of the procedure – the user Scott.

Scott:	CREATE DATABASE LINK ny USING ny.ourcompany.us.com CONNECT TO CURRENT_USER;	Scott creates a private link with the current user security option.

Scott:	CREATE PROCEDURE test (par_ID NUMBER)
	AS
	BEGIN
	    DELETE FROM Employee@ny
	    WHERE ID = par_ID;
	END;
	
	GRANT EXECUTE ON test TO John;
		Scott creates a stored procedure and grants the privilege to execute it to John.

John:	DELETE FROM scott.Employee@ny WHERE ID = 12345; *(Access is denied)*	John tries to use the private link directly and fails because the link is private.

John:	EXEC Scott.test (12345);
	              Procedure successfully
	              completed
		John uses the private link indirectly through the procedure of Scott and succeeds.

Note that with the *connected user* security option in the procedure of Scott, John will be authenticated in the remote database as John.

It is important to remember that the type of the link or its security option by themselves do not address security requirements; we always need to consider a combination of the link, and authentication and authorization of access in the remote database.

4.7. Examples: Implementing Security Measures in the Centralized and Distributed Databases

4.7.1 The Centralized Database

Consider the following security measures for the centralized implementation of the database for the Manufacturing Company case:

1. Prepare roles for users who work with local data (departments and employees) of the three cities.
2. Create a role for users who work with all data.
3. Create views to enable secure access to portions of the local data (in the example below we create views on the table Department only).
4. Create views for users of all the data. Remember that views support not only security, but also transparency of data. These views are not required by security requirements, but they

definitely enhance the transparency of the database and the applications' independence from possible database changes.

5. Grant the required privileges to the roles.
6. Create the users of local data.
7. Create the users of all the data.
8. Grant roles to the users.

1.	`CREATE ROLE Clerk_Boston;`
	`CREATE ROLE Clerk_NewYork;`
	`CREATE ROLE Clerk_Cleveland;`

2.	`CREATE ROLE Manager;`

3.	`CREATE VIEW vw_Department_Boston AS`
	`SELECT * FROM Department WHERE location = 'Boston';`
	
	`CREATE VIEW vw_Department_NewYork AS`
	`SELECT * FROM Department WHERE location = 'New York';`
	
	`CREATE VIEW vw_Department_Cleveland AS`
	`SELECT * FROM Department WHERE location = 'Cleveland';`

4.	`CREATE VIEW vw_allDepartments AS` `SELECT * FROM Department;`

5.	`GRANT SELECT, INSERT, UPDATE, DELETE ON vw_Department_Boston TO`
	`Clerk_Boston;`
	
	`GRANT SELECT, INSERT, UPDATE, DELETE ON vw_Department_NewYork TO`
	`Clerk_NewYork;`
	
	`GRANT SELECT, INSERT, UPDATE, DELETE ON vw_Department_Cleveland TO`
	`Clerk_Cleveland;`
	
	`GRANT SELECT, INSERT, UPDATE, DELETE ON vw_allDepartments TO`
	`Manager;`

6.	`CREATE USER John IDENTIFIED BY abc;`
	`CREATE USER Smith IDENTIFIED BY def;`
	`CREATE USER Scott IDENTIFIED BY uvw;`

7.	CREATE USER Adam IDENTIFIED BY xyz;
8.	GRANT Clerk_Boston TO John; GRANT Clerk_NewYork TO Smith; GRANT Clerk_Cleveland TO Scott; GRANT Manager TO Adam;

4.7.2 The Distributed Database

For the distributed solution of Chapter 3 we need to implement the local security measures in each database and the distributed security measures for users of the application that accesses all the data and is executed from the New York database. In the example below, we will discuss the security measures of the Boston and New York databases (the security measures in the

Cleveland and Boston databases are similar):

1. Consider the necessary database links. In our case, some users of the New York database access the Boston database, while users of the Boston database access only local data. We need the database link from the New York database to the Boston database. Assuming that there are a few users of the New York database who work with Boston data, we will create a connected user link.
2. Create a role for users who work with local data in each database.
3. Create a role for users who access all data in the New York database.
4. Create local views in each database.
5. Create views that implement transparency of distribution in the New York database (because only New York users need access to all the data).
6. Grant required privileges to the roles.
7. Create users of local data in each database.
8. Create users of all the data in the New York database.
9. Grant corresponding roles to the users in each database.

	Boston	New York
1.		CREATE PUBLIC DATABASE LINK boston USING Boston.ourcompany.us.com;
2.	CREATE ROLE Clerk;	CREATE ROLE Clerk;
3.		CREATE ROLE Manager;
4.	CREATE VIEW vw_Department AS SELECT * FROM Department;	CREATE VIEW vw_Department AS SELECT * FROM Department;
5.		CREATE VIEW vw_allDepartments[17] AS SELECT * FROM Department UNION SELECT * FROM Department@boston;
6.	GRANT SELECT, INSERT, UPDATE, DELETE ON vw_Department TO Clerk;	GRANT SELECT, INSERT, UPDATE, DELETE ON vw_Department TO Clerk; GRANT SELECT, INSERT, UPDATE, DELETE ON vw_allDepartments TO Manager;
7.	CREATE USER John IDENTIFIED BY abc;	CREATE USER Smith IDENTIFIED BY def;
8.		CREATE USER Adam IDENTIFIED BY xyz;
9.	GRANT Clerk TO John;	GRANT Clerk TO Smith; GRANT Manager TO Adam;

---

[17] Remember, in this demonstration we are considering only two databases, that is why the view is based on the union of two fragments. In the actual situation the view will be based on the union of all three fragments.

4.8. Summary

Securing data or preventing unauthorized access to data is a crucial feature of any database and database application. Though a database application usually features protection for data access, the most reliable way of securing of data is to provide for it in the database itself, where security measures are integrated with data and cannot be bypassed. DBMSs offer tools for implementing various security requirements.

Securing data means ensuring that only authorized users perform allowed operations on the data. Databases enforce security measures by authentication and authorizations control. Authentication is performed with the help of user names and passwords. An entitled user receives the database user name and is assigned the authentication information associated with it, such as a password and profile.

Database users have to be authorized to perform database operations. Authorization is performed through granting permissions or privileges for specific operations on particular data. Authorization can also be performed through the granting of groups of privileges, called roles.

A user who is granted privileges to create database objects is considered the owner of the objects he creates or, in other words, these objects belong to the owner's schema. The owner does not need to be granted privileges to perform legal operations on the objects, e.g. a user who created a table can alter or drop it, as well as manipulate data in it. Other users, however, cannot access an object without the owner's permission – a granted object privilege. Each type of access to an object requires a corresponding privilege, for example, if a user is granted the privilege to select from a table, this does not enable him to manipulate data in the table.

In addition to object privileges there are system privileges that enable users to perform a particular operation on all objects of a specified class. For example, a user can be given the privilege to select from any database table. In this case, to access data from a particular table the user does not need the permission of the table's owner. Other examples are the privileges to create database objects, e.g. tables, views, users, etc.

Often, it is necessary to limit a users' access to specific portions of data in a table. This is accomplished with the help of views and procedures. Users are not authorized to access the table directly; instead, they are granted privileges to access a view or use a procedure. These views and procedures are implemented in such a way that they restrict the users' access to a portion of data from the table.

Special DBMS tools support fine-grained access to data. Such tools allow for implementing security control that is context-dependent and row-based.

In the distributed database, security measures include local authentication of users and local authorization of access combined with authentication of separate databases that are communicating with each other.

A traditional sequence of steps for implementing security measures is the following:

- *Analyzing security requirements and implementation of the database*. Research the requirements on access to data in the database and how the database is implemented. Security measures depend on the implementation of the database, e.g. whether it is centralized or distributed.
- *Implementing connection of databases*. If the database is distributed, define databases that need to access other databases and implement connections. Utilize the properties of database connections of the particular DBMS to enhance security solutions depending on the needs for remote access. For example, in Oracle, use the different types and security options for links to maintain distributed security in the easiest way depending on how many local users need remote access and what their remote access needs are.
- *Creating roles*. Create roles for groups of users depending on their different needs in data.
- *Creating views and procedures*. Create views and procedures that implement transparency and maintain data security depending on the data access needs.
- *Granting privileges to roles*. Grant privileges for various types of access on the views and procedures of the previous step to the roles.
- *Creating users*. For users of the database, create user accounts with authentication information.
- *Granting roles to users*. Grant required roles to users.
- *Implementing fine-grain security*. If necessary, implement fine-grain security measures using special features of the DBMS.

Data can be additionally protected by DBMS encryption tools.

Database security measures are only a part of the complex technical security support in the IS. Technical security measures must be enhanced by various non-technical security procedures and rules.

Review Questions

- How is the database for your course project protected from access by other students?
- How can a professor get access to the data of all his or her students?
- Why is it important to implement security support in the database?
- What are basic security measures? Describe how they work and the situations in which it is reasonable to apply each of them.
- What is user authentication?
- How do roles help in managing the database security?
- What are schemas? Explain how schemas secure access to data.
- What is authorization of access?
- What are object and system privileges?
- What are the approaches to implementing fine-grain security measures?
- What are the main security problems in the distributed database?
- How does Oracle provides connections to remote databases?
- How can local data be protected from remote access?
- What is the difference between public and private links?
- How do the security options of links in Oracle implement security of access to remote data?

Practical Assignments

1. Describe the possible scenarios for using private and public links with different security options.

2. For one of your tables:
   a. Define how to protect the table from access by other users.
   b. Provide the possibility for another user to access data from the table.
   c. Provide the possibility for another user to access definite rows of the table.
   d. Provide the possibility for another user to create a table with reference to your table.

3. Specify the creation of a user with some administrative responsibilities, e.g. creating database users.

4. Consider the security requirements for students who take database courses and need to implement database projects; and professors who teach these courses and need to check the students' database projects. Suggest security measures for the students and professors.

5. Describe security measures for different scenarios of access to a table in a centralized database:
   a. All users access the same part of the table.
   b. Several different groups of users need to access different parts of the table.
   c. Numerous users have to access different parts of the table.

6. For each of the following situations describe different scenarios of security implementation and explain the benefits and disadvantages of each approach (use different types of links, replication of users, and various authorization schemes):
   a. You have table A in one database, and table B in another database. User X must have access to table A and must be prevented from access to table B.
   b. You have a table in the remote database. Local users should be able to access this table on the remote site, and should be prevented from accessing other remote objects in your or other schemas on the remote database.
   c. In the remote database, you have the table A and user X has the table B. Local users should be able to access Table A and Table B on the remote site, but should be prevented from accessing any other remote object.
   d. You must have access to any remote object of user X.
   e. Several local users need access to multiple different objects of the remote database.
   f. Most local users need access to several objects of the remote database.
   g. All local users need access to different objects of the remote database.

7. Implement the required security for one of the case assignments of Appendix 1:
   a. For a centralized solution, consider creating views, procedures, and roles.
   b. For a distributed solution, build local security measures for each database, define appropriate database links, and enable the necessary remote access.

Chapter 5.   Query Processing and Performance

The users of database applications have definite expectations about the time it will take the database to respond to their requests or the number of requests the database will be able to process per unit of time. The user requirements on performance must be met by the database and database applications, and often the success of the database is defined by its performance.

This chapter is about a special relationship between the database and database applications. Though very often we say 'database performance', actually, we mean the performance of the database applications. However, good performance of applications can be achieved only on appropriately designed and implemented databases. On the one hand, databases have to be designed and implemented with the aim of satisfying the needs of specific database applications. On the other hand, the applications have to be designed and implemented with regard to the database solution and the features of the DBMS that are responsible for the processing of the application's requests to the database.

In this chapter we will discuss requests to the database that result in retrieving and modifying queries. Improving the performance of query processing, also called *database tuning*, is one of the most important problems of database design and implementation. It is also one of the most complicated problems to solve because performance depends on many factors. This chapter discusses the general problems of query processing, the features of DBMSs that allow for improving performance, and the aspects of the database and database applications that have an impact on query processing and performance.

5.1. Problems of Query Processing

5.1.1 Goals of Query Processing

The effectiveness of query processing is usually measured with the help of the response time, throughput, and total time or cost. The objectives of query processing are minimizing the total cost and response time, and maximizing the throughput.

The *total cost (total time)* is the sum of all the times spent for processing the operations of a query. It includes the cost (time) of the Input/Output (I/O) and CPU operations. The I/O cost is the time spent on disk reading/writing operations: the system searches the disk for data, reads data blocks into memory and writes data back to disk. The CPU time is the time spent on data processing in memory (RAM).

> **Total Cost =**
> **(Number of I/O operations * Cost of one I/O operation) +**
> **(Number of RAM operations * Cost of one RAM operation).**

The cost of disk access is significantly higher than the cost of memory operations, therefore, to improve performance, it is usually important to minimize the number of disk accesses. In a distributed database, the total cost of distributed queries also includes the cost of data transfer between the databases.

The *response time* is the elapsed time for the execution of the query. The response time is composed of the actual query processing time and the waiting time, when the system waits for the needed resources to become available.

Response time = Processing time + Waiting time.

If there is no resource contention (and the waiting time is zero or insignificantly small), then the response time can be less than the total time (total cost) because some operations of a query can be processed by the system in parallel. For example, imagine that three operations are involved in the processing of a query: the first operation requires 0.1 units of time, the second – 0.3 units, and the third – 0.6 units. The total time for processing this query is 1 unit of time (0.1+0.3+0.6). If the operations are executed simultaneously, then the response time is 0.6 units. However, if some of the needed resources are unavailable, for example locked by another user (see Chapter 6 on transaction management), then the response time can be significantly higher.

The *throughput* is the number of queries processed per unit of time. The throughput can be increased by reducing the total or processing times, or by eliminating resource contention and reducing the waiting time.

Throughput = Number of executed queries per unit of time.

Different database applications have different processing goals. For example, the On-Line Transaction Processing (OLTP) applications have to perform many data requests in a limited time, and, therefore, their primary goal is to maximize the throughput. The On-Line Analytic Applications (OLAP), on the other hand, are characterized by a small number of concurrent requests. However, the requests are often complicated and resource consuming, and minimizing their response time is important. Figure 5-1 schematically illustrates how with the increase of the number of concurrent users the response time is getting worse while the throughput is getting better (until some critical number of concurrent sessions is reached).

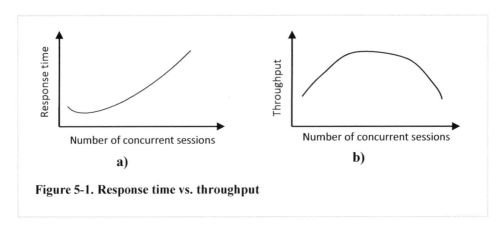

Figure 5-1. Response time vs. throughput

This chapter discusses how to achieve better performance by minimizing the processing and response times and increasing the throughput, assuming that there is no resource contention and the system is not waiting for resources to become available. Chapter 6 explains resource contention problems in the multi-user environment and approaches to improve performance of concurrent queries by minimizing the waiting time.

5.1.2 Query Decomposition

Database requests are written in a high-level language; for relational databases it is the SQL dialect of a particular DBMS. Query processing starts with the decomposition or transformation of the query into a sequence of operations of relational algebra (relational operations are explained in Appendix 2). The sequence of relational operations defines the strategy of the query execution. Most SQL queries can be transformed into more than one relational expression, and the purpose of query decomposition is to choose the expression that gives the best (or reasonably good) performance.

The discussion of query processing will be based on the Manufacturing Company case. Consider the query that finds data about employees who work in the IT departments:

```
SELECT e.*, d.*
FROM Employee e, Department d
WHERE e.deptCode = d.deptCode AND deptType = 'IT';
```

This query can be decomposed into two different relational expressions:

1. First find the Cartesian product of the tables Employee and Department, then select from the result the rows that satisfy the condition of the join of these tables, and then select the rows of the IT departments:

$$\sigma_{Department.deptType='IT'}(\sigma_{Employee.deptCode \,=\, Department.deptCode}(Employee \times Department))$$

2. First select all rows from the table Department with deptType = 'IT' and then join the result with the table Employee by deptCode:

$$Employee \blacktriangleright\!\blacktriangleleft_{deptCode} \sigma_{deptType='IT'}(Department)$$

5.1.3 Query Optimization

The second relational expression looks simpler than the first one. The following rough estimation of the processing costs for both expressions demonstrates that choosing a good execution strategy is important for good performance. To simplify the estimation we will make the following assumptions:

- The results of intermediate processing are stored on disk. Later in this chapter it is shown that the results of the intermediate operations often are kept in memory – this allows for reducing the number of I/O accesses and, therefore, improving performance.
- Rows of the tables and of intermediate results are accessed one at a time. In reality, as discussed in Chapter 2, data is read by data blocks that contain multiple rows. The number

of rows in the block depends on the rows' length, the percent of free space in the block, and the size of the block (the block size is defined by the administrator to accommodate the needs of applications in the optimal manner).

The estimation is based on 200 departments, with 40 IT type departments. 4000 employees are distributed evenly across the departments – approximately 20 employees in a department.

Because the cost of memory operations is much less than the cost of I/O operations, the cost of a strategy is estimated as the number of I/O operations.

For the first strategy:

1. For the Cartesian product, read all the rows of the tables Employee and Department: 200 + 4000 accesses. The Cartesian product results in 4000 * 200 rows.
2. For the intermediate result of the Cartesian product, write all rows to disk: 4000 * 200 accesses.
3. For the first selection (join), read the intermediate result of the Cartesian product: 4000 * 200 accesses. The first selection results in 4000 rows.
4. For the intermediate result of the first selection, write all rows to disk: 4000 accesses.
5. For the second selection (deptType = IT), read the rows of the previous result: 4000 accesses.

The cost of the first strategy is:

$$4200 + 4000 * 200 + 4000 * 200 + 4000 + 4000 = 1612200.$$

For the second strategy:

1. For the selection (deptType = IT), read all rows of the table Department: 200 accesses. The selection results in 40 rows.
2. For the intermediate result of the selection, write all rows to disk: 40 accesses.
3. For the join, read all rows of the table Employee and rows of the intermediate result: 4000 + 40 accesses.

The cost of the second strategy is:

$$200 + 40 + 4000 + 40 = 4280.$$

The difference between the processing costs of these two relational expressions (and, correspondingly, performances of the query) is striking. Choosing a good strategy is important for performance. Defining an efficient query execution strategy is called *Query Optimization*. Optimization plays an important role in query processing. The efficient decomposition of a query is only a part of the query optimization process. The following sections demonstrate how the database optimizer chooses between different ways of accessing and processing data for a given sequence of operations produced by the decomposition.

5.1.4   General Scheme of Query Processing

Figure 5-2 shows the main steps of query processing.

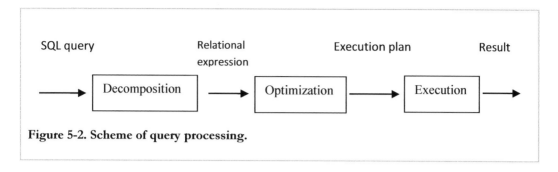

SQL query   Relational   Execution plan   Result
          expression

Figure 5-2. Scheme of query processing.

In the previous section it was shown how the query is decomposed into relational operations. In the beginning of the decomposition, the query is analyzed for correctness. First, the query must have the correct syntax; the processing of queries with syntax errors is cancelled. The decomposition step also includes analysis of the query: checking that the references to the objects of the database are correct and that the user who started the query is authorized to reference these objects (tables, views, synonyms, etc.). If the user is not authorized to access at least one of the objects of the query, the processing is cancelled.

The analysis of the query may include limited checking of the query's logic. For example, if a query condition includes the following expression:

   `WHERE ... AND deptType = 'IT' AND deptType = 'IT',`

it will be simplified into:

   `WHERE ... AND deptType = 'IT'.`

However, the programmer should not rely on the query processing capabilities of the database for improving the logic of the query. If, for example, the join conditions for the tables of a query are not specified, most DBMSs will not react to this and the query will return the Cartesian product of the tables. The main responsibility for reasonable and logically correct queries is on the programmer's shoulders. Some basic recommendations for composing "good" queries are discussed later in this chapter. In general, query processing is performed for any syntactically correct query with authorized access to all required resources. The programmer is responsible for making the query meaningful.

5.2. Types of Optimization

The optimization of a query starts with its decomposition, when the system tries to build a relational expression implementing an effective sequence of relational operations. The optimization of a query does not end there. For each relational operation in the sequence, there are different ways to search and read the necessary data, and to process the data in memory. Today's DBMSs offer two basic types of optimization: heuristic and cost-based.

5.2.1 Heuristic Optimization

Relational operations have different processing complexity (see Appendix 2). Systems with a heuristic (also called rule-based) approach to optimization use heuristic rules based on the complexity of the relational operations and the transformation rules for relational operations. The detailed description of transformation rules can be found in [Özsu]. By applying these rules, the system tries to rebuild the relational expression and make it more efficient. For the above example of query decomposition (from 5.1.3), the optimizer will choose the more efficient relational expression, which in this example happens to be the second expression.

Query optimization does not end with decomposition. After decomposing the query, the system applies definite rules for choosing the strategy of accessing the data. For example, for the discussed query the system has to read rows of the IT departments (deptType=IT) of the table Department. If there is an index on the deptType column of the table, the system will choose indexed access to the data of the table because according to heuristic rules indexed data access is preferable to full table access. Heuristic rules are formulated for the most common situations and do not take into consideration a particular state of the database, that is why they do not necessarily give the best strategy for each particular state of the database. Heuristic optimization was used in the earlier versions of DBMSs.

Heuristic optimization is based on the rules of complexity and the transformational rules of relational operations.

Some of the basic heuristic rules are:

- Perform the selection operations as early as possible. In the discussed example, the second relational expression, which started with the selection on deptType, was more efficient because fewer rows were passed to subsequent operations.
- Transform a Cartesian product that has a subsequent selection based on a join condition into the join operation. In the first discussed strategy, the Cartesian product of Employee and Department was followed by the selection with a join condition between these two tables. In the second strategy, which was more efficient, in place of the Cartesian product and the subsequent selection we used a join (recall the definition of the join operation from Appendix 2).
- Execute the most restrictive selections first – performance is better if fewer rows go to subsequent operations, e.g. on our example. first select all rows from the table Department with deptType = 'IT' and then join the result with the table Employee by deptCode:

$$\text{Employee} \blacktriangleright\blacktriangleleft_{\text{deptCode}} \sigma_{\text{deptType='IT'}}(\text{Department})$$

5.2.2 Cost-Based Optimization

Another way to find the optimal strategy for carrying out the query is to estimate the costs of the different strategies and choose the strategy with the minimum cost, similar to the approach shown earlier in this chapter. The estimation of the cost requires database statistics which are measurements of the physical properties of the database. In the above example, the estimation of strategies was based on information about the number of rows in the tables and the number of rows for the IT departments. The accuracy of cost-based optimization depends on how detailed and up-to-date the database statistics are.

The database statistics are usually kept in the database dictionary and include:

- Cardinality (number of rows) of tables.
- Number of data blocks (pages) occupied by tables.
- Number of rows per block for tables.
- Number of distinct values in columns of tables.
- Maximum and minimum values of columns of tables.

Cost-based optimization estimates costs of strategies with the help of the database statistics.

Keeping the statistics updated after every modification of data is not feasible because statistics recalculations and updates in the data dictionary create processing overhead and decrease performance. That is why statistics are gathered on a periodic basis depending on modifying activities in the database, e.g. several times a day for a database with intensive modifying activities, and less frequently for a database in which data are modified less often.

5.2.3   Static and Dynamic Optimization

There are two ways to build and execute a strategy – to accept the strategy developed *before execution* and follow it, or to start with the developed strategy, while re-evaluating and changing it *during execution* if the initial steps do not give the expected result. The first approach is called static optimization, and the second – dynamic optimization. Most DBMSs use static optimization, though there are significant efforts being performed to produce efficient dynamic query optimization.

5.3. Factors That Influence Performance

Though there was tremendous progress in query processing and query optimization capabilities of DBMSs, the performance of database applications is defined not only by the power of the query optimizer but also by many other factors.

The design of data plays an important role in the performance of the future database. The design of data has to correspond to the nature of the database applications, e.g. for OLTP databases the data model is usually normalized, while for OLAP databases, the data model is denormalized.

The implementation of the database, including the organization of data storage, has a major impact on performance. The database has to be designed and implemented considering the expected reading and modifying activities, volumes of data, number of concurrent users, and other factors.

The design and implementation of the database application have to be performed with the understanding of the database design and implementation, and the features of the DBMS. Ignoring specifics of the database implementation and not utilizing the DBMS features in the application can cause unsatisfactory performance.

The performance of the database depends upon the database environment (the hardware and software) and the degree to which the database implementation utilizes this environment.

This chapter concentrates on database-related factors that influence performance and features of the DBMS, which can be used for performance improvement. General recommendations about application design are discussed in this chapter and are discussed in more detail in Chapter 6 on transaction management.

5.3.1 Database Design

When considering a design solution for a database, it is important to remember that a particular design is rarely equally beneficial for all database requests. Therefore, the designer's efforts must be directed on achieving the best performance for the most important and frequent queries.

For OLTP databases, the primary goal of the database design methodology is to build a normalized database free of update anomalies. The performance of modifying operations benefits from the normalized design because each fact is stored in the database only once and if it is modified, the modification takes place once. However, the processing of read queries in the normalized database is often complicated because of numerous tables (compared to denormalized databases) and the necessity to join data from multiple tables in queries. The join is an expensive operation in terms of processing, and adding a table to a join query can cause performance problems. For example, if the table Title is added to the join of the query about employees of the IT departments, performance becomes several times worse.

The performance of read queries can be improved by denormalization of the database. Suppose that queries about employees of departments of different types for the Manufacturing Company database are executed often and their performance is important. Denormalization of the database by merging the tables Department and Employee can be beneficial for the performance of these queries. Denormalization results in the new table Department_Employee (deptCode, deptName, location, deptType, ID, emplName, emplType, deptCode, titleCode), which contains data about employees and the departments they are assigned to. Let us estimate the performance of the query about employees of the IT departments on the new table. The table contains 4000 rows (because one employee works in one department), and the cost of retrieving the ID and name of employees of the IT departments is the cost of reading all the rows of the new table: 4000. Denormalization improved the performance of the query.

The performance of read queries that involve multiple large tables can be dramatically improved by denormalizing the database. Note that the improvement of performance of read queries comes at the cost of performance of some update queries. For example, updating a department's name, which in the normalized database requires changing one row, causes changes in approximately 20 rows of our denormalized database. Besides, the denormalized database needs additional measures to support data consistency – in our case, it is important to ensure that the data about every department are consistently supported across multiple rows with the department's data. Denormalization of the database of the discussed case is justified if there are many read requests on the tables Employee and Department, and these tables are updated rarely. Special databases – OLAP databases or data warehouses – for which the performance of read queries from multiple very large tables is important, are designed as denormalized. Denormalization of OLAP databases is considered if required performance cannot be achieved by other means, some of which are discussed below.

The performance of some queries can be improved by denormalization of the involved tables.

Another possibility for improving performance is to consider splitting a "wide" table into several "narrower" tables. For example, if an application is often requesting the ID and name of employees of a particular department, and the performance of this application is important, then splitting the table into two: Employee1(ID, emplName, deptCode) and Employee2(ID, emplType, titleCode)will improve the performance of queries about the ID and name of employees. In Chapter 2 it is explained that data from the table is read by data blocks. The "narrower" the row of a table, the more rows fit in the block. For accessing N rows of a narrower table the system has to read fewer blocks than for a wider table. However, this solution makes retrieving and modifying of the cross-table data more complicated and expensive, which is why it is used in special situations only. This approach can be applied when a table has one or more very long columns. For example, users need to keep the resumes of employees in a database. Adding the column resume to the Employee table can have negative impact on the performance of read queries – because of this long column each block of the table will contain only a few rows, and the number of blocks, which are accessed during query processing, will be significant. If instead the new table Employee_Resume (ID, resume) is created, then performance of existing queries will not be compromised. For this example, the data about resumes will be requested separately from the other data about employees and there will not be many cross-table queries. It is recommended to keep long columns in a separate table, especially if they are accessed separately from other columns of the table.

Consider keeping very long columns in a separate table.

It is important to choose appropriate data types for columns, especially the key columns. The key columns must be simple and short – numeric data types are the best choice.

Choose correct data types for columns. Make the key columns simple and short.

A distributed design of the database (see Chapter 3) can significantly improve the performance of some applications by localizing the data.

There is no unconditionally perfect database design. The design of the database is defined by its purpose, the types and frequencies of database requests, and performance requirements.

5.3.2 Design of Applications and Queries

Often performance problems can be caused by an inappropriately designed application or by a lack of understanding of the database features by application developers. For example, an application may be programmed without considering how the DBMS handles concurrent data access and may request exclusive access to data where it actually does not need it. As a result, this application will block the processing of other applications that need the same data resource or make its concurrent execution by several users impossible (concurrent access to data and its problems are explained in Chapter 6).

In another case, an application can make multiple unnecessary accesses to the database. Reducing the number of accesses can reduce the load on the database and make the performance of this and other applications better. For example, for the Manufacturing Company case users frequently have to access data about employees of particular departments. The application shows users the list of the company's departments, allows them to select a department, and returns the data about employees of the selected department. One way to implement this application is to read the data about the departments for every such request. However, because the data about departments does not change often, a better way is to the read data about the departments once (e.g. when the application is started) and keep the data in memory (if needed, the data about the departments can be refreshed). This gives two advantages: firstly, the application will access data about the departments much faster, and secondly, there will be fewer trips to the database and less resource contention, which may improve the performance of other applications as well.

Here is another example of optimizing the performance of an application. Imagine that the application has to produce a report that requires multiple accesses to several tables retrieves and processes large amounts of data. These multiple data requests can be implemented in the application. As a result, the application performs multiple trips to the database, and data is transferred from the database to the application multiple times contributing to the network traffic. If, on the other hand, the report is implemented as a stored procedure and the application has the procedure call, then the application performs only one database access and receives only the final set of data (see Figure 5-3). This solution benefits not only the application that produces the report, but also other applications working on the database.

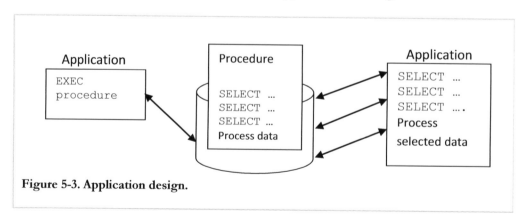

Figure 5-3. Application design.

Minimize the number of database accesses and amounts of data transferred from the database.

Queries on the database must be programmed in such a way that they benefit from the query processing features of a particular DBMS and take into consideration the design and implementation of the database. Though query optimizers today are significantly more "intelligent" than before and are less dependent on the query form to produce a good execution strategy, the role of the database programmer who understands how queries are processed and knows how the database is implemented, is very important. Here is an example of the importance of understanding of the query processing features of the DBMS. The query selects data about employees whose names start with the letter 'A' or 'a'. Assume that there is an index on the column emplName of the table Employee. Both of the following queries return the correct data. However, the first query is not able to use the index on the column emplName because of the applied function UPPER[18]. If the table Employee is large and it is necessary to use indexed access, then the first query is not a good solution:

```
SELECT * FROM Employee
WHERE UPPER(emplName) LIKE 'A%';

SELECT * FROM Employee
WHERE emplName LIKE 'A%' OR emplName LIKE 'a%';
```

Another example shows that the programming of queries requires knowledge of how the database is designed and implemented. Any of the following queries can be used for reading the data about employees of the departments '001', '002', and '003':

```
SELECT * FROM Employee
WHERE deptCode BETWEEN '001' AND '003';

SELECT * FROM Employee
WHERE deptCode IN ('001', '002', '003');

SELECT * FROM Employee
WHERE deptCode = '001' OR deptCode = '002' OR deptCode =
'003';
```

The query optimizer most probably will convert the second query into the third. Therefore, let us compare the first and third queries for different implementations of the table Employee:

- The table is stored as a heap. Whether there is an index on the column deptCode or not, the queries are processed similarly.
- The table is stored in the index cluster with deptCode as the cluster key. The queries are processed similarly.
- The table is stored in the hash cluster with the hash function applied to the column deptCode. The third query benefits from the cluster storage and accesses only blocks with data about the requested departments. However, the first query cannot take advantage of the cluster and performs full table scan. This happens because the expression deptCode BETWEEN '001' AND '003' of the first query is transformed into deptCode >= '001'

---

[18] UPPER function in Oracle returns the string value of the argument converted to the upper case, e.g. UPPER('abc') = 'ABC'.

AND deptCode <= '003', and hash clusters only can improve the performance of an exact equality queries. Therefore, for this case, the third query is the appropriate way to program the request.

These examples remind us about the effect of database transparency – we cannot rely on the application developers to know the details of the database implementation and the specifics of database processing. Therefore, it is responsibility of the database developer to provide the views or procedures that implement the application's requests in the most efficient way.

The documentation of each DBMS contains specific recommendations for writing efficient queries.

5.3.3 Data Storage

Physically data are stored in tables. The design and the implementation of tables requires attention and consideration because they have a major impact on performance. One of the goals of organizing data storage is to minimize the number of database blocks that are accessed during query processing (see the detailed discussion of data storage in Chapter 2). Several approaches help reduce the number of block accesses.

5.3.3.1 Effective Packing of Data in Tables

Data blocks must be as full as possible to store the maximum number of rows, however, there must be enough space left for updating the rows, which are already in the block. Depending on the nature of the data and database activities, database programmers and administrators have to find a compromise between partially full blocks and the risk of having migrating rows.

Keep data effectively packed and avoid row migration.

Appropriately chosen data types can improve data packing, e.g. choosing the VARCHAR2 data type for columns with variable length can result in more rows per block than when using the CHAR data type.

5.3.3.2 Clustering

The performance of queries using equality or range conditions on a column (or columns) can be improved by clustering, where rows with the same value of the column are stored in the same data blocks. This type of clustering is called *index clustering*. The index cluster needs an index to support it and is accessed through this index. For example, if the table Employee is clustered by the deptCode column, then the processing of queries with the condition …WHERE deptCode = X will result in fewer block accesses than for the heap storage of this table where rows of the department X are scattered across numerous blocks. The performance of join queries can benefit from clustering the joined tables – this is like pre-joining rows of these tables and storing them together in a cluster. Consider the query:

```
SELECT emplName, deptName
FROM Employee e, Department d
WHERE e.deptCode = d.deptCode;
```

Its performance can be improved by storing the tables Employee and Department in a cluster with the cluster key deptCode.

Note that the performance of queries on one of the clustered-together tables may become worse because records of the table will be stored across more blocks than if the table were stored by itself. For example, the performance of the following query will be worse if the table is stored in a cluster together with the table Employee:

```
SELECT * FROM Department;
```

Most DBMSs also support another type of cluster – the *hash cluster*. Rows in the hash cluster are stored not based on the value of the cluster key, but based on the result of applying the hash function to the cluster key column. The hash function applied to the cluster key defines the location of a new row when data are inserted, and the location of an existing row when data are retrieved. Appropriately defined hash clusters allow accessing the row in a single disk read.

Hash clusters are beneficial for queries that have exact equality conditions. Range or non-equality queries, like. ... WHERE deptCode <> '002' or ... WHERE deptCode > '002' cannot benefit from hash clusters.

Though clusters can significantly improve performance and increase the database throughput for read queries, they can cause performance problems for tables that have many updates and inserts because of the necessity to reorganize clusters.

Consider clustering tables for improving the performance of queries with equality conditions and joins if the tables are not modified often.

5.3.4 Indices

With the heap organization of storage, the retrieval of data in many cases requires access to most of the blocks with data (this is called full table scan). For example, to find the employee with ID = 1 (ID is the primary key and therefore unique), the system has to perform reading blocks of the table one after another until the requested row is found. The index cluster organization itself does not help much in improving performance of query processing if the system does not know in which blocks of the cluster the requested data are located. Indices are special database objects that make access to data more efficient (indices are explained in Chapter 2).

Let us perform a rough estimation of the second strategy for execution of the query about employees of the IT departments (from 5.1.2) with an index on the deptType column of the table Department and an index on the deptCode column of the table Employee. For simplicity, assume that the system performs access to one data block in the index in order to read the address of a row of the table. Remember that indexed access includes reading index blocks, finding the addresses of the needed table blocks, and then reading the respective table blocks. For the indexed execution of the discussed query:

1. For the selection, read the index on the deptType column of the table Department: 40 accesses, then read the rows of the table Department: 40 accesses.

2. For the intermediate result of the selection, write all rows to disk: 40 accesses.
3. For the join, read the result of the previous step: 40 accesses, then read the index on the deptCode column of the table Employee: 800 accesses, and then read the data of the table Employee: 800 accesses.

The total cost is significantly less than the costs of access without indices:

$$40 * 3 + 40 + 800 + 800 = 1760.$$

It is important to understand how indexed access to data is performed and that indices are not always beneficial. Let us compare the indexed and full table scan performances of the query, which requests data about employees that do not work in the IT departments:

```
SELECT ID, name
FROM Employee e, Department d
WHERE e.deptCode = d.deptCode AND deptType <> 'IT';
```

This query differs from the previously discussed query only by the condition on the deptType column. Estimation is provided for the following strategy:

$$\text{Employee} \blacktriangleright \blacktriangleleft _{\text{Employee.deptCode = Department.deptCode}} \sigma_{\text{Department.deptType<>'IT'}}(\text{Department}).$$

If there are no indices, the system performs the full scan of the tables:

1. For the selection, read the table Department:200 accesses. The selection results are 160 rows.
2. Write the intermediate result of the selection to disk: 160 accesses.
3. For the join, read the rows of the table Employee: 4000 accesses, and rows of the result of the previous step: 160 accesses.

The total cost of processing without indices is:

$$200 + 160 + 4000 + 160 = 4520.$$

The cost of index access is calculated as follows:

1. For the selection, read the index on the column deptType of the table Department: 160 accesses, then read the respective blocks of the table itself: 160 accesses.
2. Write the intermediate result of the selection to disk: 160 accesses.
3. For the join, read the rows of the result of the previous step: 160 accesses, then read the index on the column deptCode of the table Employee: 3200 accesses, and then access the respective rows of the table Employee: 3200 accesses.

The total cost of processing with indices is:

$$160 * 3 + 160 + 3200 + 3200 = 7040.$$

The total cost of the indexed access is significantly higher than the cost of access without indices. This example demonstrates that the index is not efficient when a large number of rows of the table are accessed. Indices are considered beneficial for accessing not more than 15- 25% of the rows of a table.

If indices can enhance the performance of read queries, they can decrease the performance of modifying queries, because in many cases not only does the table have to be updated, but also the indices of the table as well.

An index can be built on multiple columns, e.g. for frequent requests of the names of full-time employees working in a particular department, the following index may be useful:

```
CREATE INDEX i1 ON Employee(empType, deptCode);
```

Because the data in this index is organized by empType and within empType by deptCode (similarly to the last and first names in the phone directory), the index can be used for queries with conditions on both columns of the index or with conditions on the empType column only:

```
... WHERE empType = 'Full-time' AND deptCode = '001';
```

or

```
... WHERE empType = 'Full-time';
```

In most DBMSs this index cannot be used for queries with the condition on deptCode only:

```
... WHERE deptCode = '001';
```

If there are two groups of queries: queries of the first group are constrained by both empType and deptCode, and queries of the second group are constrained by deptCode only, then the second group of queries cannot use the previously created index i1. However, both groups of queries can benefit from the index:

```
CREATE INDEX i2 ON Employee(deptCode, empType);
```

Because indices occupy significant space[19] (some indices can be larger than their table), and because each index adds to the burden of processing of modifying queries, the number and types of indices must be carefully considered. For example, it does not make sense to keep both indices i1 and i2. The index i2 helps in the processing of the two groups of most frequent queries, and therefore we do not need to keep index i1 (note that since index i1 cannot improve the performance of all the mentioned queries, it should not be chosen in preference to i2).

The composite index is used for the processing of queries in which the leftmost part of the index columns is constrained.

Database programmers must take advantage of another important feature of indices: if a query requests only columns that are contained in the index, then there is no need to access the table

---

[19] On average, the size of the indices is about 80% of the size of the tables.

at all, and the performance of such a query will especially benefit from the index. For example, the system uses only the index i2 to process the following query about the number of employees of each type in several departments:

```
SELECT empType, COUNT(*)
FROM Employee
WHERE deptCode IN ('001', '002)
GROUP BY empType;
```

The index can be sufficient for data access of queries that reference only the columns of the index.

In some cases, in order to avoid accessing the table, it is useful to create a multi-column index and have all the needed data in it. For example, though the index i2 is unnecessarily complicated for queries that access data from the table Employee given a department code, it is sufficient for any query that involves the attributes deptCode and deptType and, therefore, can be beneficial to the query's performance.

In some cases, the optimizer can take advantage of several different table indices. Assume, for example, that there are two indices on the table Employee:

```
CREATE INDEX i1 ON Employee(deptCode);

CREATE INDEX i2 ON Employee(emplType);
```

A query about employees of a particular department and a particular type can use both indices. With the help of the first index, the optimizer finds the rows of the table that have the requested department code, with the help of the second index – the rows of the specified employee type, and then finds the intersection of the two found sets of rows.

You have to remember that the DBMS always builds an index on the columns of the primary key of a table; it is called the primary index. Indices on non-key columns are called secondary indices. When considering a secondary index, the primary index has to be taken into account. For example, if the table T (A, B, C, D) has the primary index on attributes A and B (in that order), we can have a number of situations for different query patterns based on attributes:

- A and C. Probably, instead of creating the index on the attributes A and C, a single-column index on the attribute C will suffice.
- B and C, and B and D. If queries constrained by the attribute A are not common, then changing the order of attributes in the primary index can help in building more efficient secondary indices.

It is recommended to consider a secondary index in the following situations:

- There are frequent read queries that involve constraints on certain table columns and the performance of these queries is important. Then the constrained columns could be used as the secondary index.

- Columns of the index are selective enough – queries constrained by these columns return not more than 25% of rows of the table.
- Updating activities on the table are not too heavy and their performance is less crucial than the performance of data retrieval.
- On the foreign key attribute of a child table when the child and parent tables are used together often in join queries.

Analyze the most frequent queries on a table to define the best combinations and order of columns in table's indices.

Avoid building indices for small tables and on long character columns.

Storage parameters of indices must be defined similarly to the storage parameters of tables. For better performance it is recommended to store the tables and their indices on different disks, so that the system can access the table and the index in parallel.

Index statistics must be computed on a regular basis for DBMSs that apply cost-based optimization use statistics on indices.

5.3.5 Other Factors

Taking care of the previously discussed application related factors is usually the responsibility of the developers of the database and database applications. There are other factors of a more global character, which influence the performance of the whole database and are important for multiple applications on the database. These are factors defined by the database environment, such as the storage subsystem, which includes multiple storage devices (disks or disk arrays), available memory, processing units, and the operating system.

Because of the global nature of these factors, planning, configuring and managing them is the responsibility of the system and database administrators. Tuning of the database environment is beyond the subject of this chapter, but for a better understanding of the organization of databases and query processing mechanisms, we need to discuss such parts of the database as the database buffers and log files.

5.3.5.1 Database Buffer

The database buffer and its role in the recovery of a database are discussed in more detail in Chapter 7.

Disk access is a very expensive operation in terms of performance, and the system tries to minimize the number of disk accesses. The ultimate solution to this would be to keep the whole database in memory and perform all the data processing there. Because it is not feasible for most applications, databases keep only some portion of their data in memory. The part of the memory dedicated to keeping data is called the database buffer. The size of the buffer is limited by the size of memory.

The logic of the buffer read typically is as follows:

- Go to buffer cache and look for the block.
- If the block is not there, perform physical I/O and put it into the cache.
- Return the block from cache.
- If the next user needs this block, he probably will find it in the cache.

However, there is the opportunity to do "direct I/O", normally used with parallel query - your server process will bypass the buffer cache and read right from disk into its own memory and process the blocks there. Generally used for a large table full table scan.

Because it is impossible to fit the whole database in memory, the question is, which data should be kept in the buffer? Usually the database keeps the most recently accessed data in memory. Earlier in this chapter, for estimating different strategies, it was assumed that intermediate results of the relational operations were stored on disk. In reality, intermediate results usually are kept in the database buffer. The more that data are accessed from the buffer (and not from disk), the better the performance is. Data access from the buffer is called logical access (LA), and access from disk is called physical access (PA).

When the database is started, the buffer is empty (it is said that the database is cold) and most data accesses are physical. The performance of a cold database is worse than the performance of a warm database where the database has been used for some time and part of the data is in the buffer.

The database administrator has to define the size of the buffer based on the needs of all the applications on the database and the physical parameters of the server. A larger buffer can accommodate more data, which can bring a significant improvement of performance.

5.3.5.2 Separate Storage of Tables, Indices, and Log Files

Locating tables and indices on different disks allows the system to parallelize access to the index and access to the table when leveraging indices in query processing.

Log files are discussed in more detail in Chapter 7. The purpose of log files is to protect data in the database buffer that has been modified recently from being lost, e.g. in the case of a system crash. All data modifications are recorded in log files. Writing to the log file can create a significant overhead, and hence it is important to configure log files appropriately, e.g. performance can be improved, if log files and tables are located on different disks (note that locating the log files on the same disks as tables defies the purpose of the log files to enable the data recovery – they will be lost together with the tables in case of the media crash). In some situations in order to improve performance, logging can be turned off.

5.3.6 Out of the Box Approaches

Database performance is affected by various organizational measures and activities. In some cases a simple, out-of-the-box approach helps to achieve the required performance.

For example, many times during a business day an accounting application requests yesterday's account balances. The computation of the balances is complicated and resource consuming, and tuning efforts do not give the required performance. In this situation, it may be a good idea to compute balances every day and store them in a separate table for the next day activities.

Another example shows how performance problems can be resolved by organizational measures. Pre-computing account balances for the previous example is resource consuming and creates resource contention; and hence it may be reasonable to execute it after the end of the business day when the load on the database is low. The procedure will not interfere with other important applications that have to be executed during the day.

5.4. Examples of Influence of Different Factors on Performance

The following examples are taken from [Shasha] they provide quantitative demonstrations of how different factors influence database performance.

Figure 5-4 shows how the performance of a multipoint query[20] is dramatically improved by clustering: the throughput for the clustered table is about two times higher (depending on the DBMS used) than the throughput for a heap table with an index. For the 1 million-row table, which was used for testing, the performance on the heap table without the index is extremely poor.

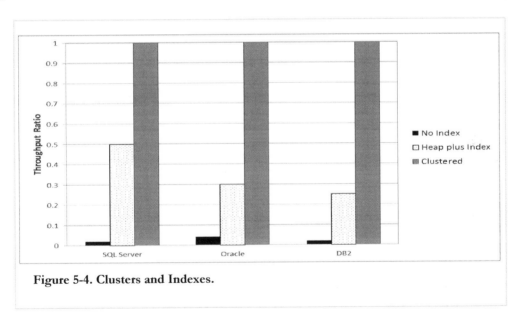

Figure 5-4. Clusters and Indexes.

Figure 5-5 shows how the index can worsen the performance of insert queries. The test involved 100,000 insertions using Oracle for a table with and without an index.

---

[20] A multipoint query is a query that returns multiple records for an equality condition.

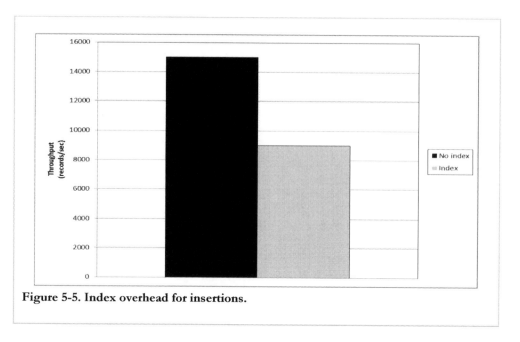

Figure 5-5. Index overhead for insertions.

Figure 5-6 demonstrates the performance improvement with an increase in the buffer size. The performance of the multipoint query increases linearly with the increasing buffer size until the whole table fits in memory.

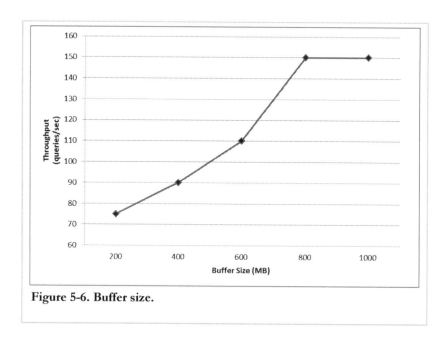

Figure 5-6. Buffer size.

Figure 5-7 shows that locating the log file and the table on different disks improves the performance of insertions and updates by almost 30%.

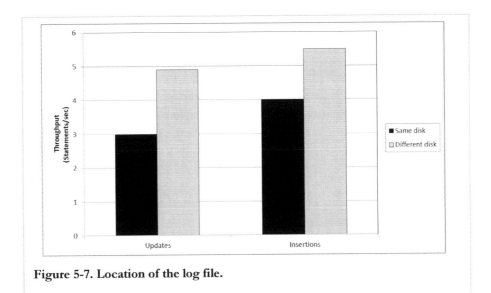

Figure 5-7. Location of the log file.

5.5. Database Tuning

Activities directed towards the improvement of database performance are called database tuning. Tuning of the database starts at the design stage and continues to the maintenance stage.

5.5.1 Proactive Tuning

Design, development and implementation efforts are directed towards achieving the performance required by users. This is proactive tuning of the database, because designers and developers, as well as administrators, try to meet users' expectations. Proactive tuning defines to a large extent the cost of further database maintenance. Figure 5-8 shows that decisions made at the earlier stages of database design and implementation have a significant impact on the performance of the database, while the cost at these stages is relatively low. Efforts directed towards the improvement of performance at the later stages have a higher cost and lower impact on database performance.

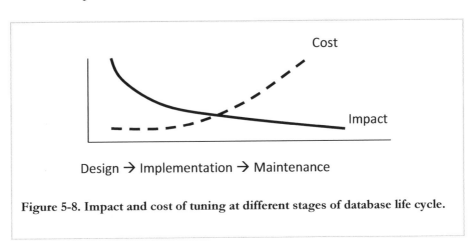

Figure 5-8. Impact and cost of tuning at different stages of database life cycle.

The recommended sequence of proactive tuning steps is the following:

- *User requirements.* Sometimes user expectations are unrealistic or unnecessarily high. Relaxing user requirements without sacrificing the functionality of the database can reduce the cost of the database design, implementation and maintenance.
- *Data design.* The design of the data must correspond to the nature of the database applications.
- *Application design.* Applications should not create an unnecessary load on the database; the number of database accesses and the amount of transferred data should be kept to a minimum.
- *Queries.* Queries must be programmed such that they take full advantage of the SQL features of the DBMS and the query optimizer, and must be developed with an understanding of the database design and implementation.
- *Access to data.* The number of physical data accesses must be minimized. All necessary indices must be created, clustering should be considered, the allocation of data in data blocks must be optimized, and the size of the database buffer must be increased.
- *Database environment.* The best configuration of memory, storage and processing units must be defined.

5.5.2 Monitoring and Troubleshooting

During the lifetime of a database, some of the database features or settings of the environment that were predefined at the development and implementation stages may become inconsistent with the current state of the database or the way the database is used. For example, a table may become very large and the performance of some queries may decrease which might require reorganizing the table storage. Or, the number of concurrent users of the database may increase and lead to lower throughput; in either case upgrading the database environment and rewriting the database transactions may be necessary.

Monitoring performance of the database is the responsibility of the database administrator. Most DBMSs provide powerful tools for performance monitoring and controlling the consumption of resources. Analyzing the results of monitoring enables the administrator to diagnose problems and bottlenecks, and to define ways of dealing with these issues. Fixing the problems may require the intervention of the database designer or developer.

Tuning the database is often a series of compromises, e.g. you may sacrifice the performance of less important queries to improve the performance of the crucial ones. Or, if the performance analysis indicates that we need an expansion of disk storage or memory and it is not possible due to technical, financial or political reasons, we may need to limit the number of concurrent users.

5.6. Performance in Distributed Databases

5.6.1 Optimization of Distributed Queries

Improving performance is the primary goal of data distribution. The appropriate distribution should significantly improve the performance of local applications and queries. Further improvements in the performance of the local databases are provided as in any centralized database.

Improving the performance of global queries, however, may require special measures. Let us discuss how query processing is performed in the distributed database and the possible ways to improve it. Making the distributed database transparent to users was discussed in Chapter 2. In the transparent distributed database, global users define their requests on global external views. To execute a query, the system has to transform the query on the views into the query on the fragments and unfragmented relations distributed across the various databases that make up the distributed database.

Let us assume that the database for the Manufacturing Company case is distributed as in the example of Chapter 3: the table Department is fragmented by the attribute location, and the fragmentation of the table Employee is derived from the fragmentation of the table Department. The global applications are executed from the New York site. The query about the ID and name of employees of the IT departments that was discussed in this chapter for the centralized database is formulated on global views for the distributed database:

```
SELECT ID, name
FROM Employee e, Department d
WHERE e.deptCode = d.deptCode AND d.deptType = 'IT';
```

Consider the global strategy similar to the second strategy for the same query in the centralized database:

$$\text{Employee} \bowtie_{\text{Employee.deptCode = Department.deptCode}} (\sigma_{\text{Department.deptType='IT'}}(\text{Department}))$$

This query must be transformed into a query on fragments and relations in different locations using the fragmentation reconstruction rules:

$$(\text{Employee}_1 \cup \text{Employee}_2 \cup \text{Employee}_3) \bowtie_{\text{deptCode}} (\sigma_{\text{deptType='IT'}}(\text{Department}_1 \cup \text{Department}_2 \cup \text{Department}_3))$$

Since the global query is run in New York, data are requested from the New York database, and there are several ways to execute the query. For example:

- Send all necessary data to the New York database and then perform all processing there following the expression above.
- Distribute the query, perform local processing on each involved site, then send the results to the New York database and finish the processing there. For this approach, the strategy may be rewritten as (the detailed explanation of how the following expression is obtained is given in 5.6.2.2):

$$\text{Employee}_1 \bowtie_{\text{deptCode}} (\sigma_{\text{deptType='IT'}}(\text{Department}_1)) \cup$$

$$\text{Employee}_2 \bowtie_{\text{deptCode}} (\sigma_{\text{deptType='IT'}}(\text{Department}_2)) \cup$$

$$\text{Employee}_3 \blacktriangleright\!\!\blacktriangleleft_{\text{deptCode}} (\sigma_{\text{deptType='IT'}} (\text{Department}_3)))$$

This strategy performs local selections on the Department fragments and joins the results to the local fragments of Employee:

$$\text{Local result}_i = \text{Employee}_i \blacktriangleright\!\!\blacktriangleleft_{\text{deptCode}} (\sigma_{\text{deptType='IT'}}(\text{Department}_i)) \text{ [for i=1,2,3]}$$

Then the results of the local processing are transferred to the New York database; the New York database performs the union of the local results:

$$\text{Local result}_1 \cup \text{Local result}_2 \cup \text{Local result}_3$$

The cost of processing of distributed queries includes the cost of data transfer between the databases.

The total Cost =
(the number of I/O operations * the cost of one I/O operation) +
(the number of RAM operations * the cost of one RAM operation) +
(the number of transferred bytes * the byte transfer cost)

The data transfer cost is usually considerably higher than the cost of I/O operations, therefore the following rough estimation of the strategies does not consider the cost of memory and I/O operations. The cost of data transfer is calculated as the number of transferred rows.

Assume that the data are distributed evenly across the sites and on each site there are approximately 65 departments and 1330 employees. The first approach results in approximately 2660 row transfers for data of employees and 130 row transfers for the departments from both the Boston and Cleveland sites. The total cost is 2790.

For the second approach, each site performs the local selection of the IT departments and joins the result of the selection with the data about the local employees. For each site, there are 13 IT departments with 20 employees in each of them. The total cost of data transfer from the Boston and Cleveland sites is 520. Obviously, this approach gives better performance. Besides, in this case smaller amounts of data are transferred across the network – this reduces resource contention and improves the performance of other applications.

Distributed query processing includes two additional steps (Figure 5-9):

- *Data localization.* The query on global views is transformed into a query on fragments and unfragmented relations (or replicas).
- *Global optimization.* The system develops a global strategy for distributed query processing. The strategy is directed towards the minimization of the data transfer cost.

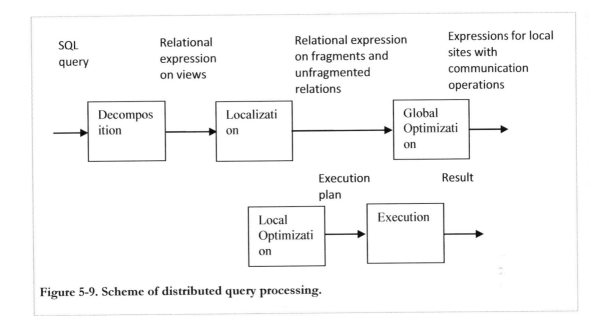

Figure 5-9. Scheme of distributed query processing.

5.6.2 Reduction

The localization of the distributed query in the previous section was performed by application of the reconstruction rules: the query on global views was transformed into a query on fragments. The resulting query is called the *generic* query.

For some distributed requests, generic queries can be simplified or reduced – this results in creation of new, reduced views. The following sections provides some examples of reduction.

5.6.2.1 Reduction of the Primary Horizontal Fragmentation

Let us consider the query, which requests data about the New York and Cleveland departments:

```
SELECT * FROM Department
WHERE location IN ('Cleveland', 'New York');
```

The query is decomposed into the following relational expression on global views:

$$\sigma_{\text{location IN ('Cleveland', 'New York')}}(\text{Department}).$$

The view Department is implemented as the union of the horizontal fragments:

$$\sigma_{\text{location IN ('Cleveland', 'New York')}}(\text{Department}_1 \cup \text{Department}_2 \cup \text{Department}_3).$$

One of the transformation rules for the relational operations says that the selection on the union of relations is equal to the union of selections on relations, therefore the generic query can be rewritten as:

$$\sigma_{location\ IN\ (`Cleveland',\ `New\ York')}(\ Department_1)\cup$$

$$\sigma_{location\ IN\ (`Cleveland',\ `New\ York')}(Department_2)\ \cup$$

$$\sigma_{location\ IN\ (`Cleveland',\ `New\ York')}Department_3).$$

Because the condition of the selection from the fragment Department₁ (location = 'Boston') is conflicting with the predicate of the fragment, the result of applying the selection on the fragment Department₁ is always empty. Therefore, the generic query can be reduced to:

$$\sigma_{location\ IN\ (`Cleveland',\ `New\ York')}(Department_2)\ \cup$$

$$\sigma_{location\ IN\ (`Cleveland',\ `New\ York')}Department_3).$$

5.6.2.2   Reduction of the Derived Horizontal Fragmentation

In some cases, the processing of distributed queries that involve both primary and derived fragments can be significantly simplified. Consider the query about the ID and name of employees from the IT departments from 5.1.2. The generic query for this query is:

$$Employee_1 \cup Employee_2 \cup Employee_3 \bowtie_{deptCode} (\sigma_{deptType='IT'}(Department_1 \cup Department_2 \cup Department_3))$$

The transformation rule for the join of unions says:

$$(R_1 \cup R_2)\bowtie(S_1 \cup S_2) = R_1 \bowtie S_1 \cup R_1 \bowtie S_2 \cup R_2 \bowtie S_1 \cup R_2 \bowtie S_2$$

With the help of this rule, the generic query is transformed into:

$$Employee_1 \bowtie Department_1 \cup Employee_1 \bowtie Department_2 \cup$$

$$Employee_1 \bowtie Department_3 \cup Employee_2 \bowtie Department_1 \cup$$

$$Employee_2 \bowtie Department_2 \cup Employee_2 \bowtie Department_3 \cup$$

$$Employee_3 \bowtie Department_1 \cup Employee_3 \bowtie Department_2 \cup$$

$$Employee_3 \bowtie Department_3.$$

Because of the nature of the derived fragmentation, any join $Employee_i \bowtie Department_j$, where $i \neq j$ produces an empty result. Therefore, the above expression can be reduced to the expression that was mentioned in 5.6.1:

$$Employee_1 \bowtie_{deptCode} (\sigma_{deptType='IT'}(Department_1)) \cup$$

$$Employee_2 \bowtie_{deptCode} (\sigma_{deptType='IT'} (Department_2)) \cup$$

$$Employee_3 \blacktriangleright\!\!\blacktriangleleft_{deptCode} (\sigma_{deptType='IT'} (Department_3)).$$

5.6.2.3 Reduction of the Vertical Fragmentation

Let us discuss the vertical fragmentation of the relation Employee from the Case 3.6 of Chapter 3. Let's say that the New York users need data about the names of all employees and the codes of the departments to which employees are assigned. In addition, let's assume that the Cleveland users are working with data about the types and title codes of all employees.

$$Employee_1 = \Pi_{ID, empName, deptCode} (Employee)$$

$$Employee_2 = \Pi_{ID, empType, titleCode} (Employee).$$

The query requests all titles that are used by employees of the company:

```
SELECT DISTINCT titleCode
FROM Employee;
```

This query is decomposed into:

$$\Pi_{titleCode}(Employee).$$

Reconstruction of the global relation from vertical fragments produces the following generic query:

$$\Pi_{titleCode}(Employee_1 \blacktriangleright\!\!\blacktriangleleft_{ID} Employee_2).$$

One of the transformation rules says that the projection on the join of relations is equal to the join of projections on relations:

$$\Pi_{titleCode}(Employee_1 \blacktriangleright\!\!\blacktriangleleft_{ID} Employee_2) =$$

$$\Pi_{titleCode}(Employee_1) \blacktriangleright\!\!\blacktriangleleft \Pi_{titleCode}(Employee_2).$$

It is easy to see that the projection on the fragment Employee$_1$ produces the empty result and can be eliminated from the query. The resulting reduced query is:

$$\Pi_{titleCode}(Employee_2).$$

5.6.2.4 Reduction of the Hybrid Fragmentation

The reduction of the hybrid fragmentation is provided by the application of the discussed reduction approaches:

1. Remove the selection on a horizontal fragment if the selection condition conflicts with the predicate of the fragment.
2. Remove the projection on a vertical fragment if the fragment does not contain any of the columns of the projection.
3. Remove joins, which produce empty relations.

For distributed queries that allow reduction, it is useful to apply the reduction rules and build reduced global views, i.e. views that include only fragments or relations that are relevant for the query.

5.7. Query Processing in Oracle

5.7.1 Types of Optimization in Oracle

Oracle supports two types of optimization: the rule-based (RBO) and the cost-based (CBO). CBO was first introduced in Oracle 8 and now is considered the main optimization type. However, CBO can be applied only if the necessary statistics are available.

5.7.1.1 Rule-Based Optimization

To produce a strategy of query execution, RBO applies heuristic rules. It uses information about the structure and integrity constraints of the tables involved in the query, existing indices and their types (primary, secondary, cluster, single-column, composite). Rules rank different types of access to data: the lower the rank, the better the performance is expected. The highest rank is for a full table scan (all rows of the table are accessed), the lowest – direct access to a row with the help of the physical address of the row (ROWID). The optimizer tries to apply the lowest-rank operations first. For example, if there is an index on the column deptType of the table Department and an index on the column deptCode of the table Employee, then for the query

```
SELECT *
FROM Employee e, Department d
WHERE e.deptCode = e.deptCode AND deptType = 'Business';
```

RBO decides to use the index on the column deptType of the table Department because the rank of the single-column index is lower than full table scan. Further, to access respective rows of the table Employee for selected department rows, the optimizer uses the index on the column deptCode.

5.7.1.2 Cost-Based Optimization

CBO is recommended for most applications and is used as the default when possible (the optimizer can apply it only if database statistics are available). Statistics can be calculated by the statement ANALYZE or with the help of the supplied package DBMS_STATS. For example, the following statements gather the statistics for the table Department and one of its indices:

```
ANALYZE TABLE Department COMPUTE STATISTICS;

ANALYZE INDEX i0 COMPUTE STATISTICS;
```

Statistics must be refreshed on a regular basis because obsolete statistics can cause the optimizer to not choose the best strategy for the query execution for the current state of the database.

In addition to the statistical data mentioned in 5.2.2, Oracle supports histograms. Histograms contain the most detailed information about the distribution of data in columns and they allow for a more accurate estimation of execution strategies than regular statistics. For example, suppose there are 10 different department types and that of the 200 departments, only 60 departments are of the business type. Regular statistics on the table Department say that for 200 rows of the table there are 10 distinct values of the column deptType. Based on this information, the optimizer estimates that there are approximately 20 rows for each department type, and when building the strategy of execution of the query about employees of the business departments from the previous section, decides to use the index on deptType assuming that approximately 10% of the rows of the table will be accessed.

The histogram on the column deptType of the table Department (Figure 5-10) shows that there are 60 rows of the table, for which the column deptType is equal 'Business'. The optimizer may choose not to use the index and perform a full table scan of Department because based on the histogram it makes a conclusion that more than 25% of the table rows will be accessed.

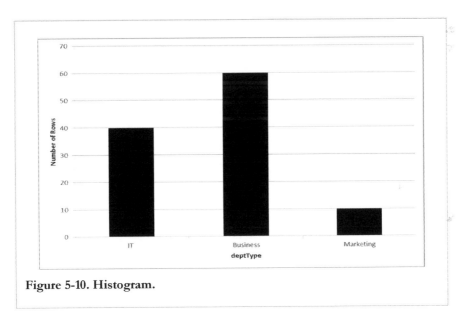

Figure 5-10. Histogram.

Information about statistics is available in the views of the database dictionary. Some of these views are:

- USER_TABLES contains the statistics of the tables owned by the user.
- USER_TAB_HISTOGRAMS contains the information about the histograms for the tables.
- USER_TAB_COL_STATISTICS contains statistics on the columns of the tables.

The following query returns basic statistics (the number of rows, the number of blocks, the average row length, and the date when the statistics were gathered) on the tables Department and Employee:

```
SELECT TABLE_NAME, NUM_ROWS, BLOCKS, AVG_ROW_LEN,
```

```
              TO_CHAR(LAST_ANALYZED, 'MM/DD/YYYY HH24:MI:SS')
FROM USER_TABLES
WHERE TABLE_NAME IN ('DEPARTMENT','EMPLOYEE');
```

TABLE_NAME	NUM_ROWS	BLOCKS	AVH_ROW_LEN	LAST_ANALYZED
DEPARTMENT	200	30	449	07/29/1999 00:59:51
EMPLOYEE	4000	50	663	07/29/1999 01:16:09

5.7.1.3   Reusing Execution Strategies

Often many database queries have the same execution pattern. For example, in the Manufacturing Company case users often need to get data about an employee given the employee's ID. Obviously, the execution strategy for all queries of this type is the same. Optimization of each query adds to the query execution cost, therefore, performing optimization once and then reusing the produced strategy in subsequent queries of the same type can additionally improve performance.

The optimizer can reuse the execution strategy after an authorization check (that has to be performed for each query). Imagine that two users John and Scott try to execute the same query:

```
SELECT * FROM John.Table1;
```

If Scott does not have authorization to access John's Table 1, the authorization check will stop further processing; if Scott does have the authorization the optimizer will use the same execution strategy.

Oracle stores execution strategies of the most recent queries in a special part of memory, called the shared pool. When a new query is processed, Oracle performs syntax, semantic, and authorization checks of the query, and then checks the shared pool. If the same query was executed not long ago and its strategy is still stored in the shared pool, Oracle reuses the execution strategy and saves on optimization and generation of the execution strategy. Such processing is called soft parsing (as opposed to hard parsing when all the steps of query processing must be performed). Reducing the number of hard parses is very important for performance on a database with a large number of concurrent users issuing numerous requests of the same type. Utilizing this feature requires a special approach to queries programming.

The database cannot recognize that two requests have the same execution strategy if they are not identical strings. For example, a user is requesting data about the employee with ID = 1:

```
SELECT *
FROM Employee
WHERE ID = 1;
```

If the user requests data about an employee with the different ID later on, the optimizer will fail to match the query with the previously executed one, though the strategy of access definitely can be reused. Therefore, it is recommended to submit similar queries in the same form using the Oracle feature of bind variables. Instead of hard coding the value of an employee's ID in each query, the value is passed to the query through a variable; the variable is assigned the value before every query execution. The above query is rewritten with the help of a simple PL/SQL block with the bind variable:

```
VARIABLE v_id NUMBER;    -- Declaring the variable
BEGIN
    :v_ID := 1;          -- Assigning the value to the variable
END;

SELECT *                 -- Using the variable in the query
FROM Employee
WHERE ID = :v_ID;

BEGIN
    :v_ID := 2;          -- Assigning a new value to the variable
END;

SELECT *                 -- Re-executing the query
FROM Employee
WHERE ID = :v_ID;
```

The request for data about another employee is formulated in exactly the same form as the first request, and the optimizer is able to apply the soft parse.

Most programming interfaces to Oracle support this feature, e.g. JDBC – Java Database Connectivity.

5.7.2 Data Storage

Different types of data storage and storage parameters are described in Chapter 2. The organization of data storage plays an important role in database tuning. Table storage is defined in the CREATE TABLE statement:

```
CREATE TABLE Department (
    deptCode CHAR(3) PRIMARY KEY,
    deptName VARCHAR2(20) NOT NULL,
    location VARCHAR2(25) CHECK (location = 'New York'),
    deptType VARCHAR2(15))
PCTFREE 10
PCTUSED 40
TABLESPACE users
STORAGE (  INITIAL 50K
           NEXT 50K
           MAXEXTENTS 10
           PCTINCREASE 25 );
```

The TABLESPACE clause specifies the tablespace where the table is located, and the STORAGE parameters specify the initial size and expansion of the table.

Parameters PCTFREE and PCTUSED specify how rows of the table are stored in data blocks. PCTFREE defines the percent of free space left in each block for possible future updates of rows of the block in order to avoid migrating or chained rows. PCTUSED sets the percent of used space in the block; a block with its percent of used space above the setting of PCTUSED is not considered available by the system for inserting new rows. The settings of the both parameters depend on the nature of the data in the table and the operations on the data, and they have an impact on the performance of read and write queries.

The value of PCTFREE cannot be set too high or the block space will be used inefficiently, and to prevent migrating rows it cannot be set too low. A too high value for PCTUSED will prevent unused space in the database but will result in more overhead for insert and delete operations because the block will be moved more frequently d from and to the list of blocks available for insertions. If the value for PCTUSED is too low, it will reduce the overhead of handling the list of available blocks, but will cause unnecessary expansion of the table.

For a table with a fixed row length and not many updates, the setting of PCTFREE has to be low; if a table has columns with variable length and their updates are possible, then the value of this parameter has to be higher. For a table with no or little deleting and inserting activities, the setting of PCTUSED can be high; for a table with many inserts and deletes, PCTUSED has to be lower. For example, for a table with a fixed row length and many expected delete and insert operations PCTFREE = 5 and PCTUSED = 50 are recommended; for a large read-only table PCTFREE = 5 and PCTUSED = 90 are recommended; for a table with a variable row length, frequent updates and no delete operations PCTFREE = 30 and PCTUSED = 70 are recommended. The total of these two settings should not exceed 100.

Index storage parameters are defined similarly to storage parameters of tables.

5.7.3 Clusters

Oracle supports two types of clusters: index and hash. Clusters improve the performance of some read queries, but intensive updating activity can result in the necessity to reorganize clusters and will negatively affect the performance of updating queries. Oracle clustered storage is explained in Chapter 2.

In index clusters, rows of a table that have the same value for a column (which is called the cluster key) are stored in the same blocks. Such storage is beneficial for read queries with equality or range conditions on the cluster key attribute. For example, queries about employees of a particular type:

```
SELECT * FROM Employee WHERE emplType = X;
```

can benefit from a cluster with the column emplType as the cluster key because rows with the same employee type will be stored together, and the system can read all requested rows from one or several blocks. Clustered storage is prepared in accordance with storage parameters for the cluster that are similar to the storage parameters of tables:

```
CREATE CLUSTER Employee_type (emplType VARCHAR2(10))
TABLESPACE users
PCTUSED 80
PCTFREE 10
SIZE 40
```

The parameter SIZE specifies the length of the row and defines the number of rows in the block of the cluster. An unreasonably high value of the parameter can cause rows of the cluster to be stored across more blocks than necessary. A low value of the parameter can lead to chained data.

After the cluster is prepared, it is used for storing tables:

```
CREATE TABLE Employee (
      ID NUMBER PRIMARY KEY,
      . . .
      emplType VARCHAR2(10),
      . . . )
CLUSTER Employee_type (emplType);
```

Index clusters are supported by the index on the cluster key:

```
CREATE INDEX i0 ON CLUSTER Employee_type;
```

Index clusters are also useful for join queries when the parent and child tables are stored in the cluster with the foreign key as the cluster key.

Hash clusters are created similarly to index clusters, however, they do not need the cluster index. The hash function, applied to the cluster key, defines the address of the row. Hash clusters are beneficial for queries with exact equality conditions only. To improve the performance of read queries that request data about employees of a particular type, the table Employee can be stored in a hash cluster with the hash function applied to the column emplType:

```
CREATE CLUSTER Employee_type_hash (emplType VARCHAR2(10))
TABLESPACE users
PCTUSED 80
PCTFREE 10
HASHKEYS 3;
```

Here are some recommendations about using clusters:

- Cluster together tables that often participate in join queries; in this case the foreign key column is chosen as the cluster key. However, clustering can make the performance on one of the clustered tables worse than when the table were stored separately.
- Index clusters can improve the performance of queries with range or equality conditions on the cluster key attribute.

- Hash clusters can be beneficial for queries with equality conditions on the cluster key attribute; they do not enhance performance of range queries.
- Clustering of tables with high modifying activity is not recommended.

5.7.4   Indices

The role of B-tree and hash cluster indices in improving performance was discussed before in this chapter. Oracle also supports a special – bitmap – type of index.

5.7.4.1   Bitmap Indices

Bitmap indices are beneficial for columns with low cardinality. They can dramatically improve query performance. Their additional advantage is that they are considerably smaller than B-tree indices.

The column emplType in the Employee table that has only three values is a good candidate for the bitmap index:

```
CREATE BITMAP INDEX i1 ON Employee(emplType);
```

The table below illustrates the bitmap index for the emplType column of the table Employee of our case. It consists of three separate bitmaps, one for each employee type.

emplType = 'Full-time'	emplType = 'Part-time'	emplType = 'Consultant'
1	0	0
0	0	1
0	1	0
1	0	0
0	0	1
1	0	0
0	1	0

Each entry or bit in the bitmap corresponds to a single row of the Employee table. The value of each bit depends on the value of emplType in the corresponding row in the table. For instance, the bitmap **emplType = 'Full-time'** contains '1' as its first bit in the first entry of the index because the first row of the Employee table contains data about a full-time employee. The bitmap **emplType = 'Full-time'** has '1' in the fourth and the sixth rows of the index.

The bitmap index can efficiently process the following query about the number of full-time employees by counting the number of '1' in the **emplType = 'Full-time'** column of the bitmap. This query will not need to access the table at all:

```
SELECT COUNT(*)
FROM Employee
WHERE emplType = 'Full-time';
```

Because of specifics of their storage, bitmap indices can create performance problems for modifying queries. These indices are widely used in data warehouses (OLAP databases).

It is important to remember that indices enhance data retrieval; however, they can cause performance problems for modifying queries. Here are some general recommendations for using indices:

- Consider bitmap indices for columns with low cardinality.
- Create the index on the foreign key of a child table if the parent and the child tables are often used together in queries.
- Create the B-tree index for queries with equality or range conditions (e.g. salary < 30000) and prefix match queries (e.g. emplName LIKE 'A%').
- Avoid indexing long columns and creating indices on small tables.
- Do not create indices for queries that access more than 25% of rows in a table.

5.7.4.2 Function-Based Indices

Before Oracle 8, a function applied to an indexed column in a query disabled indexed access to data. For example, though we have the index on the column emplName of the table Employee, the following query will result in a full table scan because of the function UPPER:

```
SELECT * FROM Employee WHERE UPPER(emplName) = 'A%';
```

This simple query can be rewritten to enable using the index, however, in situations that are more complicated, such limitation creates inconveniences. Now Oracle supports function-based indices that are created not on columns of a table, but on functions applied to columns. Such indices can be utilized by the optimizer to access the table's data for queries with conditions that include functions. The following function-based index can be used for improving the performance of the above query:

```
CREATE INDEX i0 ON Employee(UPPER(emplName);
```

Function-based indices can be based on both built-in and user-defined functions.

5.7.5 Partitions

Oracle partitions implement separate and physically independent storage for parts of a table. Such a storage arrangement is beneficial for queries that access rows from a particular part – the system's data search is more directed and efficient. For example, queries about employees of a particular type can benefit from partitioning the table Employee by emplType:

```
CREATE TABLE Employee (
  ...
)
PARTITION BY HASH(emplType)

PARTITIONS 3;
```

This was an example of hash partitioning. Range partitioning can be applied to numeric and date columns. Partitioning by dates is very efficient in historical databases or data warehouses. For example, if a table stores data about daily activities of the business, then the analysis of the business activities for different years can benefit from partitioning the table's rows by year.

Storage parameters of each partition are specified similarly to storage parameters for tables. Local indices on a partition enforce a search on that partition. In addition to local indices, global table indices support a search on the whole table.

5.7.6 Index-Organized Tables

The index-organized table can be perceived as storing the primary index on a table with all the table's columns. Index-organized tables are extremely beneficial for queries with conditions on the key columns of the table – the system performs an indexed search and gets all the needed data in one read operation (compared to a table with an index, where the system reads the index and then reads the table). Another advantage of the index-organized table is that it occupies much less storage space than the table with its primary index.

Queries constrained by the non-key columns of the index-organized table do not benefit from such storage.

5.7.7 Tuning of Queries

5.7.7.1 Understanding How Oracle Processes Queries

By default, Oracle uses CBO and the default goal of CBO is increasing the *throughput*. If needed, the goal of CBO can be set to minimizing the *response time*.

The default behavior of the Oracle optimizer is defined by the initialization parameter OPTIMIZER_MODE, which can have one of the following values:

- CHOOSE. The optimizer chooses between CBO and RBO. If statistics are available for at least one of the tables involved in the query, the optimizer will use CBO. If no statistics are available for the tables of the query, then the RBO approach will be used. This is the default value of OPTIMIZER_MODE.
- ALL_ROWS. The optimizer uses CBO regardless of the presence of the statistics. The goal of the optimization is increasing the throughput.
- FIRST_ROWS. The optimizer uses CBO regardless of the presence of statistics. The goal of optimization is minimizing the response time.
- RULE. The optimizer uses RBO regardless of the presence of statistics.

This parameter can be defined for all sessions using the database or for a particular database session. For example, the following statement changes the default behavior of the optimizer to RBO for the current session only

```
ALTER SESSION SET OPTIMIZER_GOAL = RULE;
```

5.7.7.2 Hints

The application developer or user who understands the nature of the data and the database queries can suggest a better strategy than the one chosen by the optimizer in some cases. For example, if the optimizer has general statistics on the index on the deptType column for the table Department, but it does not have histograms on this column, then the optimizer may decide that the index is not selective enough and choose not to use it for processing of the query:

```
SELECT * FROM Department WHERE deptType = 'Marketing';
```

The application developer, on the other hand, knows that there are only a few departments with this department type and that using the index on the column can improve performance.

The developer can prompt the optimizer to choose another strategy with the help of hints. Hints are used to change the optimization approach, the goal of optimization, the type of access to data, and the way joins are processed. The hint affects the optimizer's behavior only for a particular query. Hints are inserted in the statement as comments with the sign '+'. For example, the hint RULE changes the approach of the processing of the previous statement from CBO to RBO, and it can force the optimizer to use the index on the column deptType:

```
SELECT /*+ RULE */ * FROM Department WHERE deptType =
'Marketing';
```

The developer can explicitly specify the index to be used (assume that the name of the index on the column deptType for the table Department is i0):

```
SELECT /*+ INDEX (Department, i0) */ * FROM Department WHERE
deptType = 'Business';
```

The following example shows how to specify the order of joining tables in a query. For example, in the following query it is beneficial to join the selected rows of the table Department with the table Employee, and then join the result with the table Title. The hint prompts the optimizer to join tables in the order in which they are mentioned in the query:

```
SELECT /*+ ORDERED */ e.ID, e.name, t.salary
FROM Department d, Employee e, Title t
WHERE d.deptCode=e.deptCode AND e.titleCode=t.titleCode AND
    d.deptType = 'IT';
```

Oracle has more than 20 hints.

5.7.7.3 Monitoring

The previous section discussed how to change the optimizer's strategy for query executions. To do this, the developer has to be able to see how the optimizer executes a query.

The EXPLAIN PLAN statement displays the execution strategy for a query. Strategies are stored in the table PLAN_TABLE. The main columns of interest of this table are:

- OPERATION. The name of the operation performed, e.g. TABLE ACCESS.
- OPTIONS. The name of the operation (options) associated with the OPERATION, e.g. FULL.
- OBJECT_NAME. The name of the object of the operation, e.g. Department.

- ID. The number of the step.
- COST. The estimated cost of execution of the operation (NULL when RBO is used).
- CARDINALITY. The estimated number of rows accessed by the operation.
- STATEMENT_ID. Identifies the rows of PLAN_TABLE that refer to a particular query.

The following statement writes the execution strategy into the table PLAN_TABLE:

```
EXPLAIN PLAN SET STATEMENT_ID = 'P1' FOR
SELECT * FROM Department
WHERE location = 'Cleveland';
```

We can see the execution plan by selecting from PLAN_TABLE. The following statement selects from the PLAN_TABLE the estimated cost, operations with options, and objects of operations and formats the output:

```
SELECT ID || ' ' || PARENT_ID || ' ' ||
           LPAD(' ',2*(LEVEL - 1)) || OPERATION || ' ' ||
OPTIONS ||
           ' ' || OBJECT_NAME "Execution Plan"
FROM Plan_table
START WITH ID = 0 AND STATEMENT_ID = 'P1'
CONNECT BY PRIOR ID = PARENT_ID AND
           STATEMENT_ID = 'P1';
```

The result of this request shows that the query will be executed as a full-table scan:

```
Execution Plan
--------------------------------------------------
0         SELECT STATEMENT
1    0    TABLE ACCESS FULL DEPARTMENT
```

The *actual* performance of a database can be traced by turning the tracing of database performance on:

```
ALTER SESSION SET SQL_TRACE = true;
```

The trace file contains not only the execution strategies of queries, but also the detailed information about the consumption of resources. Using the generated trace file, the utility TKPROF produces a formatted output file that is used for performance analysis and for finding problems and bottlenecks.

5.7.8 The Performance of Distributed Queries

A query is distributed if it accesses data from a remote site. The local site (the site, which initiates the query) breaks the query into portions and sends them to remote sites for execution. The remote site executes its portion of the query and sends the result back to the local site. The local site then performs all the necessary post-processing and returns the results to the user or application.

The most effective way of optimizing the distributed query is to minimize the number of accesses to the remote databases and the amount of data retrieved from them.

Let us discuss a query on the distributed design of the Manufacturing Company case from Chapter 3. The query is originated in the New York database and has to return the names of those New York employees, whose salary is more than $20000 (the table Title is located in the Boston database):

```
SELECT name
FROM Employee e, Title@boston t
WHERE e.titleCode = t.titleCode AND
        t.salary > 20000;
```

To execute the query, for each row of the local fragment of Employee, the local site (New York) will access the remote site (Boston) to get the salary of the corresponding title. For each of these multiple trips to the remote site, the table Title will be searched for the corresponding title. A more efficient way to execute the query would be to access the remote site once, retrieve only the required rows, and then use these rows at the local site to produce the result.

In order to "prompt" Oracle on how to work with the remote site more efficiently and to optimize the execution of distributed queries, it is recommended to use collocated inline views (two or more tables of a query located in the same database are called collocated). The purpose of the collocated inline view is to define within the query a subquery that needs data only from one remote site. The conditions on the remote tables must be included in the view. The above distributed query can be rewritten with the inline view:

```
SELECT name
FROM Employee e,
        (SELECT titleCode
        FROM Title@boston
        WHERE salary > 20000) t
WHERE e.titleCode = t.titleCode;
```

The Boston site and the table Title there will be accessed once. Only the required rows of the table Title (with salary more than 20000) will be transferred to the New York database where the query processing will be completed.

Oracle's optimizer can transparently rewrite some distributed queries to take advantage of the performance gains offered by collocated inline views. However, you should remember that the form of the query still plays an important role in the query's execution.

5.8. *Examples: Tuning Query Processing*

5.8.1 Manufacturing Company Case

Let us consider tuning the centralized database for the Manufacturing Company case. Assume that the company has several hundred departments and several hundred thousand employees. Storage solutions for the case were suggested in Chapter 2. Here, we will discuss the usefulness of some indices.

According to the case description, users of each city need to work with data about local departments and employees of these departments. Access to local data (e.g. in Boston) is performed with the help of the queries:

```
SELECT * FROM Department WHERE location = 'Boston';

SELECT e.* FROM Employee e, Department d
WHERE e.deptCode = d.deptCode AND location = 'Boston';
```

The table Department is often accessed by queries with conditions ... WHERE location = ?'. Such queries can benefit from an index on the column location:

```
CREATE INDEX i0 on Department(location);
```

Because the attribute location has only three values, we could consider a bitmap index instead of the B-tree index. However, the table Department is small (only several hundred rows), and Oracle will not use an index (of any kind), rather performing a full scan of the table. Therefore, the index is not needed.

The table Employee is involved in queries together with the table Department. For join queries, it is recommended to create the index on the foreign key of the child table, in our case, on the attribute deptCode of the table Employee:

```
CREATE INDEX i1 ON Employee(deptCode);
```

The application that requests data about employees of particular departments will also benefit from this index.

There is another application that processes data about employees of a specific type, for example full-time employees:

```
SELECT * FROM Employee WHERE emplType = 'Full-time';
```

To improve the performance of such queries, we will consider the index on the column emplType. Because this column has only three values, we choose the bitmap index:

```
CREATE BITMAP INDEX i2 ON Employee(emplType);
```

5.8.2 Analyzing Performance in Oracle

Appendix 5 shows a session of work in Oracle. Oracle execution strategies are analyzed for different queries that are executed on a table with several hundred thousand rows with and without indices, and with and without database statistics. The role of the database buffer is demonstrated.

5.9. Summary

The performance of queries is one of the main features, which define the quality of a database. Achieving good performance is a complicated problem, and its solution depends on the design, implementation, and management of the database.

Usually, the performance of queries is measured by response time and throughput. Minimizing the response time and maximizing throughput are different goals of performance management and they depend on the type of application.

Query processing consists of several steps: decomposition, optimization, and execution. Optimization is a very important part of query processing and it produces a strategy of query execution. The performance of the query depends on the strategy that is built by the optimizer. DBMSs apply two types of optimization: the heuristic or rule-based and cost-based. Heuristic optimization is based on rules of complexity of relational operations and does not take into consideration the current state of the database. Cost-based optimization estimates different strategies by calculating costs of their execution and chooses the cheapest strategy; to perform estimation database statistics are needed. For the same query, cost-based optimization may produce different strategies for different states of the database. Statistics are gathered by special utilities and are stored in the data dictionary.

Data design defines performance of the future database. The normalized data model is free from data modification anomalies and usually delivers better performance for modification queries. Retrieval of data on the normalized database, however, can suffer from bad performance because often multiple tables need to be joined. Denormalization of the database performed by merging tables is a common approach for improving the performance with the help of design. Storing very long columns in a separate table is another possibility that may be considered by designers. The distribution and localization of data can improve performance, especially for large databases.

The physical data design and implementation of the database largely define performance. The main goal of physical design is to minimize the number of disk accesses for query processing. Developers should decide how the data of each table are stored in data blocks and what type of storage is used for the table – heap or organized. Choosing the appropriate data types for columns of the table is also important for efficient query processing.

There are several ways to organize the storage of data. The most common approach is clustering – storing rows of the table that are often accessed together in the same data blocks. The index cluster stores together rows that have the same value of a particular attribute, which is called the cluster key. The index cluster has to be supported by an index on the cluster key. The hash cluster organizes rows with the same value of the hash function in the same blocks. Access to data in hash clusters is very efficient – the system calculates the value of the hash function and goes directly to the blocks with the requested data. However, while index clusters can facilitate queries with equality and range conditions, hash clusters are beneficial for queries with exact equality conditions only. Clusters should not be used for tables with intensive updating, inserting and deleting activity.

Data storage parameters that define where data has to be stored, how data is packed in data blocks, how the system maintains data, (and other parameters) have to be specified for each table, cluster and index.

Some DBMSs support other ways of organizing data storage. For example, in Oracle, tables can be partitioned or index-organized.

Access to data can be enforced by special objects – indices. Table indices are beneficial for selective read queries (which access not more than 25% of the rows of a table). Multi-column indices are involved in the processing of queries constrained by attributes of the left-most part of the index. Accessing indices only can be sufficient and, therefore, especially useful for the processing of queries that reference only indexed columns.

The successful design and implementation of a database do not guarantee good database performance. Performance depends on the database environment – capacity of the database server, and available memory and storage. Queries and applications on the database have to be implemented with knowledge of the query processing features of the DBMS and with an understanding of the database design and implementation.

Tuning a database starts with database design and continues into database maintenance:

- *Analyzing the nature of the data and the database requests*. Database professionals have to understand the purpose of the database, the nature of the data and the database requests.
- *Designing for performance*. Database design serves the purpose of the database and the nature of data and the database activities. The Physical design has to utilize the data storage capabilities of the DBMS. Consider distributing data, clustering, partitioning, or other ways of organizing the data storage. Define the storage parameters of each table in correspondence with how the data of the table will be used.
- *Implementing for performance*. Configure the database environment and implement the database according to the design. Design and implement indices for important queries.
- *Tuning applications and queries*. Applications and queries have to utilize the data processing features of the DBMS and the design and implementation of the database.

Review Questions

1. What factors influence the performance of queries?
2. How is performance measured? Describe the relationships between different performance measures.
3. What factors affect the performance of distributed queries?
4. What are the steps of query processing and what is the purpose of each step?
5. Define what effective storage of data is?
6. What are the benefits of clustering? When does clustering have to be considered?
7. What are the different types of optimization? Under what circumstances are these different types of optimization used?
8. What are the prerequisites of cost-based optimization?
9. How does data design affect database performance?

10. What is the impact of the physical data model on performance?
11. How can application design improve the performance of the database?
12. Define the strategies of indexing.
13. How can composite indices improve the performance of some queries?
14. How can the database environment influence performance?
15. Why is the performance two hours after the start of a database better than immediately after the start?
16. How is data storage organized in Oracle? What types of storage organization are supported in Oracle?
17. What types of indices are supported in Oracle? In what situations is each index type beneficial?
18. What database statistics does the Oracle optimizer use? How can histograms improve performance?
19. What is the role of hints in Oracle queries?
20. How can one learn about Oracle's strategy for execution of a particular query?
21. Will indexed access be beneficial for a query that accesses 70% of rows of the table?

Practical Assignments

1. For the centralized database design for the Manufacturing Company case:
    a. Define the types of storage and storage parameters of the tables. Explain any assumptions and decisions you had to make. .
    b. Build indices for improving the performance of the mentioned applications. Explain any assumptions and decisions you had to make..
    c. Build queries for the mentioned requests in Oracle SQL.
    d. Check the execution plans for the queries for RBO and CBO.

2. Perform the tasks of the previous assignment for the other case studies.

3. Several queries are executed on the Manufacturing Company database. One query accesses the data about employees of a particular employee type and a particular department, another – about the employees of a particular employee type. Which index may improve performance of both queries?
    a. Composite index on emplType, deptCode.
    b. Composite index on ID, emplType, deptCode.
    c. Composite index on deptCode, emplType.
    d. Single-column index on emplType.

4. Describe the conditions under which clustering the table T(A, B, C, D) with the column C as the cluster key is beneficial.

5. Explain when you may consider adding the table S (X, Y, Z) to the cluster of the previous assignment.

6. On the table T(A, B, C, D) we have several queries. One query accesses data from T given the values of the attributes B and D, another – given the value of D, and the third query – given the value of the attribute C. What indices on the table T can improve the performance of the queries?

7. Partition the table T(A, B, C, D).

    a.   Explain any assumptions you had to make.

    b.   Write queries that will benefit from the partitioning.

8. For the distributed design of the Manufacturing Company database, build a query that returns data about all employees of a particular title (the query is executed from New York). Rewrite the query using inline collocated views and explain why the new query will be more efficient.

9. Build reduced views for the following requests on the Manufacturing Company database (the requests are executed from New York). When writing the queries, use inline collocated views where appropriate.

    a.   Retrieve data about employees of marketing departments of Boston and New York.

    b.   Retrieve data about Boston and Cleveland employees with titles T1 and T2.

10. The table T($\underline{A}$, B, C, D) has a B-tree index on the column B. Which of the following requests may benefit from the index? Where necessary, define additional conditions under which the index will be beneficial. If the query cannot benefit from the index, suggest other solutions for improving its performance.

```
a. SELECT * FROM T WHERE B = x;
b. SELECT * FROM T WHERE B <> x;
c. SELECT * FROM T WHERE B LIKE 'x%';
d. SELECT * FROM T WHERE SUBSTRING(B, 1, 1) = 'x';
```

11. Assume that the table Employee of the Manufacturing Company case includes the column gender.

    a.   Describe situations when using the index on the column will be beneficial.

    b.   What type of index would you will recommend?

    c.   Explain when the index will be beneficial if 95% of employees of the company are men, and 5% are women.

12. For a table, e.g. Employee of the Manufacturing Company case, describe data access scenarios and conditions under which you would organize the storage of the table as:

    a.   Cluster.

    b.   Partition.

    c.   Index-organized.

    d.   Distributed.

Chapter 6.   Transaction Management

This chapter continues the discussion of the relationship between databases and database applications started in Chapter 5. Concurrent execution of database requests can cause problems with performance and data consistency. The application has to be implemented with an understanding of these problems and the ways they are resolved by the database.

6.1. *Problems of Concurrent Access and Failures*

The discussion of database performance in the previous chapter concentrated on the performance of separate queries and did not consider the performance issues that could occur if queries are processed concurrently. Imagine the situation where your query is updating a row of a table, and at the same time, another user wants to make updates to the same row. If another query has to wait for your query to finish the update (and as will be shown in this chapter is a common scenario), then the performance of the second query will be definitely degraded. The waiting time component of the *response time* of the query, which was mentioned in Chapter 5, depends on concurrent queries.

Degrading performance of multiple applications working simultaneously on the database is not the only problem of concurrent query processing. Consider a simple case of concurrent actions.

Case 6.1.

> *A bank database keeps data about balances on checking and savings accounts of customers. John and Mary have a joint checking account, and the current balance is $100. At some moment, both of them need to withdraw money: John – $50, and Mary – $75.*

Here are two possible scenarios for the case: in the first, John and Mary perform their bank operations one after another, and in the second, they happen to do it simultaneously from different ATM machines.

Time	Scenario 1
1	John tries to withdraw $50. The application reads the balance on the account; the balance is $100.
2	Money is withdrawn.
3	The balance is updated to $50.
4	Mary tries to withdraw $75. The application reads the balance on the account; the balance is $50.
5	Withdrawal is rejected, because the balance cannot be negative. The balance remains $50.

Time	Scenario 2	
	John	**Mary**
1	John tries to withdraw $50. The application reads the balance on the account; the balance is $100.	Mary tries to withdraw $75. The application reads the balance on the account; the balance is $100.
2	Money is withdrawn.	
3		Money is withdrawn.
4	The balance is updated to $50.	
5		The balance is updated to $25.

In the second scenario, John and Mary access the same data concurrently, and, as we can see, concurrency causes problems – the correctness of the data is compromised. The resulting state of the data is inconsistent with bank business requirements.

We may imagine another scenario of concurrent access to the account, when the application performs additional checking of the account balance before updating it:

Time	Scenario 3	
	John	**Mary**
1	John tries to withdraw $50. The application reads the balance on the account; the balance is $100.	
2		Mary tries to withdraw $75. The application reads the balance on the account; the balance is $100.
3	Money is withdrawn.	
4		Money is withdrawn.
5	The application re-reads the balance on the account; the balance is $100.The balance is updated to $50.	
6		The application re-reads the balance on the account; the balance is $50.The balance is updated to -$25.

The concurrent scenarios show that we cannot guarantee the correctness of the results of our actions and, moreover, cannot foresee what the results would be. This definitely would be unacceptable for the businesses relying on the databases and database applications (please note that we discuss hypothetical scenarios to introduce the problems of concurrent access and then illustrate how these problems are resolved by DBMSs).

Another example shows how concurrent operations can compromise data integrity.

Case 6.2.

   The database contains information about departments and employees:

```
Department (deptCode, deptName)

Employee (ID, emplName, deptCode)
```

Referential integrity of deptCode of the table Employee is not supported through the foreign key constraint, but in the application. Let us consider a situation when one user – John – tries to assign a new employee to the existing department '555' that does not have any employees at the time, while another user – Scott – is deleting this department. Both John and Scott use an application that performs all the corresponding checks of data integrity.

Time	John	Scott
1	Tries to assign an employee to the department '555' (updates the deptCode attribute row for the employee). Application ensures integrity – checks the table Department and finds the department '555'.	
2		Tries to delete the department '555' from the Department table. Application ensures integrity – checks the table Employee and does not find any employees assigned to the department '555'.
3	The deptCode attribute of the employee is updated to '555'.	The row of the department '555' is deleted from the table Department.

The resulting state of the database violates data integrity – an employee is assigned to a non-existing department '555'. Note that this would not happen if the integrity rules were specified in the database (the attribute deptCode of the table Employee defined as the foreign key to the relation Department).

The next two cases demonstrate concurrent actions on the database that do not cause any problems with the correctness of data.

Case 6.3.
   John and Mary simultaneously check the balance of their account.

Time	John	Mary
1	John checks the account: The balance is $100.	Mary checks the account: The balance is $100.
2	The balance remains $100.	The balance remains $100.

Case 6.4.

> *Scott has a checking account with the balance of $200 in the same bank. He needs to withdraw money simultaneously with John.*

Time	John	Scott
1	John tries to withdraw $50. The application reads the balance on the account; the balance is $100.	Scott tries to withdraw $75. The application reads the balance on the account; the balance is $200.
2	Money is withdrawn.	Money is withdrawn.
3	The balance is updated to $50.	The balance is updated to $125.

Whichever scenario we choose for execution of actions of these two situations, the resulting state of data always will be correct. Concurrency does not create problems when: (a) Concurrent operations read the same data and (b) Concurrent operations access different data.

The above examples show that in some cases simultaneous actions of several users can lead to incorrect or inconsistent database states (we understand the correctness of a database state as its correspondence to business rules). Does this mean that concurrent execution of transactions should not be allowed? On the other hand, we understand that concurrency significantly increases the performance of database applications, e.g. if in the above examples, operations were executed serially (one after another), the throughput of the database would be lower or, in other words, the execution of all operations would require more time. Besides, as we see from Cases 6.3 and 6.4, for some operations concurrent execution does not cause database inconsistencies. Operations involving concurrent executions that might result in incorrect states of the database are called *conflicting*.

Concurrent execution of multiple operations often is the only possibility for the database to satisfy performance requirements. For example, even with the best possible performance of the bank application, if customers' requests were processed serially, this would cause many users to wait for their turn to perform a bank operation, which, of course, is unacceptable for this business. Hence databases are required to have mechanisms for executing operations concurrently. Concurrent mechanisms have to recognize conflicting operations and regulate their simultaneous execution, so that the resulting state of the database is consistent with business rules.

The consistency of a database can be also endangered by database failures.

Case 6.5.

> *John also has a savings account, and he wants to transfer $50 from his savings account to his checking account. Before the transfer, his savings and checking balances are $100.*

Here is one of the possible scenarios:

Time	Scenario
1	John tries to transfer $50. The application reads the balance on the savings account; the balance is $100.
2	$50 are withdrawn from the savings account. The savings balance is updated to $50.
3	The database (or the application) fails.
4	...
5	After the database (or the application) is recovered, the savings balance is $50, and the checking balance is $100.

In this scenario, the incorrect state of the database happened because of the failure that interrupted the sequence of operations. To preserve data consistency, the database must be able to recover from failure either by finishing the sequence of operations, or by undoing the withdrawal from the savings account and returning to the initial state.

Let us summarize the discussion of the cases. A database state may become inconsistent with business rules if:

1. *Conflicting* operations are executed *concurrently*. Therefore, to enable concurrent execution, the database has to recognize conflicting concurrent operations and organize their execution to prevent inconsistency. The organization of concurrent processing has to be aimed at preserving data consistency and achieving appropriate performance.
2. The *sequence* of operations is interrupted by *failure*. To prevent inconsistency, the database must be able to recover from failure to a consistent state either by undoing the performed operations and returning to the initial state before the sequence started, or by finishing the sequence.

For each sequence of operations on the database, business rules define the correct final state of the database. For example, in *Case 6.5* we see that money transfer operations have to result in the balance of one account being decreased by $50 and the balance of another increased by $50. The resulting state of the database has to be consistent with the logic of operations and business rules. Figure 6-1 shows two sequences of operations T1 and T2, which start from states $State_1$ and $State_2$ and must take the database into states $State_3$ and $State_5$, respectively. Any other final state of the database is incorrect ($State_4$) and has to be prevented by the database. In case the correct final state cannot be achieved, the database must be returned to the previous correct state, from which the sequence of operations started.

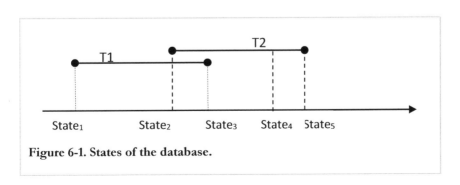

Figure 6-1. States of the database.

6.2. *The Concept of a Transaction*

In the cases of the previous section, sequences of database actions that implemented the logic of business processing were executed incorrectly either because of the harmful impact of concurrent operations or because some operations of the sequence were not executed. Hence, the concept of a transaction, as a *logical unit* of work in the database, was introduced.

Transactions support consistent database computing.

A transaction is a sequence of operations on the database (reads, writes, and calculations), which takes the database from one consistent state to another, and if this is not possible, returns the database into the initial consistent state.

A transaction is different from a separate operation (query). The operations of a transaction do not act independently – each operation belongs to the transaction. The successful execution of a particular operation does not guarantee that the result of this operation will be applied to the database – this happens only if all other operations of the transaction are executed successfully. If a transaction includes only one operation, then the success of the transaction depends on the success of this single operation.

The transaction is a tool of *consistent and reliable* database processing. By reliability we mean that a system is resilient to various types of failures and is capable of *recovering* from them to a consistent database state without data loss.

This chapter discusses transactions and database consistency under the conditions of concurrent access to data. The next chapter is dedicated to the role of transactions in the recovery of databases.

The consistency of the database depends not only on how the system processes transactions, but also on the correctness of the transactions. If the database programmer incorrectly implements the business logic in a transaction, then the database will always become inconsistent with the business rules. For example, if a money transfer transaction is implemented in such a way that a particular amount of money is deposited to one account and a different amount is withdrawn from another account, then the database will become inconsistent even if the transactions are executed serially and there are no failures. In this discussion, we assume that the transactions correctly implement the business logic.

The support of data consistency can affect the performance of some transactions. When designing transactions, database programmers have to utilize transaction management features of the DBMS in such a way that the consistency of data is preserved, and the performance of concurrently executed transactions is not compromised.

The sequence of operations in a transaction is finished by the commands COMMIT or ROLLBACK. Committing the transaction means that all operations were executed successfully and there was no threat of inconsistency caused by other transactions. Rolling back means that the transaction is aborted and the results of all performed operations are disregarded. The transaction explicitly defines consistent states of the database – the next consistent state is achieved after a COMMIT, and the database is returned to the previous consistent state in the case of a ROLLBACK. In some DBMSs the beginning of a transaction is defined by a special statement, e.g. BEGIN TRANSACTION in MS SQL Server. In other DBMSs, including Oracle, the new transaction is immediately started after COMMIT or ROLLBACK.

The following is an example of using COMMIT and ROLLBACK in Oracle on a newly created table:

```
CREATE TABLE test (f1 NUMBER);
```

SELECT * FROM test; *0 rows returned* INSERT INTO test VALUES (1); COMMIT;	The first transaction inserts a record into the table and commits.

SELECT * FROM test;
    1 row returned (with f1 equal 1)
 	
INSERT INTO test VALUES (2);
 	
SELECT * FROM test;
    2 rows returned (with f1 equal 1 and 2)
 	
ROLLBACK;
	The SELECT statement starts the second transaction and shows that the INSERT of the first transaction is permanent.
	
	The transaction inserts the second record, and the following SELECT shows it.
	
	The transaction performs ROLLBACK.

SELECT * FROM test; *1 row returned (with f1 equal 1)*	The third transaction starts after the ROLLBACK. The result of the action of the second transaction has not been recorded in the database – the database returned into the initial state of the second transaction.

Let us consider organizing the actions of *Case 6.5* in a transaction, but in a different order than before: first, we deposit $50 into the checking account, and then withdraw $50 from the savings account. Also, assume that the balance of the savings account has been changed to $30.

Time	Scenario
1	John tries to transfer $50.
2	$50 is deposited on the checking account; the balance of the checking account is updated to $150.
3	The application reads the balance on the savings account; the balance is $30.
4	Money cannot be withdrawn from the savings account.

5	The depositing of $50 on the checking account has to be undone.
6	The transaction is finished with ROLLBACK.

The above scenario shows that the design of a transaction plays an important role in the database performance. Because depositing is executed first, without checking that the money transfer is possible, the system wastes resources on executing this operation and then rolling it back.

The following scenario shows a more efficient transaction design; it is executed successfully because the initial savings balance is changed to $100:

Time	Scenario
1	John tries to transfer $50. The application reads the balance on the savings account; the balance is $100.
2	$50 is withdrawn from the savings account. The savings balance is updated to $50.
3	The balance of the checking account is updated to $150.
4	The transaction is finished with COMMIT, and the new balances on the accounts become permanent.

For system failures during the execution of concurrent transactions, most DBMSs roll back all uncommitted transactions if the database processing was interrupted abnormally. It is important to understand that if operations were not organized in transactions, the system would not know which operations to roll back. Transaction processing, failures and database recovery are also discussed in the next chapter.

Let us take a closer look at the problems of concurrent execution and how these problems can be prevented or resolved with the help of transactions.

Assuming that database processing is reliable, serial execution of transactions does not cause any inconsistencies. We will check the correctness of the concurrent execution of transactions by comparing the results with the results of the serial execution of the same transactions – the results that we know are correct and the ones we expect. The following problems – they are called phenomena – are recognized in transaction processing. Please note that the following scenarios are not the only possible scenarios of concurrent execution of the involved transactions – these scenarios were specifically chosen to illustrate the phenomena. Even if not every data processing situation results in a phenomenon, the system needs to recognize the problematic situations and prevent the phenomena from happening.

Lost Update.

Initially $x = 100$. The transaction T1 adds 1 to x; the transaction T2 subtracts 1 from x. Serial execution of the transactions results in $x = 100$. Concurrent execution of the transactions in the following scenario results in $x = 99$.

Time	T1	T2
1	Read (x) x = 100	
2	x ← x + 1	Read (x) x = 100
3	Write (x) x = 101	x ← x - 1
4	Commit	Write (x) x = 99
5		Commit

The update of the transaction T1 was not seen by the transaction T2.

Dirty Read.

Initially x = 100. The transaction T1 adds 1 to x and then rolls back; the transaction T2 subtracts 1 from x. Serial execution of the transactions results in x = 99. Concurrent execution of the transactions in the following scenario results in x = 100.

Time	T1	T2
1	Read (x) x = 100	
2	x ← x + 1	
3	Write (x) x = 101	
4		Read (x) x = 101
5	Rollback	x ← x − 1
6		Write (x) x = 100
7		Commit

The dirty read happens because T2 is dependent on the changes performed by T1. If T1 is rolled back, T2 continues with dirty, "non-existing" data. To prevent the inconsistency caused by the dirty read, T2 should have been rolled back.

Fuzzy (non-repeatable) read.

Initially x = 100. The transaction T1 reads x two times; between the reads of the transaction T1, the transaction T2 subtracts 1 from x. In serial execution, T1 will always read the same value – 100 or 99 – depending on the order of the transactions. For concurrent execution, reads of T1 are inconsistent (non-repeatable).

Time	T1	T2
1	Read (x) $x = 100$	
2		Read (x) $x = 100$
3	…	$x \leftarrow x - 1$
4		Write (x) $x = 99$
5	Read (x) $x = 99$	…
6	Commit	Commit

Phantom.

The transaction T1 reads 100 rows, which satisfy some condition F, and then updates these rows. However, because the transaction T2 deletes one of the rows while T1 processes the read records, T1 does not write 100 rows as it intended, but only 99 – it updated the deleted phantom row. If T2 added a new row, T1 would have a new phantom row that it did not update. Phantoms are similar to fuzzy reads.

Time	T1	T2
1	Read all x_i for which $F(x_i) = $ TRUE 100 rows read	Read (x_j)
2		Delete (x_j)
3	Update all x_i 100 rows updated	
4	Write all x_i for which $F(x_i) = $ TRUE 99 rows written	
5	Commit	Commit

Another example of phantom would be if T1 in the above scenario was finding the sum of all x_i (moment 3). Then, the result of T1 will include the record that has been deleted.

6.3. Properties of Transactions

The examples of the phenomena show that just organizing operations into transactions does not protect the database from inconsistency. A transaction itself cannot foresee and prevent the above phenomena; that is why the DBMS contains a transaction manager that coordinates the concurrent execution of transactions. The consistency of the database is defined by how the transaction manager supports properties of transactions. The following are the properties of transactions defined by the ANSI/ ISO SQL standards (http://webstore.ansi.org):

- Atomicity

- Consistency
- Isolation
- Durability

Atomicity defines the transaction as a unit of processing: either all actions of the transaction are completed or none of them. If the transaction fails, then the database has to be recovered either by undoing the performed actions and returning into the starting consistent state or by completing the remaining actions and going to the next consistent state.

Consistency defines the degree of correctness of transactions or, in other words, what phenomena, if any, can occur during transaction processing. When we discuss the correctness of the transaction, we mean the correct concurrent execution of the transaction by the system, assuming that when executed separately, the transaction is correct. ANSI defines four levels of consistency of concurrent transactions:

1. Transaction T sees degree 3 consistency if:
    - T does not overwrite dirty data of other transactions.
    - T does not commit any writes until it completes all its writes.
    - T does not read dirty data of other transactions.
    - Other transactions do not dirty any data read by T before it completes.

2. Transaction T sees degree 2 consistency if:
    - T does not overwrite dirty data of other transactions.
    - T does not commit any writes until it completes all its writes.
    - T does not read dirty data of other transactions.

3. Transaction T sees degree 1 consistency if:
    - T does not overwrite dirty data of other transactions.
    - T does not commit any writes until it completes all its writes.

4. Transaction T sees degree 0 consistency if:
    - T does not overwrite dirty data of other transactions.

Transaction consistency is maintained by the transaction manager. In the above scenarios of phenomena, inconsistencies are caused by *uncontrolled* executions of transactions that are reading and writing dirty data of other transactions.

Isolation defines how the transaction is protected from the impact of operations of other transactions. Insufficient isolation does not provide for high consistency. If there is not enough isolation, transactions can be executed incorrectly, or have to be aborted and rolled back to avoid inconsistency.

ANSI defines four levels of isolation:

- *Read uncommitted.* The transaction can read uncommitted changes of other transactions. With this level of isolation, all phenomena are possible, as we could see from the previous examples.

- *Read committed.* The transaction can read only committed changes of other transactions. With this level of isolation, fuzzy reads and phantoms are possible.
- *Repeatable read.* The transaction performs repeatable reads regardless of any committed changes of other transactions. With this level of isolation, only phantoms are possible.
- *Anomaly serializable.* The transaction is executed as if it were the only one in the database. With this level no phenomena happen.

In the examples of phenomena introduced above, transactions are not isolated enough – they interfere with each other while performing operations on the same data. Therefore, these transactions are not consistent enough. For the lost update T2 is allowed to read data before T1 has committed it; in the dirty read, T2 reads data that was previously written and not committed by T1; in the fuzzy read, T1 reads uncommitted data of T2, and T2 writes data, which was previously read by T1; in the phantom T2 changes the number of data values while T1 is trying to process and update the data.

Durability means that when the transaction is completed, the changes cannot be undone.

We may say that Atomicity and Durability are trivial transaction properties as they follow from the definition of the transaction. We will focus on Consistency and Isolation (that defines Consistency) and the way they are maintained in general and in Oracle in particular.

6.3.1 Isolation Level of Transactions in Oracle

The following simple test allows us to determine the isolation level of transactions in the Oracle DBMS. The table test was populated with 100 rows containing sequential numbers in both fields (to generate the numbers we use and illustrate the sequence object of the Oracle database and a simple insert query that uses one of the existing database objects – the view user_objects from the data dictionary):

```
CREATE TABLE test (f1 NUMBER, f2 NUMBER);

CREATE SEQUENCE seq_test;

INSERT INTO test
      (SELECT seq_test.NEXTVAL, seq_test.NEXTVAL
      FROM user_objects
      WHERE ROWNUM < 101);
```

Time	T1	T2
1	SELECT COUNT(*) FROM test; *Returns COUNT(*) = 100*	
2		DELETE FROM test WHERE f1 <= 50; *50 rows deleted*
3	SELECT COUNT(*) FROM test; *Returns COUNT(*) = 100*	
4		COMMIT;
5	SELECT COUNT(*) FROM test;	

		Returns COUNT(*) = 50	
6	`COMMIT;`		

7			`UPDATE test SET f2 = 1`
			`WHERE f1 = 51;`
			1 row updated

8	`SELECT f2 FROM test`
	`WHERE f = 51;`
	Returns f2 = 51		

9			`COMMIT;`

10	`SELECT f2 FROM test`
	`WHERE f1 = 51;`
	Returns f2 = 1		

This test shows that:

- There are phantoms: T1 reads 100 rows at moment 3 (after some rows were deleted by another transaction) and 50 rows at moment 5.
- There are fuzzy reads: T1 reads the value of the field of a particular row at moment 8 and gets 51, then it reads the value of the field of the same row at moment 10 and gets 1.
- There are no dirty reads: at moment 8, T1 does not see the uncommitted change of T2, which was performed at moment 7.

We can conclude that the isolation level in Oracle is READ COMMITTED.

6.4. Serializability Theory

The safest way to execute transactions is to execute them serially; however, most database applications need better performance than could be provided by serial execution. Besides, in many cases concurrent access does not endanger the consistency.

All previous examples show that *uncontrollable* concurrent access to data can cause serious problems. Therefore, transaction management is directed at finding some *regulated* way of concurrent execution of transactions, which would be a trade-off between data consistency provided by the serial execution and better performance provided by the concurrent execution.

To regulate the execution of transactions, the database builds schedules. A schedule is an interleaved order of execution of operations of concurrent transactions. For a pair of transactions, the system can generate multiple schedules. Let us consider the following transactions:

$$T1: \{O_{11}, O_{12}, \ldots, O_{1n}\}$$

$$T2: \{O_{21}, O_{22}, \ldots, O_{2m}\}$$

and one of the possible schedules of their concurrent execution:

$$S1: \{O_{11}, O_{21}, \ldots, O_{1i}, O_{2j}, \ldots, O_{1n}, O_{2j+1}, \ldots, O_{2m}\}$$

The database appears in an inconsistent state only when transactions concurrently access the same data. Such transactions are called conflicting. Not every pair of concurrent accesses to a particular data is conflicting:

- The read of one transaction never conflicts with the read of another transaction (*Case 6.3*).
- The read of one transaction conflicts with the write of another transaction (*Case 6.1*, phenomena).
- The write of one transaction conflicts with the write of another transaction (lost update phenomenon).

For conflicting operations, the order of these operations (the schedule) is important and defines the result. Scenarios for the *Case 6.1* demonstrate the correct result for the first schedule (serial execution), and different incorrect results for the two concurrent schedules.

Case 6.6.

> *Let us combine the cases 6.1 and 6.4: John transfers $50 from the savings account to the checking account and then withdraws $50 from the checking account. Mary withdraws $75 from the checking account.*

Consider several different scenarios:

Time	Scenario 1	
	John	**Mary**
1	John tries to transfer $50. The application reads the balance on the savings account; the balance is $100.	Mary tries to withdraw $75 from the checking account: The application reads the balance on the account; the balance is $100.
2	$50 is withdrawn from the savings account.	$75 is withdrawn from the checking account.
3	The savings balance is updated to $50.	The checking balance is updated to $25.
4	$50 is deposited on the checking account.	
5	The checking balance is updated to $75.	
6	John tries to withdraw $50. The application reads the balance on the checking account; the balance is $75.	
7	$50 is withdrawn.	
8	The checking balance is updated to $25.	

Time	Scenario 2	
	John	**Mary**
1	John tries to transfer $50. The application reads the balance on the savings account; the balance is $100.	

2	$50 is withdrawn from the savings account.	
3	The savings balance is updated to $50.	
4	$50 is deposited into the checking account.	
5	The checking balance is updated to $150.	
6	John tries to withdraw $50: The application reads the balance on the savings account; the balance is $150.	
7	$50 is withdrawn.	Mary tries to withdraw $75 from the checking account: The application reads the balance on the account; the balance is $150.
8	The checking balance is updated to $100.	$75 is withdrawn
9		The checking balance is updated to $75.

The first scenario of concurrent execution of John and Mary's transactions results in the same database state as the serial execution would have. Different schedules that result in the same database state are called conflict equivalent. Concurrent schedules that are conflict equivalent to serial schedules are called serializable.

The goal of concurrent transactions management is to build serializable schedules of execution of transactions, combining the benefits of performance of concurrent execution with the correctness of serial execution.

Here is the example with two transactions which perform the following actions:

T1
Read (x)
x ← x + 1
Write (x)
Commit

T2
Read (x)
x ← x + 1
Write (x)
Commit

We can build different schedules for execution of these transactions: serial schedules, in which operations of one transaction are followed by operations of another transaction, and concurrent schedules, in which operations of one transaction are interleaved with operations of another transaction. In the following schedules, the operations of the transactions are defined with their first letters: R is for Read, W – for Write, U – for Update, C – or Commit, and RB – for Rollback, and indexes define the transaction to which the operation belongs:

S1 = {R1, U1, W1, C1, R2, U2, W2, C2}

S2 = {R2, U2, W2, C2, R1, U1, W1, C1}

S3 = {R1, U1, W1, R2, U2, W2, C1, C2}

S4 = {R1, U1, R2, W1, U2, W2, C1, C2}

S5 = {R2, U2, R1, W2, U1, W1, C2, C1}

If before the execution of the transactions x = 0, then the result of the first three schedules is x = 2, and the result of the last two schedules is x = 1.

We have two sets of the conflict equivalent schedules: (S1, S2, S3) and (S4, S5). Schedules S1 and S2 are serial, the schedule S3 is conflict equivalent with serial schedules and, therefore, is serializable. Schedules S4 and S5 are conflict equivalent with each other, but are not equivalent to serial schedules, and, therefore, are non-serializable. Serializable schedules take the database into the consistent state, while non-serializable schedules result in an inconsistent database state.

Here is another example of transactions:

T1
Read (x)
x ← x + 1
Write (x)
Read (y)
y ← y + 1
Write (y)
Commit

T2
Read (x)
x ← x * 2
Write (x)
Read (y)
y ← y * 2
Write (y)
Commit

For two transactions Ti and Tj, Ti → Tj means that Ti is followed by Tj. Initially, x = 10 and y = 10. For T1 → T2, the result of transactions is x = 22 and y = 22. For T2 → T1, the result is x = 21 and y = 21.

Let us discuss several possible concurrent schedules. Schedule S1 results in x = 22 and y = 22; it is serializable for T1 → T2:

S1 = {R1(x), U1(x), W1(x), R2(x), U2(x), W2(x), R1(y), U1(y), W1(y), R2(y), U2(y), W2(y), C1, C2}

Schedule S2 results in x = 21 and y = 21; it is serializable for T2 → T1:

S2 = {R2(x), U2(x), W2(x), R1(x), U1(x), W1(x), R2(y), U2(y), W2(y), R1(y), U1(y), W1(y), C1, C2}

Schedule S3 results in x = 20 and y = 22; it is not serializable:

$$S3 = \{R1(x), U1(x), R2(x), W1(x), U2(x), W2(x), R1(y), U1(y), W1(y), R2(y),$$
$$U2(y), W2(y), C1, C2\}$$

The next example shows the schedule for the concurrent execution of three transactions:

T1
Read(x)
x ← x + 1
Write(x)
Commit

T2
Read(x)
x ← x + 1
Write(x)
Read(y)
y ← y + 1
Write(y)
Read(z)
Commit

T3
Read(x)
Read(y)
Read(z)
Commit

For x, y, z that initially are equal to 0, the serial schedule T2 → T1 → T3 results in x = 2, y = 1, z = 0.

The following schedule is serializable for T2 → T1 → T3:

$$\{R2(x), W2(x), R1(x), W1(x), C1, R3(x), R2(y), W2(y), R3(y), R2(z), c2, R3(z), C3\}$$

6.5. Concurrency Control Approaches

Approaches for managing concurrent transactions i.e. building serializable schedules of their execution – can be divided into two groups:

- *Locking.* Locking is a mechanism, which controls access to data for conflicting operations in transactions. To sustain serializable execution of transactions, locking causes some operations to be postponed or be denied access to data.
- *Scheduling.* Scheduling, or timestamping is another mechanism that performs ordering of transactions' operations in a serializable manner based on rules or protocols.

6.5.1 Pessimistic and Optimistic Approaches to Transaction Management

Approaches to transaction management are also classified into pessimistic and optimistic.

Pessimistic approaches assume that the conflict between concurrent transactions is possible and try to prevent inconsistency of the database as early as possible.

Optimistic approaches, on the other hand, are based on the assumption that the conflict is unlikely. These approaches try to schedule operations in transactions and postpone checking of the correctness of the schedule until its execution. If executing an operation violates the rules of consistency, then the transaction, which contains the operation, is aborted.

6.5.2   Locking

Case 6.4 showed that concurrent transactions which access different data do not cause inconsistency. We say that these transactions are not conflicting for the data. Execution of non-conflicting transactions does not require special rules; and further discussion will be provided for conflicting transactions, that is, transactions concurrently accessing the same data.

Case 6.3 showed that if one transaction reads data, another transaction can read the same data without compromising data consistency. Two (or more) transactions can read the same data concurrently, or we say, can share reading access to data.

The read operation does not conflict with the read operation of another transaction.

The example with the fuzzy read shows that if a transaction reads data, it cannot allow another transaction to write this data because of possible inconsistency. The example with the dirty read shows that if a transaction writes data, it cannot allow another transaction to read it. The example with the lost update shows that if a transaction writes data, it cannot allow another transaction to write the same data.

The read operation conflicts with the write operation of another transaction. The write operation conflicts with the write operation of another transaction.

Two transactions cannot share read – write or write – write access to the same data. In this case, only one transaction can get exclusive access to the data.

6.5.2.1   Types of Locks

Depending on the type of access to the data, the transaction leaves a trace (or a mark), which shows what type of access to this data is allowed for concurrent transactions. This trace is called a lock. There are two types of locks: *Shared* and *Exclusive*.

If a data item receives a shared lock from one transaction, this item can be read by other transactions, but none of the other transactions can write in this data item. If a data item receives an exclusive lock from a particular transaction, this transaction can read this data item and write it, but other transactions can neither read nor write it. In other words, two reads can be performed concurrently on a data item, but a read and a write or a write and a write cannot.

If a transaction involves reading data, it tries to obtain a read lock (shared lock) on the data. This is possible if the data item does not have an exclusive lock of another transaction. However, the data item can have a shared lock of another transaction or not have any lock.

If the transaction involves writing data, it tries to obtain a write lock (exclusive lock). This is possible, if the data item does not have a lock of another transaction. If the data item has a shared or exclusive lock of another transaction, the transaction cannot get an exclusive lock on the data item.

For example:

Time	T1	T2
1	Read (x) *Applies a shared lock to x.*	
2		Read (x) *Is allowed because T1 has a shared lock of x. Applies a shared lock.*
3	Write (x) *Cannot apply an exclusive lock because of the shared lock of T2.*	

And another example:

Time	T1	T2
1	Write (x) *Applies an exclusive lock to x.*	
2		Read (x) *Is not allowed to apply the shared lock because of the exclusive lock of T1.*

For a data item, more than one transaction can hold a shared lock, but only one transaction can have an exclusive lock.

Some systems allow the transaction to upgrade its shared lock to an exclusive lock or downgrade the exclusive lock to a shared lock. For example, if the transaction first reads a data item and applies a shared lock, and then writes the data item, then the shared lock of the data item is changed to an exclusive lock. This could happen if other transactions do not have any lock of this data item.

6.5.2.2   Releasing Locks

A transaction locks a data item when it accesses it. This makes the item completely or partially (depending on the type of the lock) unavailable to other transactions. When should the lock be released to allow other transactions to proceed with access to the data item?

Let us assume that the transaction locks an item when it performs an operation and releases the lock immediately after the operation is finished to make the item available to other transactions. Then the transaction proceeds with its other operations. This approach does not postpone other transactions for long, but does it work for data consistency?

The following schedule represents our example with dirty reads:

S = {R1, U1, W1, R2, RB1, U2, W2, C2}

This schedule with locks will look like (a shared lock is shown as SL, an exclusive lock – as EL, and a lock release as LR):

$$S = \{SL1, R1, LR1, U1, EL1, W1, LR1, SL2, R2, LR2, RB1, U2, EL2, W2, LR2, C2\}$$

The result of this schedule is the same as it was without locking – we have a dirty read. Releasing the lock of an operation immediately after the operation is finished does not solve the inconsistency problem because it does not isolate the transactions and allows them to interfere with each other.

Consistent concurrent transaction management uses a *two-phase locking* mechanism (2PL). The rules of the 2PL mechanism are:

- No transaction can request a lock after it releases a lock.
- A transaction cannot release a lock until it is sure that it will not need another lock.

With the 2PL mechanism, every transaction is executed in two phases: the growing phase, when it accesses data items and locks them, and the shrinking phase, where the transaction releases the locks. At a certain point called the *lock point, when* the transaction is finished with locking, but has not released the locks yet, there are two possibilities: to release locks one by one, or to release all locks at one time when the transaction is terminated.

The two-phase locking mechanism with a "gradual" shrinking phase (Figure 6-2) reorganizes the schedule for the dirty read example in the following way:

$$S = \{SL1, R1, U1, EL1, W1, LR1, SL2, R2, RB1, U2, EL2, W2, LR2, C2\}$$

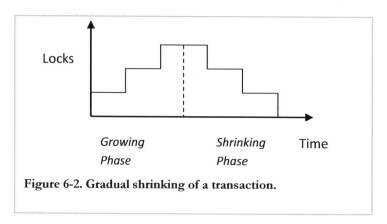

Figure 6-2. Gradual shrinking of a transaction.

This schedule is not serializable and it still results in a dirty read. After the first transaction has finished all its operations, it started releasing the locks. The second transaction got access to the data item before the first transaction was finished, read the data item, and because it was before the end of the first transaction, it was a dirty read. The first transaction rolled back and created the dirty read phenomenon in the database. Note that in this case the first transaction upgraded the lock on the data item from the shared to exclusive. This was possible because no other transaction was holding any lock on the data item.

Locking protects database consistency if the shrinking phase is implemented as an "immediate" lock release for all locks when the transaction is finished (Figure 6-3).

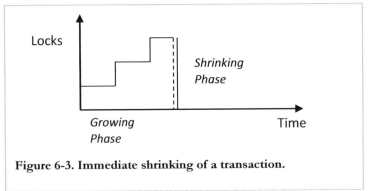

Figure 6-3. Immediate shrinking of a transaction.

All locks of a transaction are released at the same time when the transaction is finished.

The schedule for the dirty read example is changed. Because the lock release of the first transaction is performed when the transaction is finished, the second transaction cannot apply the shared lock where it had it before. The second transaction waits for the first transaction to release the lock. Actually, the locking forces the transactions to be executed serially:

S = {*SL1*, R1, U1, *EL1*, W1, *LR1*, RB1, *SL2*, R2, U2, *EL2*, W2, *LR2*, C2}

Here is an interesting example about serializability and locking: locking enforces serializability, however, not every serializable schedule is possible with locking:

T1
Read(x)
x ← x + 1
Write(x)
Read(x)
y ← y * 10
Write(y)
Commit

T2
Read(x)
Commit

T3
Read(y)
Commit

For x = 1 and y = 1 and T3 → T1 → T2 we will get x = 2, y =10.

The following schedule (locks are implied) is serializable with T3 → T1 → T2, but it would not be allowed by the 2PL mechanism (because T1 will need a lock on y after it is finished with processing x, it cannot release the lock on x and make x available to T2 and T3). The operation of T2, which is not allowed by locking, is shown in italic.

S= {R3(x), R1(x), U1(x), W1(x), *R2(x)*, R3(y), R1(y), U1(y), W1(y), C1, C2, C3}

In general, locking supports serializability of the concurrent execution of transactions in the following way: for two transactions

$$T1: \{O_{11}, O_{12}, \ldots, O_{1n}\}$$

$$T2: \{O_{21}, O_{22}, \ldots, O_{2m}\}$$

the system builds a concurrent schedule until it encounters an operation which conflicts with an already executed operation of another transaction:

$$S: \{O_{11}, O_{21}, \ldots, O_{1i}, O_{2j}, \ldots, O_{1i+1}$$

The next operation O_{1i+1} of T1 cannot be executed because it conflicts with the operation O_{2j} of T2 (it means that O_{2j} holds a lock on the data item requested by O_{1i+1}). Execution of T1 cannot be continued and is postponed until the end of T2, when T2 releases all its locks:

$$S: \{O_{11}, O_{21}, \ldots, O_{1i}, O_{2j}, O_{2j+1}, O_{2m}, O_{1i+1} \ldots, O_{1n}\}$$

Let us revise the examples of phenomena under the locking approach.

Lost Update:

Time	T1	T2
1	Read (x)	
2	x ← x + 1	Read (x)
3	Write (x) *Waits because T2 holds a shared lock (read at moment 2).*	x ← x − 1
4		Write (x) *Waits because T1 holds a shared lock (read at moment 1).*
5	*Deadlock: one of transactions has to be canceled.*	
	Transaction is interrupted, the write operation is cancelled.	*Waits*
6	Rollback	
7		*Write is performed*
8		Commit

This example demonstrates the disadvantage of the locking approach: it can cause situations where one transaction is waiting for another transaction to release a lock, while the other transaction is waiting for the first transaction to release its lock. Such situations are called *Deadlocks*. A deadlock cannot be resolved by the transactions themselves. The database transaction manager detects a deadlock situation and aborts one of the operations that caused the deadlock: in the above example it was the Write of the transaction T1. As one of the operations of the transaction T1 is cancelled, the transaction has to be rolled back (remember the atomicity property!).

Dirty Read:

Time	T1	T2
1	Read (x)	
2	x ← x + 1	
3	Write (x)	
4	…	Read (x) *Waits because T1 holds an exclusive lock (write at moment 3)*
5	Rollback	
6		*Reads x=100*
7		x ← x − 1
8		Write (x)
9		Commit

The transaction T2 is stopped at moment 4. After T1 rolls back, T2 reads the initial value of x. Note that if T1 were committed instead of rolling back, T2 would read the updated value of x after commitment of T1.

Fuzzy read:

Time	T1	T2
1	Read (x)	
2		Read (x)
3	…	x ← x − 1
4		Write (x) *Waits because T1 holds the shared lock (read at moment 1)*
5	Read (x)	*Waits*
6	Commit	
7		Commit

Transaction T2 is stopped by the lock, and T1 continues with repeatable reads.

Phantoms:

Time	T1	T2
1	Read all x_i for which $F(x_i)$ = TRUE *100 rows read*	
2	Update all x_i *100 rows updated*	Read (x_j) (x_j is one of x_i)
3		Delete (x_j) *Waits because T1 holds a shared lock (read at moment 1)*
4	Write all x_i for which $F(x_i)$ = TRUE *Waits because T2 holds a shared lock (read at moment 2)*	
5	*Deadlock: one of transactions has to be canceled.*	

6	*Transaction is interrupted, the write operation is cancelled.*	
7	Rollback	
8		*Delete is performed*
9		Commit

The transactions are in deadlock. The transaction T1 is cancelled and the phantom phenomenon is prevented. Note that if T2 were inserting a row instead of deleting it, then the phantom effect would depend on the granularity of locking which will be discussed next.

6.5.2.3   Granularity of Locking

In our discussion, we were applying the operations to data items, but never discussed what the data item was. The data item used for concurrency management defines the *Granularity of locking*. The data item can be (from the larger to finer grain):

- Whole database
- Table
- Data block
- Row
- Attribute in a row.

The granularity of locking determines concurrent performance in the database: the finer the grain, the higher the level of concurrency. DBMSs usually lock data blocks or rows. Oracle locks rows of a table. Later in this chapter, we will show how Oracle applies locking of a larger grain in some special situations.

For the above example of the phantom, if the grain is smaller than a table, the insertion is allowed and the phantom phenomenon happens.

6.5.2.4   Locking in Oracle

Here are some examples on the previously used table test that demonstrate how Oracle applies locking:

Time	T1	T2
1	SELECT * FROM test; *100 rows returned*	
2		SELECT * FROM test; *100 rows returned*
3		DELETE FROM test WHERE f1 =1; *1 row deleted*
4	UPDATE test SET f1 = 110 WHERE f1 =10; *1 row updated*	
5		UPDATE test SET f1 = 120

		WHERE f1 =20; *1 row updated*

6	`UPDATE test SET f1 = 111`
	`WHERE f1 = 20;`
	Waits	

7		`COMMIT;`
8	*0 rows updated*	

We can make the following conclusions about locking in Oracle:

- Read operations share locks: T1 reads rows of the test table at moment 1, and then T2 reads the same rows at moment 2.
- The granularity of locking is a row: T1 updates a row at moment 4, and then T2 updates another row at moment 5 (please note that this is not totally conclusive as this could happen if Oracle locked data blocks and the involved rows were in different blocks; but Oracle does lock rows).
- Write operations apply exclusive locks: T2 applies an exclusive lock to the row at moment 5, then T1 wants to write the same row, but has to wait for the lock to be released.
- Once again we can see that Oracle has the READ COMMITTED isolation level: T1 does not find any rows for its last update because the row with f1 = 20 was updated and committed to f1 = 120 by T2.
- And the last interesting conclusion: Oracle does not apply any reading lock! At moment 3, T2 deleted a row. If Oracle applied a shared lock on rows of the table, then T2 would not be able to apply the exclusive lock to these rows (could not delete the rows) after T1 had read them.

6.5.3 Timestamping

Unlike locking approaches, timestamping does not maintain the serializability of schedules by exclusion. It tries to build a serializable schedule by specific ordering of the operations of transactions.

To order operations, the transaction manager assigns to every transaction T a timestamp that we will denote as ts(T). Timestamps must be unique and monotonically increasing. If ts(Ti) < ts(Tj), we say that Ti is older than Tj (i.e. Tj is younger than Ti).

6.5.3.1 The Basic Timestamping Algorithm

The main idea of timestamping is that for each pair of conflicting operations, the operation of the older transaction must be executed before the operation of the younger transactions. If O_{1i} and O_{2j} are two conflicting operations from transactions T1 and T2, respectively, and ts(T1) < ts(T2), then O_{1i} has to be executed before O_{2j}.

If the transaction manager receives two sets of operations $\{O_{11}, O_{12}, ..., O_{1n}\}$ and $\{O_{21}, O_{22}, ..., O_{2m}\}$, it can build a serializable schedule. For example, if O_{1i} and O_{1k} are conflicting with O_{2j} and ts(T1) < ts(T2), then O_{1i} and O_{1k} will be placed before O_{2j} in the schedule.

Because not all the operations of transactions are available when their concurrent execution starts, the operations are scheduled when they are ready to be executed: the transaction manager checks a new operation against conflicting operations that have been already scheduled. If the new operation belongs to a transaction that is younger than the transaction with the conflicting operations, then the operation in the younger transaction is scheduled for execution. Otherwise, it would be impossible to put the operation in the schedule without violating the rules of timestamping causing the operation to be rejected, and causing the entire transaction to roll back (remember the atomicity property of transactions).

Compare the following execution of transactions to the locking scenario of 6.5.2.1:

Time	T1	T2
1	Read (x)	
2		Read (x) *Is allowed because there is no conflict.*
3	Write (x) *Is not allowed because the conflicting operation was performed by the younger transaction.*	

Time	T1	T2
1	Write (x)	
2		Read (x) *Is allowed because the conflicting operation of the older transaction was executed before.*

In the following example (because we will refer to it several times, we label it as the Timestamping Example) x = 10 and y = 10. For T1 → T2, which means that T2 is younger than T1 and ts(T1) < ts(T2), the result of a serial execution is x = 12 and y = 22.

Time	T1	T2
1	Read(x)	
2	x ← x + 1	
3	Write(x)	
4		Read(x)
5		x ← x + 1
6		Write(x)
7		Read(y)
8		y ← y * 2
9		Write (y)
10	Read (y) *Is cancelled because the younger T2 wrote to y*	

11	y ← y +1 *Is not executed*	
12	Write(y) *Is not executed*	Commit
13	Rollback	

The read operation of the transaction T1 at moment 10 was cancelled because a younger transaction already wrote to y, and all previously executed operations of T1 have to be rolled back. T1 may be restarted with a different timestamp. If the Read(x) operation of T1 were allowed at moment 10, then the result of the execution of the transactions would be incorrect: x = 12, y = 21.

In the case that these transactions were submitting their operations as in the following scenario, then they both would be executed.

Time	T1	T2
1	Read(x)	
2	x ← x + 1	
3	Write(x)	
4	Read (y)	Read(x)
5	y ← y +1	x ← x + 1
6	Write(y)	Write(x)
7	Commit	Read(y)
8		y ← y * 2
9		Write (y)
10		Commit

Note that this scenario will be impossible under the locking approach. For the timestamping approach, when operations of the concurrent transactions come to the transaction manager one at a time, the manager has to be able to recognize a conflict. For example, in the first – unsuccessful – scenario of the Timestamping example, at moment 10 the scheduler has to know that the data item y has been updated by a younger transaction.

To maintain timestamp ordering, the system assigns timestamps to data items. A data item receives read and write timestamps (we will define them with the help of RTS and WTS, respectively). The timestamp of an item is the largest timestamp of all transactions that read or write this data item. Comparing the timestamp of an item with the timestamp of the transaction, the transaction manager can detect the situation when a younger transaction has reached the item before the older one.

The rules of scheduling the operations are the following.

For a transaction T that issues *Read(x)*:

- If ts(T) < WTS(x), then T is aborted. In other words, if a younger transaction has already updated the item, the transaction T cannot read it.

- Otherwise T continues. The read timestamp of an item is reassigned to RTS(x) = max(ts(T), RTS(x)) – either the read timestamp of T or the timestamp of a younger transaction that has read x.

For a transaction T that issues *Write(x)*:

- If ts(T) < RTS(x) or ts(T) < WTS(x), then T is aborted. It means that if a younger transaction has read the item and is using it or has updated the item, then the write of the transaction T is not allowed.
- Otherwise T continues. The write timestamp of x is reassigned to WTS(x) = ts(T).

By applying these rules, the timestamping approach always produces serializable schedules. The disadvantage of the ordering approach is the aborting of transactions, which may create significant overhead. However, timestamping is free from deadlocks.

One more thing has to be said about timestamping. In the second scenario of the Timestamping example, which was serializable, both transactions were successfully completed. What if for some reason transaction T1 is rolled back? This will create a dirty read situation. Timestamping does not prevent dirty reads. That is why timestamping usually is used either in combination with some kind of locking or finalizing the transactions is postponed – the transaction manager delays the execution of the conflicting operation until it receives the notification of how the older conflicting transaction ended.

Let us see how timestamping prevents the phenomena (in all examples below, assume that T1 is older than T2):

Lost Update:

Time	T1	T2
1	Read (x)	
2	x ← x + 1	Read (x)
3	Write (x) *Is aborted because RTS(x) > ts(T1)*	x ← x – 1
4	Rollback	Write (x)
5	*T1 has to be restarted*	Commit

The write operation of the transaction T1 is aborted and T1 has to roll back. T2 ix successfully completed and there is no lost update.

Dirty Read:

Time	T1	T2
1	Read (x)	
2	x ← x + 1	
3	Write (x)	

4	...	Read (x)
		Is allowed because ts(T2) > WTS (x)
5	Rollback	x ← x − 1
6		Write (x)
		Dirty read
7		Commit

As was mentioned, timestamping does not protect from dirty reads.

Fuzzy read

Time	T1	T2
1	Read (x)	
2		Read (x)
3	...	x ← x − 1
4		Write (x)
		Is allowed because ts(T2) > RTS(x) and ts(T2) > WTS(x)[21]
5	Read (x)	...
	Is aborted because WTS(x) > ts(T1)	
6	Rollback	Commit
7	*T1 has to be restarted.*	

Transaction T1 has to be restarted, and if the next time it does not experience concurrent conflicting transactions, it would have repeatable reads (but the value of x would be different, of course).

Phantoms

Time	T1	T2
1	Read all x_i for which $F(x_i)$ = TRUE	
	100 rows read	
2	Update all x_i	Read (x_j)
3		Delete (x_j)
		Is allowed because ts(T2) > RTS(x).
4	Write all x_i for which $F(x_i)$ = TRUE	
	Is aborted because ts(T1) < RTS(x)	
5	Rollback	Commit
	T1 has to be restarted	

---

[21] WTS (x) is less than ts(T2) because we assume that the last writing to x was performed before T1 and T2.

The phantom phenomenon was prevented; the transaction T1 has to be restarted.

6.5.3.2   The Multiversioning Algorithm

To reduce the overhead of restarting transactions, often systems use a special modification of timestamping – multiversioning. Under this approach, write operations do not modify the database directly. Instead, each update creates a new version of the data item. Each version of the data item is marked by the timestamp of the transaction that created it. The existence of versions is transparent to users. Users refer to an item without knowing with which version of it they are working – the appropriate version is chosen by the system.

The rules of multiversioning are the following:

For a transaction T that issues *Write(x)*:

- If the version x_i that has the largest write timestamp $WTS(x_i)$ satisfies $WTS(x_i) <= ts(T)$ and $ts(T) < RTS(x_i)$, then T is aborted. In other words, if a younger transaction has already read the data item (the version of the item which T has to write), the transaction cannot write the item.
- Otherwise, the transaction T continues and creates a new version x_j with $WTS(x_j) = ts(T)$.

For a transaction T that issues *Read(x)*:

- T reads the version x_i of x, where $WTS(x_i)$ is the largest write timestamp less than or equal to $ts(T)$.

The last rule makes multiversioning different from basic timestamping – theoretically, reads never fail. In practice, however, some reads may fail because the storage space for multiple versions is limited – see the explanation below.

Figure 6-4 shows several versions of data items x, y, and z with their timestamps. The timestamp of a version is the timestamp of the transaction which created this version. From the figure we can say that the earliest versions of x (timestamp 90) was x = 10. Then some transaction with the timestamp 95 updated x and created another version x = 11. After that the transaction with the timestamp 100 again updated x to x = 12. The same transactions updated the data item y. The data item z was updated by older transactions with the timestamps 71 and 86.

Consider three transactions: T1 with $ts(T1) = 101$, T2 with $ts(T2) = 90$, and T3 with $ts(T3) = 70$. Each of them has to read items x and z and then increase them by 1.

T1 is younger than any transaction, which recently accessed items x and z, that is why it will be executed without any problems. T1 will read the latest version of x with the timestamp 100 and then create a new version of x with its own timestamp. It will similarly process the item z.

T2 is able to read from the version of x with the timestamp 90. This is, actually, the version created by T2 itself, as we can see from the timestamp. However, when T2 tries to write the new version of x, the transaction manager discovers that the latest version of x has a higher read timestamp than T2 – 100 – which means that a younger transaction read and wrote the item (actually, the transaction with the timestamp 95 read the version of x available to T2, and after that, the transaction with the timestamp 100 read the version with the timestamp 95), and therefore T2 is aborted.

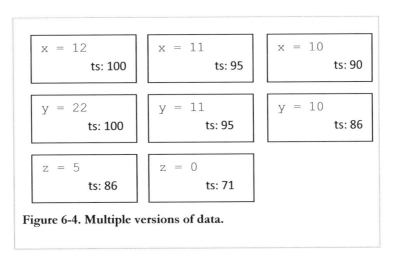

Figure 6-4. Multiple versions of data.

T3 cannot find appropriate versions of x and z that it can read because its timestamp is smaller than the timestamp of any version of these data items, that is why it has to be aborted as well.

Versions of data are stored in special memory – *rollback segments*. Rollback segments contain versions of data from committed or still uncommitted recent transactions. Because the size of rollback segments is limited, data versions of new updates overwrite data versions of updates that happened earlier. That is why some long-running transactions, such as T3 in the example above, which started long before other transactions, can fail to find the required version of data and have to be aborted.

Let us analyze multiversioning scenarios for the examples of phenomena (T1 is older than T2):

Lost Update

Time	T1	T2
1	Read (x)	
2	x ← x + 1	Read (x)
3	Write (x) *Is aborted because ts(T1) < RTS(x)*	x ← x − 1
4	Rollback	Write (x)
5	*T1 has to be restarted*	Commit

The transaction T1 is aborted because a younger transaction already read the data item.

Dirty Read

Time	T1	T2

1	Read (x)	
2	x ← x + 1	
3	Write (x)	
4	...	Read (x) *Is allowed because ts(T2) < WTS (x)*
5	Rollback	x ← x − 1
6		Write (x) *Dirty read*
7		Commit

After T1 rolls back, T2 is successfully completed. However, T2 used dirty data of T1 and wrote the dirty result in the database.

Fuzzy read

Time	T1	T2
1	Read (x)	
2		Read (x)
3	...	x ← x − 1
4		Write (x)
5	Read (x) *Reads the version of x as it was at moment 1*	...
6	Commit	Commit

The transaction T1 does not encounter the fuzzy read because it can only read the version of data which is consistent with its timestamp.

For the phantom example, the processing is performed in the same manner as for the basic timestamping approach.

Under multiversioning, phenomena examples have less aborted transactions than for the basic timestamping: in the fuzzy read example under the timestamping approach one transaction was aborted, while for the multiversioning approach both transactions were processed and produced a consistent database state.

Multiversioning changes one of the scenarios of the concurrent execution of transactions for the case 6.1 with bank accounts.

Time	Scenario 2	
	John	**Mary**
1	John tries to withdraw $50. The application reads the balance on the account; the balance is $100.	Mary tries to withdraw $75. The application reads the balance on the account; the balance is $100.

2	Money is withdrawn.	
3		Money is withdrawn.
4	The balance is updated to $50 *Is aborted because Mary's* *transaction has read the account's* *row at moment 1, RTS(balance) >* *ts(John's transaction)*	
5	Rollback	The balance is updated to $25.

Preventing inconsistency, multiversioning causes rollback of one of the transaction.

In the multiversioning approach, storage space is traded for performance – though the system has to use more space for storing multiple versions of data, there is less overhead of aborted transactions.

6.5.3.3   Timestamping in Oracle

The following is another example of the execution of concurrent transactions in Oracle:

Time	T1	T2
1	SELECT * FROM test; *returns 100 rows*	
2		SELECT * FROM test; *returns 100 rows*
3		DELETE FROM test WHERE f1=1; *1 row deleted*
4	SELECT * FROM test; *returns 100 rows*	
5	DELETE FROM test WHERE f1 =2; *1 row deleted*	
6	SELECT * FROM test; *returns 99 rows*	
7		COMMIT;
8	SELECT * FROM test; *returns 98 rows*	

From this example we can conclude that Oracle uses multiversioning. At moments 4 and 6 the transaction T1 reads the version of data consistent with its own timestamp: at moment 4 it is the same version as in the beginning of the transaction though the transaction T2 has deleted one row, and at moment 6 it is its own new version of data. However, at moment 8, after T2 commits the update of data, the transaction T1 reads the current version of data and not the version consistent with its timestamp. We remember that Oracle uses the READ COMMITTED isolation level, which makes transactions see committed changes of other transactions.

The special behavior of multiversioning in Oracle is also seen at moment 5, when T1 is allowed to write data (delete a row), which was previously read by the younger transaction T2 at moment 2. By the rules of multiversioning, this delete operation had to be aborted. This situation shows that Oracle does not use read timestamps.

6.6. Transaction Management in the Distributed Database

6.6.1 Serializability in the Distributed Database

Let us discuss how serializability is supported in the distributed database. First, as the following example shows, the definition of serializability has to be changed for the distributed replicated database.

Consider the data item x = 10 that is replicated on two sites. Two transactions T1 and T2 are executed concurrently.

T1	T2
Read(x)	Read(x)
x ← x+1	x ← x*2
Write(x)	Write(x)
Commit	Commit

Here are the two serial schedules: S1 is generated on the first site, and S2 is generated on the second site:

$$S1 = \{R1(x), U1(x), W1(x), C1, R2(x), U2(x), W2(x), C2\}$$
$$S2 = \{R2(x), U2(x), W2(x), C2, R1(x), U1(x), W1(x), C1\}$$

As you can see, the order of transactions in these schedules is different. After the transactions are finished, on the first site x = 22 (because T1 preceded T2), and on the second site x = 21 (because T2 preceded T1). These states of replicated data violate the mutual consistency of local databases in the replicated database.

Distributed replicated database schedules that maintain mutual consistency are called *one-copy serializable*. A one-copy schedule is serializable if:

- Each local schedule is serializable.
- Each pair of conflicting operations is executed in the same order in all local schedules (in our example, the order of execution of conflicting operations W1 and W2 on the second site was different from the order of these operations on the first site).

6.6.2 Locking Approaches

In the distributed database, locking has to be applied to all replicas of accessed data and to remotely accessed data. Distributed lock management can be performed in several ways:

- *Centralized.* One site is defined as the primary site and it is in charge of locking all replicated or remotely accessed data.
- *Primary copy locking.* One copy of shared data is designed for locking; all other sites must go to this site for permission to access data.
- *Decentralized locking.* All sites share lock management and execution involves coordination of schedulers of all sites.

6.6.3 Timestamping Approaches

Generating timestamps for a distributed database can be implemented with the help of a global monotonically increasing counter (which is difficult to maintain in a distributed environment) or with autonomous counters on each site. With autonomous counters, to preserve the uniqueness of identifiers, the site's number is usually attached to the transaction timestamp.

6.7. Transactions and Performance

The design of transactions and making them correspond to business rules is the responsibility of the application programmer. In a multi-user environment, the correctness of transactions requires the appropriate use of concurrency support mechanisms of the particular DBMS. Because the support of consistency of the database comes at the cost of performance, application programmers must carefully use the concurrency support features of the database. The design of transactions can have a significant impact on the performance of database applications.

> **The design of transactions has to be based on the business rules and take into consideration the features of the DBMS and the conditions under which transactions are executed.**

We will discuss some basic recommendations for the design of transactions.

6.7.1 Reduce Locking

Locking reduces concurrency on the database. Most DBMSs provide locking of different granularity. Use locking of the finest granularity allowed by the correctness conditions of your transaction. For example, your transaction has to produce a report based on data from a table, and it is important that the data remain unchanged while the report is being built. The simplest way to do it is to lock the whole table. In many DBMSs this would be unnecessary and inconsiderate to other transactions. Because our transaction only reads data from the table, the better way to preserve the transaction's consistency is to utilize multiversioning and the appropriate isolation level of the DBMS. For example, in Oracle you may define the transaction as READ ONLY (this elevates the isolation level from the default READ COMMITTED), and the transaction will see the version of data consistent with its timestamp.

6.7.2 Make Transactions Short

The length of the transaction affects database performance. The longer a transaction is, the longer other transactions may have to wait for the transaction to finish and release the locks. On the other hand, for a longer transaction it is more probable that it would be locked by other transactions that keep locks.

However, breaking a transaction into several smaller transactions should not endanger the consistency of the database. For example, in *Case 6.5*, if we consider dividing the money transfer transaction into two: one for withdrawal and another for depositing, then it will compromise the consistency of the database. If a failure happens between these two smaller transactions, then we will not be able to rollback the result of the first transaction and will end up with an inconsistent database.

In a different situation, when a bank transaction includes performing some operation (e.g. depositing money into an account) and then requesting a report on the account's activity, the corresponding database transaction can be broken into two: one for updating the row with the account's data, and another for reading data about the account's activity. In this case, locks applied for updating the account will be released immediately after the update and make the data available for other transactions.

6.7.3   Choose Isolation Level

Most DBMSs support several isolation levels. Higher isolation levels guarantee better consistency, but provide less concurrency than the lower ones. Choose the lowest isolation level without compromising the consistency of your transaction. For example in Oracle, if your transaction performs read operations only, and you want the reads to be consistent with respect to some moment, then there is no need to execute the transaction in SERIALIZABLE mode, it is sufficient to declare the transaction as READ ONLY. Because the READ ONLY isolation level is lower than SERIALIZABLE, your transaction will allow for more activities on the database by other transactions.

Figure 6-5 shows the relationship between consistency and throughput for different isolation levels. For this example, a summation query was executed concurrently with swapping transactions (a read followed by a write). Oracle's multiversioning guarantees the correctness of the summation query regardless of the isolation level.

6.7.4   Evaluate the Importance of Consistency

In the cases with bank operations, the correctness of transactions is required by business rules. However, there are situations when absolute correctness is desirable but not required. For example, imagine an application for flight reservations. Each reservation transaction includes: 1) requesting the list of available seats, 2) asking a customer about the seat he/she wants, and 3) booking the seat. If all these actions are organized in one transaction, then while a customer is thinking about the seat, all other reservation transactions are locked. If we agree to occasional inconsistencies in the flight reservation processing, we may break the transaction into two by making the request for available seats a separate transaction. The worst thing that can happen is that while a customer is thinking about the seat and decides to book a particular one, another customer takes this seat. In this case, a customer needs to restart the reservation process. This approach, though it causes some inconsistencies in business processing, does not compromise the consistency of data.

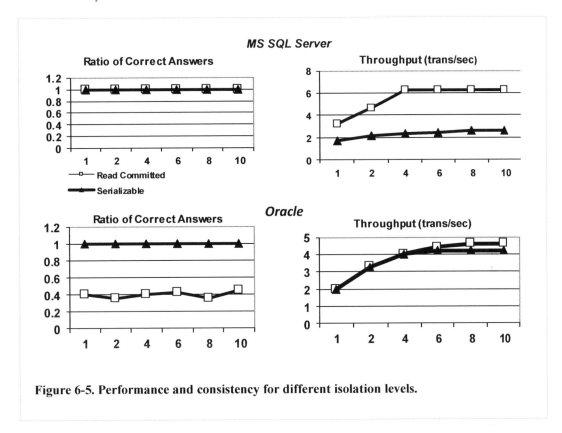

Figure 6-5. Performance and consistency for different isolation levels.

6.7.5   Apply Other Measures

In some cases, concurrency issues can be resolved with the help of other measures.

Conflicts for data can be resolved with the help of organizational routines. For example, if a long transaction has to be executed fast, and we do not want other transactions to interfere with its execution and lock the data, instead of locking the whole tables used by this transaction, we may execute this transaction at night, when there is no other updating activity on the database.

The consistency of transactions can be enforced by database design. For example, suppose a long transaction has to perform changes to most of the rows of the table T every day. The changes are based on data from the table S. If we do not organize these updates as one transaction, then in case of failure during the execution of the updates, the table T may become inconsistent – part of the rows that were successfully modified will be as of the current day, while another part will remain as of the previous day. Such a transaction, however, can cause serious performance problems for other transactions because during its execution many rows of the table T will be locked, or it may experience problems itself because there is a possibility that another transaction will try to read or modify data from T. We may choose another approach and add a column, which will keep the date of the last update of a row, to the table T. Now we can organize the update of the table T as a series of transactions, each of which updates one row if the date of the last update of the row is not the current day. If the updating procedure fails, we can restart it as many times as necessary.

We discussed distributed design as an effective way to improve performance. When data is efficiently localized, the possibility of transaction conflicts for data is reduced.

6.8. How Oracle Manages Data Concurrency and Consistency

Oracle maintains data consistency in the multi-user environment with the help of combining the multiversioning consistency model, various types of locks and different isolation levels of transactions.

A transaction begins with the first executable SQL statement (except for transactions not using the default isolation level). The transaction ends when any of the following happens:

- COMMIT or ROLLBACK statement.
- DDL statement (such as CREATE, DROP, RENAME, ALTER). The current transaction commits any DML statements and then DDL statement is executed and committed.
- The user disconnects from Oracle (the current transaction is committed).
- The user process terminates abnormally (the current transaction is rolled back).

After a transaction ends, the next executable SQL statement automatically starts the next transaction.

6.8.1   Query Consistency

Oracle *automatically* provides *read* consistency for separate *queries*. This means that the query will see all the data it needs, the way the data was when the query started. This is called *statement-level read consistency*. If necessary, Oracle also provides read consistency of all queries in the transaction – called *transaction-level read consistency*.

To provide these consistent views of data, Oracle uses multiple versions of data maintained in rollback segments. The rollback segment contains older values of data that have been changed by uncommitted or recently committed transactions. Figure 6-6 shows how Oracle provides statement-level read consistency using data in rollback segments.

When the query is submitted, it is assigned a timestamp, which in Oracle is called the current system change number (SCN). The query in Figure 6-6 has SCN = 102 and it will retrieve the versions of the requested rows with SCN less than or equal to its own SCN (highlighted in the figure). The third and fourth rows of the table were modified by younger transactions, and the system retrieves appropriate versions of data from the rollback segment. Therefore, each query sees the latest changes that have been committed before the query began. If other transactions that occur during the query execution perform changes to the requested data, then the versions of data consistent with the SCN of the query are reconstructed from the rollback segments, guaranteeing that consistent data is returned for each query. A query never sees dirty data or any of the changes made by transactions that commit during the query execution.

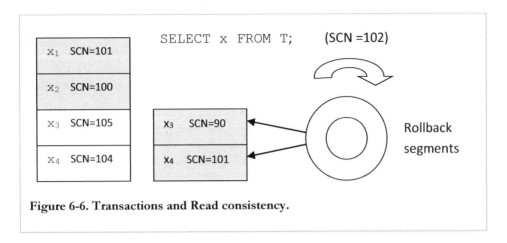

Figure 6-6. Transactions and Read consistency.

In rare situations, Oracle cannot return a consistent set of results for a long-running query. This occurs when the versions of data needed by the query are overwritten in the rollback segment by versions of younger updates because of the limited storage in the rollback segments. This can be avoided by creating more or larger rollback segments.

If at any time during execution an SQL statement causes an error, all effects of the statement are rolled back. For example, the query UPDATE T SET x = x*1.1 needs to read consistent versions of x to perform its update. If for some row, an appropriate version of x is unavailable from the rollback segment (e.g. due to the situation described above), the query is aborted and all updates that took place are rolled back.

With the help of the SERIALIZABLE isolation level (see details below) Oracle can enforce transaction-level read consistency. When the transaction is executed in the serializable mode, it sees all data as of the time when it started and the changes performed only by that transaction without seeing the committed changes of other transactions. Transaction-level read consistency produces repeatable reads and does not expose the query to phantoms.

Oracle provides three isolation levels: READ COMMITTED, SERIALIZABLE, and READ ONLY.

6.8.2   READ COMMITTED Isolation Level

This is Oracle's default isolation level. Each query executed by a transaction sees only data that was committed before the query (not the transaction) began. The query will never read dirty (uncommitted) data. Oracle does not prevent other transactions from modifying data read by the transaction because read operations do not apply locks. Therefore, data read by the transaction can be modified by other transactions, and as a result, if the transaction executes a particular read query several times, it may experience both non-repeatable reads and phantoms.

Let us analyze examples of phenomena in Oracle with READ COMMITTED isolation level:

Lost Update

Time	T1	T2
1	SELECT x FROM T; *Returns 0*	
2		SELECT x FROM T; *Returns 0*

3	UPDATE T SET x = 1;
	    Is allowed because the read of T2 did
	    not apply a lock	

4	COMMIT;	

5		UPDATE T SET x = - 1;
		    Is allowed because T1 committed and
		    released locks

6		COMMIT; *Lost update of T1*

In this particular modification of our initial scenario the lost update phenomenon is not prevented because Oracle SELECT operations do not apply locks (compare with lost update under the theoretical locking approach in 6.5.2.2). Note that the lost update of the first transaction could be prevented by executing it with the SERIALIZABLE isolation level (see 6.8.3).

Dirty Read

Time	T1	T2
1	SELECT x FROM T; *x = 100*	
2	UPDATE T SET x = x + 1;	

3		SELECT x FROM T;
		    No dirty reads, because it does not
		    see the uncommitted write of T1; it
		    reads x = 100 from the older version

4	ROLLBACK;	
5		. . .

Oracle lowest isolation level – READ COMMITTED – prevents transactions from seeing dirty data of other transactions.

Fuzzy read

Time	T1	T2
1	SELECT x FROM T; *x = 100*	
2		UPDATE T SET x = x - 1;
3	SELECT x FROM T; *x = 100. No fuzzy because T1 does*	

	not see uncommitted changes of T2	
4		COMMIT;
5	SELECT x FROM T; *x = 99. Fuzzy read because T1 sees* *committed changes of T2*	...
6	COMMIT;	

The fuzzy read does not happen at moment 3 because of the READ COMMITTED isolation level. However, this isolation level does not prevent the fuzzy read at moment 5, after T2 committed its changes. READ COMMITTED does not prevent phantoms as well.

6.8.3 SERIALIZABLE Isolation Level

The SERIALIZABLE isolation level can be set for the instance, session, or a particular transaction. The serializable transaction sees only those changes that have been committed at the time the transaction began, and the changes made by the transaction itself through INSERT, UPDATE, and DELETE statements. Serializable transactions do not encounter non-repeatable reads or phantoms. In situations when Oracle cannot serialize a transaction due to a committed delete, insert or update of a younger transaction, it generates an error. The following is an example using the table test introduced earlier in this chapter:

Time	T1	T2
1	SET TRANSACTION ISOLATION LEVEL SERIALIZABLE;	
2	SELECT f2 FROM test WHERE f1 <10;	
3	...	UPDATE test SET f2 = 101 WHERE f1 = 1;
		COMMIT;
4	UPDATE test SET f2 = 101 WHERE f1 = 1; *Cannot serialize access*	

Serializability in Oracle is implemented as a complete isolation of the transaction from other transactions. Each serializable transaction is executed as if it were the only transaction. The following is an example that shows that the result of two serializable transactions executed concurrently does not necessarily agree with the result when these transactions are executed serially (from [Kyte 2005]). The two transactions shown perform operations on the empty tables A(x) and B(x):

Time	T1	T2
1	SET TRANSACTION ISOLATION LEVEL SERIALIZABLE;	
2		SET TRANSACTION ISOLATION LEVEL SERIALIZABLE;

3	INSERT INTO A SELECT COUNT(*) FROM B;	
4		INSERT INTO B SELECT COUNT(*) FROM A;
5	COMMIT;	
6		COMMIT;
7	SELECT x FROM A; $x = 0$	
8		SELECT x FROM B; $x = 0$

In the serial execution of these transactions, one of them will return x = 1. The concurrent execution of transactions returns a result that is inconsistent with serial execution.

6.8.4   READ ONLY Isolation Level

The read-only transaction cannot include INSERT, UPDATE, and DELETE statements; it sees only those changes that have been committed at the time the transaction began. It behaves as a serializable transaction with only SELECT statements. If read consistency of the transaction is important and the transaction does not contain modifying statements, then it is recommended to use this isolation level. The following is an example of the fuzzy read scenario for a transaction with read-only isolation level:

Time	T1	T2
1	SET TRANSACTION ISOLATION LEVEL READ ONLY;	
2	SELECT x FROM T; $x = 100$	
3		UPDATE T SET x = x - 1;
4	SELECT x FROM T; $x = 100$. *No fuzzy read because T1 does not see uncommitted changes of T2*	
5		COMMIT;
6	SELECT x FROM T; $x = 100$. *No fuzzy read because of the read only isolation level.*	...
7	COMMIT;	

6.8.5   SELECT FOR UPDATE

Some of the phenomena (e.g. lost update) happen in Oracle as it does not apply read locks by default. However, we can explicitly request a read lock with the statement SELECT ... FOR UPDATE. For example, the lost update phenomenon example with SELECT FOR UPDATE will be processed in the following way:

Time	T1	T2
1	`SELECT x FROM T WHERE x = 100 FOR UPDATE;`	
2		`SELECT x FROM T WHERE x = 100 FOR UPDATE;`
3	`UPDATE T SET x = x + 1 WHERE x =100;` *Waits because of the read lock applied by T2*	
4		`UPDATE T SET x = x - 1 WHERE x =100;` *Waits because of the read lock applied by T1*
5	*Deadlock is resolved by aborting the last operation of T1.*	
6	`ROLLBACK;` *T1 has to rollback. The lock of x is released*	
7		*1 row updated*
		`COMMIT;`

Transactions behave similar to the basic locking approach: one of the transactions has to be aborted, and the consistency of the database is preserved.

6.8.6 Locking Data in Oracle

6.8.6.1 Row-Level Locking

Both read committed and serializable transactions use row-level locking. Oracle uses fine-grain locking to provide a high degree of concurrency. Oracle's row locking is fully automatic and requires no user action. Implicit locking occurs for all modifying statements. The read lock has to be applied manually with the help of the SELECT FOR UPDATE statement. Oracle also allows users to manually apply several table locks, which are discussed later.

The combination of multiversioning and row-level locking produces the following outcomes for concurrent executions of transactions in Oracle:

- Readers of rows do not wait for writers of the same rows.
- Writers of rows do not wait for readers of the same rows (unless SELECT...FOR UPDATE is used).
- Writers only wait for other writers if they attempt to update the same rows.

The transaction acquires the exclusive DML lock for each individual row modified by one of the following statements: INSERT, UPDATE, DELETE, and SELECT with the FOR UPDATE option.

Oracle automatically detects deadlock situations and resolves them by aborting one of the statements involved in the deadlock, in this way releasing one set of the conflicting row locks.

6.8.6.2   Table Locking

The only DML locks that Oracle acquires automatically are row-level locks. There is no limit to the number of row locks held by a statement or a transaction.

The following simple example shows that row locks are accompanied by table locks:

Time	T1	T2
1	UPDATE T SET x = 0 WHERE x =100;	
2		ALTER TABLE T ADD (y NUMBER); *Is waiting*
3	ROLLBACK;	
4		*Table is altered*
5	UPDATE T SET x = 0 WHERE x =100;	
6		DROP TABLE T NOWAIT; *Error message*

The transaction T1 locks rows of the table T. When the transaction T2 tries to perform a DDL operation on the table at moment 2, it has to wait because this operation requires locking the whole table exclusively, which is impossible at the time. When the transaction T2 issues a DDL statement at moment 6 with the option NOWAIT (execute immediately if possible), the system returns an error message because the transaction T1 locked some rows of the table and it is impossible to execute the DROP TABLE operation immediately. Row locks are preventing the whole table from being dropped.

Table locks caused by DML statements are imposed on the table transparently to users. Additionally, Oracle allows users to explicitly apply table locks.

Table locks can be held in one of several modes of different restrictiveness starting with the least restrictive: row share (RS), row exclusive (RX), share (S), share row exclusive (SRX), and exclusive (X). A lock mode applied by a transaction defines what operations can be executed on the table by other transactions and in what modes other transactions can lock the table.

The table below shows table lock modes caused by different statements and operations that these locks permit and prohibit.

SQL Statement	Mode of Table Lock	Lock Modes Permitted				
		Row Share	Row	Share	Share Row	Exclusive

		(RS)	Exclusive (RX)	(S)	Exclusive (SRX)	(X)
SELECT...FROM table...	none	Y	Y	Y	Y	Y
INSERT INTO table ...	RX	Y	Y	N	N	N
UPDATE table ...	RX	Y*22	Y*	N	N	N
DELETE FROM table ...	RX	Y*	Y*	N	N	N
SELECT ... FROM table FOR UPDATE OF ...	RS	Y*	Y*	Y*	Y*	N
LOCK TABLE table IN ROW SHARE MODE	RS	Y	Y	Y	Y	N
LOCK TABLE table IN ROW EXCLUSIVE MODE	RX	Y	Y	N	N	N
LOCK TABLE table IN SHARE MODE	S	Y	N	Y	N	N
LOCK TABLE table IN SHARE ROW EXCLUSIVE MODE	SRX	Y	N	N	N	N
LOCK TABLE table IN EXCLUSIVE MODE	X	N	N	N	N	N

In most cases, database programmers only need to properly define transactions, and Oracle will automatically manage locking. However, overriding default locking can be useful in some situations such as:

- We know that our transaction will lock most of the rows of a table. Then locking the whole table in the beginning of the transaction gives better performance than applying locks to individual rows.
- The business logic of the transaction prohibits any phenomena, and the transaction is important and cannot be aborted. We had an example showing that the serializable isolation level, though it prevents inconsistencies, can cause an abortion of the transaction. Using exclusive table locks that do not allow other transactions any updating activity on the table (e.g. X or SRX) will protect the transaction from the phenomena.
  - The transaction has to have exclusive access to the table to prevent other transactions from any modifying actions that can cause delays in the transaction execution.

An interesting illustration of Oracle locking is its handling of referential integrity. For the Manufacturing Company case let us consider the situation when for one of the rows of the table Department the value of the primary key is modified or the row is deleted. The problem

---

22 Y* means that only the rows affected by the operation are locked.

we can run into here is violation of the foreign key constraint when a concurrent transaction tries to use the old or new value of the deptCode in one of the rows of the child table Employee.

Figure 6-7 illustrates the locking on the parent and child tables when a user attempts to change the value of the deptCode (for the deptCode = '001').

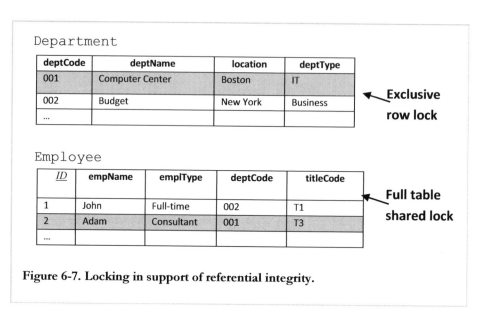

Figure 6-7. Locking in support of referential integrity.

The following steps take place:

- The updated row is locked exclusively in a regular manner.
- The database acquires a *full table shared lock* on all rows of the table Employee during the primary key modification of department '001'.
- This lock enables other sessions to query but not modify the table Employee. For example, neither attributes of the table can be updated nor a new record can be inserted. The table lock on Employee releases *immediately* after the primary key modification on the departments table completes (note that in Oracle 8 the lock was released at the end of the transaction). If multiple rows in departments undergo primary key modifications, then a table lock on employees is obtained and released once for each row that is modified in departments.

Let us analyze what happens in different situations:

- Update of deptCode = '001'or delete of this row. Because there are dependent rows in the child table, the update or delete will not happen.
- Update of deptCode or delete of the row that are not referenced in the child table. Updates or inserts on the child table that might reference the old values of the deptCode wait for a row-lock on the parent table to clear.

- Insert of a new row in the parent table. Updates or inserts on the child table that might reference the new value of the deptCode will not happen until the first transaction on the parent table commits.

In Appendix 5 there is an example of the concurrent behavior of two transactions that apply different types of locks.

6.9. Preventing Phenomena in Oracle Transactions

When we design transactions for database applications, we pursue the following goals:

- Maintain consistency of the business data or, in other words, avoid phenomena
- Minimize the chance of the transaction of being delayed or interrupted
- Minimize imposition on other transactions.

For example, to avoid the lost update illustrated in several scenarios, we can explicitly apply shared row lock (FOR UPDATE), or lock the table in the ROW SHARED lock, or execute the transaction with the SERIALIZABLE isolation level. The first approach seems to be most appropriate as it is less imposing on other transactions than the second approach and does not create potential problems for the transaction itself when it can be interrupted by younger transactions.

If we need to prevent fuzzy read, then the most appropriate would be to use the READ ONLY isolation level: we prevent fuzzy reads without preventing other transactions from reading or modifying data we deal with. If our transaction has modifying operations, then we can lock data (rows or the whole table) in the SHARED lock. Using SERIALIZABLE isolation level has the same shortcomings as in the case of the lost update.

6.10. Examples: Implementation of Transactions and the Design of the Database for Performance and Consistency

6.10.1 Transactions in Applications

Earlier in this chapter, we discussed examples of interactive transactions, where a user submitted a transaction consisting of several operations, waited for the response of the database, and then continued executing the transaction depending on the results of the previous operations. Recall, for example, transferring money from one account to another. A user withdrew money from one account, and then deposited the same amount to another account. If both operations were correct, the user committed the actions. If at least one of the operations was aborted, then executed operations were rolled back. Transactions in applications are implemented as sequences of commands, and when a transaction is started, the system tries to execute all the commands one after another. The logic of the transaction and different actions that have to be performed depending on the results of the operations need to be programmed. The following is an example of a bank money transfer transaction implemented with the help of an Oracle stored procedure:

```
CREATE OR REPLACE PROCEDURE transfer
      (par_account1 NUMBER, par_account2 NUMBER, par_amount NUMBER)
AS
   nAmount NUMBER;
BEGIN
   -- Check whether the amount can be withdrawn
   SELECT Balance INTO nAmount FROM Accounts WHERE account =
par_account1;

IF nAmount >= par_Amount THEN
      UPDATE Accounts
      SET Balance = Balance - par_amount
      WHERE account = par_account1;

      UPDATE Accounts
      SET Balance = Balance + par_amount
      WHERE account = par_account2;
END IF;
-- If we are here, then all actions were successfully executed
-- and must become permanent.
COMMIT;

EXCEPTION
   WHEN OTHERS THEN
   -- If we are here, then something happened
   -- during execution of the procedure. Any actions that were
   -- executed should be undone.
  ROLLBACK;
END;
```

If anything happens during the execution of the procedure, e.g., one of the update statements is aborted because of a deadlock, and Oracle raises an exception and takes the procedure to the exception handling section. In our procedure, this section of the procedure ensures that any performed actions are undone by issuing ROLLBACK. In case all actions were successful, the procedure gets to the end, where the actions are made permanent with the help of COMMIT. A bank application contains the call for the execution of the procedure. For example, for transferring $100 from the account 1234 to the account 5678, the application will execute the call:

```
EXEC transfer (1234, 5678, 100);
```

Though this transaction prevents inconsistency in case of failure or possible errors, it does not consider problems of concurrent access to data. Because Oracle does not apply read locks, after the check of the balance on the first account, another transaction may change the value of the balance and cause data inconsistency, for example, as in the *Case 6.1*. To guarantee data consistency, the statement with the check of the balance has to be rewritten in the following way:

```
-- Check whether the amount can be withdrawn
```

-- Apply FOR UPDATE option to prevent balance from being updated by another user

> SELECT Balance INTO nAmount FROM Accounts WHERE account = par_account1
> FOR UPDATE;

With the help of this simple example, we once again want to remind readers that the database application and the transactions included in it have to be implemented with a deep understanding of the features of the DBMS and knowledge of how the database is organized.

This transaction can be implemented in the application in any application language, e.g. in Java. The logic of the Java program will be similar to the logic of the Oracle procedure: it will contain read and write accesses to the database, analyses of the results of each operation and corresponding actions on finishing the transaction either by rollback or commit.

6.10.2 Concurrency and the Design of Tables

The way the DBMS provides data processing can cause performance problems in the case of concurrent transactions. Chapter 2 explains the basics of data storage, packing of data, and how the system uses storage parameters to manipulate the data. For example, if a row is to be inserted into a table, the system checks the list of available blocks for the table (called FREELIST) and inserts the row in a block from the list. If after doing this operation the block becomes full (no more rows can be inserted), the system deletes the block from the FREELIST. When data are deleted from the table, the FREELIST is also involved – some blocks may be returned to it depending on the setting of the parameter PCTUSED. Therefore, when processing data from a table, the system performs manipulations on the table's FREELIST, and to maintain consistency of the FREELIST in the case of concurrent actions, it has to apply locks on the FREELIST, as with any other resource. For intensive concurrent inserting and deleting activities on the table, performance can degrade because concurrent actions will be waiting for each other to release the locks of the FREELIST. That is why for the tables with expected concurrent insert and delete actions it is recommended to increase the number of free lists of the table. With multiple lists, more operations, each working with a separate list, can be executed concurrently. The number of free lists of a table is defined in the table's definition:

```
CREATE TABLE test (. . .) STORAGE (FREELISTS 3);
```

6.11. Summary

Consistency of the database can be violated by concurrent execution of database operations or by failure of the system. The concept of a transaction as a logical unit of work is introduced to prevent incorrect states of the database. The transaction is a tool of consistent and reliable database processing. Four properties define transaction management: atomicity, consistency, isolation, and durability. Consistency of a transaction in the multi-user environment depends on the isolation property – how well the transaction is shielded from the interference of other transactions. ANSI defines four levels of isolation: READ UNCOMMITTED, READ COMITTED, REPEATABLE READ, and SERIALIZABLE. With different levels of isolation, concurrent transactions can experience such phenomena as lost updates, dirty reads, fuzzy reads, and phantoms. The Serializable level guarantees excluding all phenomena.

The goal of transaction management is to produce serializable schedules of execution of concurrent transactions. Serializable schedules result in the same database state as when transactions are executed serially, and they combine the correctness of serial execution with the better performance of concurrent execution. The transaction manager maintains serializable schedules with the help of locking and timestamping mechanisms.

The transaction applies locking to prevent concurrent transactions from accessing the same data.. Different DBMS apply locking of different granularity, from the row to the whole database. Granularity of locking defines the level of concurrency – the smaller the grain, the higher the level of concurrency. The disadvantage of locking is the possibility of a deadlock. Deadlocks are resolved by the transaction manager.

Under the timestamping approach, operations of concurrent transactions are executed in an ordered, serializable manner. If the transaction manager cannot generate a serializable schedule for the transaction, then the transaction is aborted. Multiversioning is a modified version of timestamping, which allows reducing the number of aborted transactions with the help of storing multiple versions of data.

The design of transactions for database applications plays an important role in database performance. General recommendations for transaction design include using fine grain locking, lowering the isolation level, and splitting long transactions into shorter ones.

Oracle transaction management is based on combinations of locking, multiversioning, and different isolation levels.

Review Questions

1. How can concurrent operations interfere with each other and cause incorrect database states?
2. Why can a system failure cause data inconsistency? Give an example of inconsistent database computing caused by failure.
3. What is a transaction?
4. How is a transaction defined by its properties?
5. What inconsistencies can occur during concurrent database access? Describe situations with different phenomena.
6. What levels of transaction isolation are defined by ANSI? What phenomena can happen for different isolation levels?
7. What types of access to data are conflicting?
8. What types of locks are applied by the database?
9. Can two transactions share a lock? What type of lock is it?
10. What is a deadlock? Give an example of a deadlock between two transactions.
11. What happens if data needed by a transaction are locked by another transaction?
12. What is the goal of the timestamping approach? Define the rules of read and write operations for timestamping approach.

13. Is it possible that a transaction cannot be executed in a serializable manner under the timestamping approach? When does it happen, and how does the transaction manager resolves the situation?
14. What is multiversioning? Explain how multiversioning reduces the number of aborted transactions.
15. What is limiting the possibilities of multiversioning?
16. Which approach is more pessimistic, locking or timestamping?
17. How does the isolation level of the transaction influence performance?
18. What are the special features of transaction management in Oracle?
19. What isolation levels can you define for transactions in Oracle?
20. How are read locks implemented in Oracle?
21. When can manual table locks be useful? What are the disadvantages of table locks?

Practical Assignments

The assignments are defined on the Manufacturing Company case. Implement the assignments in Oracle or another DBMS.

1. You need to increase salaries for all titles by 2%. How should you implement this operation in Oracle to prevent inconsistency caused by interruptions of the operation?

2. Build a transaction for transferring an employee from one department to another in:
   a. A centralized database.
   b. A distributed database for the example presented in Chapter 3.

   Explain your transactions and show that they preserve business consistency of the database.

3. Assume that deptCode of the table Employee is not defined as the foreign key to the table Department. Build two transactions in Oracle: one for deleting an existing department, another – for adding a new employee to this department. Implement referential integrity checks in these transactions. Will your transactions guarantee referential integrity? What changes you will make to your transactions to ensure referential integrity?

4. In the example of the distributed database from Chapter 3, distributed referential integrity is supported with the help of a trigger. Explain how referential integrity can be violated by concurrent actions. Show what changes you can make to the trigger to preserve referential integrity in the concurrent environment.

5. An important transaction repeatedly reads data from the table Employee. How will you protect read consistency of this transaction? Show how you can prevent this transaction from being locked by other transactions.

6. An important transaction updates data in most of the rows of the table Employee. How can you protect the consistency of this transaction? Show how you can prevent this transaction from being locked by other transactions.

7. Execute concurrently a pair of transactions T1: $x \leftarrow y$ and T2: $y \leftarrow x$ for arbitrary values of x and y. Compare to the serial execution of these transactions and explain the result. Suggest how to change the transactions to ensure consistency of their results.

8. A bank database contains the table Balance(<u>acctNumb</u>, Balance) with data about accounts and balances on them, and the table BankOperation(<u>acctNumb, operationDate, operationNumb</u>, amount)with data about operations on accounts, which includes operation date and number and the amount of money involved in the operation (positive for deposits and negative for withdrawals). At the end of the business day, the table Balance is updated by data from the table BankOperations. Implement this updating procedure in Oracle and demonstrate that the procedure will preserve consistency of data in the case of concurrent access or failure.

9. For each of the following situations, describe what Oracle transaction management tools you would use and explain your choice:
    a. A report with calculations on data from multiple tables.
    b. A report based on several records of one table.
    c. Analysis and processing of all records of a table.
    d. Analysis and processing of data from several tables.

Chapter 7. Transactions and the Database Recovery

One of the examples from the previous chapter showed that inconsistency of a database may be caused by system failures. Recovery tools of the database systems are responsible for preventing database inconsistency by bringing a database into a consistent state after a failure: if the destination state of the transaction that was interrupted by the failure cannot be achieved, then the database has to be returned to the state which it was in before the transaction began.

The role of the database recovery tools is also to prevent data losses. Failures that cause memory losses result in the loss of the data that were kept in memory during processing. Media failures endanger the stability and persistency of a database. In this chapter, we will discuss database recovery to a consistent state and prevention of data loss in cases of software and/or hardware crashes that result in the loss of memory content, and media crashes, which result in the loss of data on disk.

7.1. Recovery from a System Failure

To understand the problems and the mechanisms of database recovery, we need to discuss data processing in even more detail.

As we know, operations on data are performed in memory. Chapter 5 discussed the part of memory called the database buffer that plays an important role in data processing. The buffer keeps the results of the most recent database operations. Figure 7-1 shows interactions between the database and the buffer during data processing.

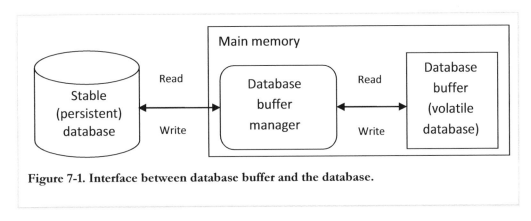

Figure 7-1. Interface between database buffer and the database.

To perform a database operation, the system requests the database buffer manager to read the needed data from the database into a part of memory dedicated to data processing – the database buffer. When modified data has to be written to the stable database[23], the buffer manager performs the corresponding write from the buffer to disk.

---

[23] For example, when the buffer has to be freed for the data of the new transactions.

Let us consider a simple transaction, which increases the values of data items x and y by 1. One of the possible scenarios is:

- Detect the address of the data block containing the data item x on disk
- Transfer x to the buffer
- Update x
- Write x back to disk
- Detect the address of the data block containing the data item y on disk
- Transfer y to the buffer
- Update y
- Write y back to disk.

Imagine a situation when a failure that causes a memory loss occurs between the update of y and writing it back to disk. At this point, the updated value for y which is kept in memory will be lost. During the database recovery, the actions of the system depend on whether the transaction was ready to commit. If the transaction was ready to commit its action, the update of y has to be redone and written to the stable database because of the durability property of transactions. If the transaction did not plan to commit, then the update of x has to be undone and the initial value of x has to be written to disk (rolled back) because of the atomicity property of transactions. Otherwise, the recovered database may lose committed data – a violation of the durability property of transactions (Figure 7-2a, the ready to commit case) or may contain uncommitted data – a violation of the atomicity property (Figure 7-2b, the rolled back case).

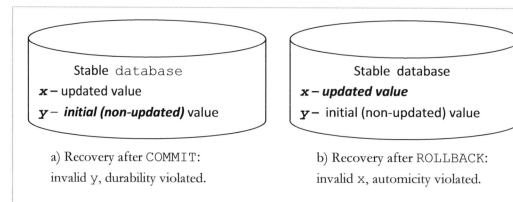

a) Recovery after COMMIT:
invalid y, durability violated.

b) Recovery after ROLLBACK:
invalid x, automicity violated.

Figure 7-2. Possible states of the stable database in the case of a buffer loss.

Before discussing how the recovery of a database is implemented, we will show that the actual interaction between the buffer and the stable database is more complicated than described in the above example. The database buffer occupies a substantial part of memory and usually contains more data than that is being processed at the moment. In Chapter 5 it was mentioned that the buffer is one of the factors that influence database performance – the larger the buffer, the more data the system can keep in it and, therefore, in more cases the system can retrieve needed data from the buffer without searching the disk. This results in more accesses to the data in memory (logical reads) and reduces the number of disk accesses (physical reads). When a transaction requests data, the database buffer manager performs the following actions:

1. Searches the buffer for the data block with the requested data
2. If the data block is not in the buffer, then the buffer manager allocates a free buffer block, fetches the block from the stable database and loads it into the block of the buffer
3. If there is no free space in the buffer, the manager decides which block of the buffer must be written (flushed) to the stable database and replaces this block with the fetched one Usually, the manager flushes the least recently used blocks.

Therefore, at any moment, the data that defines the actual state of the database are contained either in the stable database, or in the buffer, or in both.

The current database state is defined by the stable database and the database buffer.

The above example shows that some failures can result in the loss of the database buffer and the inability of the database to recover properly. By data loss we understand either the unavailability of results of committed transactions or the inability to return to initial states of uncommitted transactions.

To prevent data loss in case of failure, the database must ensure the following:

1. The results of all committed transactions become permanent or, in other words, these results should persist in the database after the completion of each transaction. In the case of failure and memory loss, results of committed transactions will be stored on the stable database.
2. If a transaction is unable to finish its work, the results of all performed operations must be erased from the database. In the case of failure and memory loss, the database will be able to restore the state in which it was before the transaction started.

Such management of the database guarantees the atomicity and the durability properties of transactions.

The purpose of the recovery subsystem is to support the atomicity and durability of transactions.

However, the above two goals of the recovery subsystem cannot be achieved with the described schema of data processing (Figure 7-1) because:

1. Committed changes may be lost with memory loss
2. Uncommitted changes cannot be undone, because initial data may be overwritten by the updated data.

To prevent the loss of the committed changes, they must be stored not only in the buffer, but also in the stable database. Committed changes of transactions are called *after-images* of data[24].

For initial data to be restored, it should not be overwritten, but must be preserved in the stable database until the transaction is completed. The copies of the initial data of uncommitted transactions are called *before-images* of data.

Therefore, the stable database and the buffer are not enough to provide the recovery of the database. The recovery mechanisms need another stable storage for before- and after-images. Such additional stable storage in the database is called *log files*. All changes to the data in the database are registered in the log files.

Figure 7-3 schematically shows interaction among the database, the buffer, and the log files during data processing.

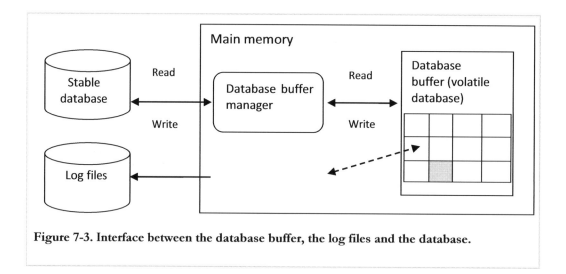

Figure 7-3. Interface between the database buffer, the log files and the database.

To ensure the persistence of the committed changes, the recovery subsystem writes the after-images of committed transactions into the log file. To protect the committed data, writing in the log file happens immediately after the commit and before writing to the stable database.

To guarantee the restoring of the initial data of the uncommitted transactions, the recovery mechanism also writes the before-images of transactions into the log file. Writing in the log file takes place prior to updating the stable database. In some cases, the recovery system uses the previous committed change of the data item as the before image of this item.

The current database state is defined by the stable database and log files.

The current database state is the state after all committed transactions. The stable database itself does not reflect the current state because it may not contain all committed changes or may contain some uncommitted changes.

---

[24] Note that before- and after-images are stored as change vectors.

Figure 7-4 shows two transactions at the time of failure.

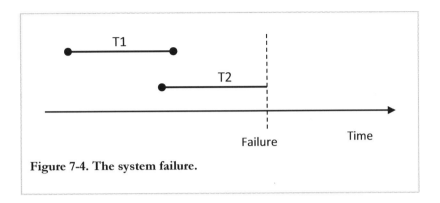

Figure 7-4. The system failure.

All data needed for recovery after the failure is available in the stable database and the log file. To restore the committed changes of the transaction T1, the recovery subsystem uses the after-image of T1 from the log file to write it in the stable database, which after the failure is in the old state. This is called the *redo* of the transaction (Figure 7-5):

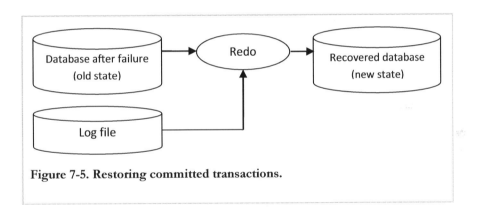

Figure 7-5. Restoring committed transactions.

To erase the results of the uncommitted transaction T2, the recovery subsystem uses the before-image of T2 from the log file and writes it in the database, which after failure is in the new state. This *undoes* the transaction T2 (Figure 7-6):

For each transaction, the log file contains the following information:

- The identifier of the transaction
- Type of the logged action (e.g. insert, delete, transaction start, commit, etc)
- The identifier of the data item
- The before-image of the data item

- The after-image of the data item.

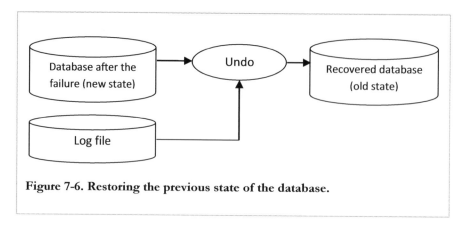

Figure 7-6. Restoring the previous state of the database.

To control the size of the log file and prevent it from becoming too large, the recovery subsystem periodically writes committed data from the log file into the stable database. This is called a *checkpoint*. It is important to properly define the time interval between the checkpoints – more frequent checkpoints create some overhead, however the database can be recovered faster because fewer transactions will need to be redone.

The recovery manager interacts with the transaction manager in the following way:

1. At the start of a transaction, the *'transaction start'* action is recorded in the log file.
2. When the update is performed, all the data mentioned above for a transaction except the before-images are written to the log file.
3. When the transaction is ready to commit, the *'transaction commit'* action is written into the log file. Then, the buffer is updated from the log file.
4. If the transaction aborts, the *'transaction abort'* action is recorded in the log file.

Such an approach is called the *deferred* update. If the system fails, the only actions that should be performed are the redoing of committed transactions (the transaction, which have 'transaction commit' in the log file) that took place after the last checkpoint. The transactions are applied in the order, in which they are written in the log file. The uncommitted transactions do not need any recovery, because for them no actual changes were performed on the database.

There is another approach, which is called the *immediate* update:

1. At the start of a transaction, the *'transaction start'* action is recorded in the log file.
2. When the update is performed, all data is written to the log file.
3. After being written to the log file, updated data is written to the database buffer. Note this approach differs from the deferred state because the database buffer is updated before the commit is made and that before images are written to the log.
4. When the transaction is ready to commit, the *'transaction commit'* action is written in the log file.

If the system fails, all transactions that were committed must be redone similarly to how it is performed by the deferred approach. The transactions that do not have a "transaction commit" record in the log file, are undone with the help of before-images that were written to the log. Actions from the log file are undone in reverse order.

Note that data is written to the log before it is written to the database. If the database were written before the log file, then in case of failure after writing to the database, the system would not be able to restore the database.

7.2. *Recovery from a System Failure in a Distributed Database*

A distributed transaction involves several sites. Failure of a distributed transaction can be caused by:

- Failure of an operation on one of the sites (e.g. due to a deadlock)
- A system failure on one of the sites
- Failure of the communication link between databases.

The atomicity of the distributed transaction requires that in case of one of these events all actions of the transaction on all participating sites be aborted and rolled back. The atomicity of the local parts of the transaction is managed by the local recovery managers as was described in the previous section.

Atomicity of distributed transactions is managed by the *two-phase commit* (2PC) protocol (Figure 7-7). The 2PC protocol ensures that all sites participating in the transaction execution are ready to commit their part of the transaction before the sites start committing the actions.

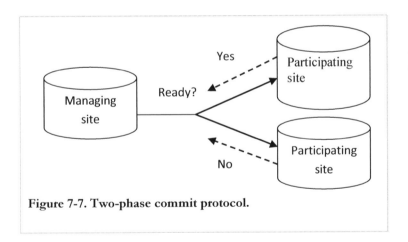

Figure 7-7. Two-phase commit protocol.

Assume that a distributed transaction has one site acting as the transaction manager (usually this is the site where the transaction is initiated).

During the first *voting* phase, the manager asks all participating sites whether they are ready to commit their part of the transaction. If at least one site votes to abort the transaction (or fails to respond within some time), the manager decides to abort the distributed transaction. If all participating sites are ready to commit their actions, then the manager agrees to commit the distributed transaction.

During the second *decision* phase, the manager informs all participating sites about the decision to commit or rollback the transaction and waits for their acknowledgement.

The following is the description of the actions of the global and local transaction managers and their communications with the recovery subsystem and log files during the committing of the distributed transaction.

Managing site:

1. Writes the *'begin commit'* record into the log, sends PREPARE to all sites, and goes to the WAIT state.
2. At receiving an ABORT vote, writes *'abort'* in the log. Sends GLOBAL_ABORT message to all sites and waits for the participants to acknowledge.
3. If all sites voted with READY_COMMIT, writes *'commit'* in the log file, sends the GLOBAL_COMMIT message to all sites, and waits for the participants to acknowledge.
4. After acknowledgement is received, writes *'end transaction'* action in the log file.

Participating site:

1. At receiving the PREPARE message, either writes *'ready commit'* in the log file and sends READY_COMMIT to the managing site, or writes *'abort'* in the log file and sends ABORT to the managing site. In the case of an abort (which site is calling the abort? I assume the participating), the participant proceeds with aborting the transaction and does not wait for the global decision.
2. If the GLOBAL_ABORT message is received from the managing site, writes *'abort'* in the log file and aborts the transaction.
3. If the GLOBAL_COMMIT message is received, then writes *'commit'* in the log file and commits the transaction. Only at this moment are all data locks released.

The distributed transaction can be interrupted by a failure of any participating site or the network communication. In these cases, the sites involved in processing do not receive the expected response of the failed or cut off site within the defined time period and have to terminate their actions, while the failed site has to recover from the failure.

Termination procedures of the managing and participating sites are shown in Figure 7-8 and Figure 7-9 (in these and the following figures the dashed line shows responses (or actions) that are expected but not received).

Figure 7-8 shows the actions of the managing site in case it has timed out and must terminate its processing. Timing out can happen during one of two waiting steps:

- The manager is waiting for votes from participants. If the vote is not received from one of the participating sites, then the manager decides to abort the transaction (Figure 7-8b).
- The manager is waiting for the acknowledgement of successful completion of the participant's part of the transaction. If there was no acknowledgement from some participants, then the manager again sends the decision to the sites that did not respond (Figure 7-8c).

- Figure 7-8a shows the normal completion of the transaction when the manager receives the votes from all participants and has acknowledgement from all participants either after the initial or additional sending of the global decision.

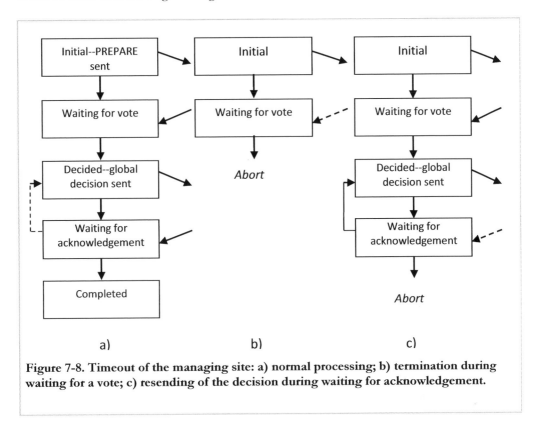

Figure 7-8. Timeout of the managing site: a) normal processing; b) termination during waiting for a vote; c) resending of the decision during waiting for acknowledgement.

Figure 7-9 demonstrates the behavior of the participating site in case it does not receive the message from the manager:

- If the timeout happens during the initial step, then the participant decides to abort the transaction without further participation in the distributed transaction (Figure 7-9b).
- If the participant fails to receive the global decision (if it is waiting for the decision, it means that it voted for commit), then the participant is blocked and has to continue waiting for the decision (Figure 7-9c). If a timeout happens at this point, the participant has to abort the transaction.
- Figure 7-9a shows the normal processing of a transaction at the participating site.

In case of a failure during recovery, the failing sites use records from their log files. Recovery of the managing site after failure is shown in Figure 7-10:

- Recovery during the initial step requires a restart of the commit process (Figure 7-10a).
- If a failure happens while waiting for the vote, it means that the site has not received the abort vote yet and after a restart it can try to commit again (Figure 7-10b).

- If after a restart while waiting for acknowledgements the site receives acknowledgements from all participating sites, it finishes the transaction. If some of the acknowledgements are missing, the site has to resend the global decision (Figure 7-10c).
- Figure 7-10a shows the normal recovery of the managing site.

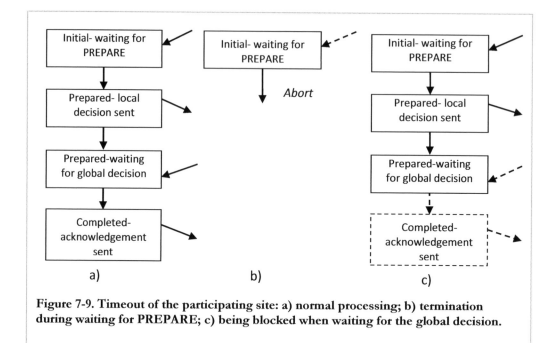

Figure 7-9. Timeout of the participating site: a) normal processing; b) termination during waiting for PREPARE; c) being blocked when waiting for the global decision.

The participating site recovers from failure as in Figure 7-11:

- If a failure happens during the initial state, then the site aborts the transaction because the managing site could not achieve a global commit without the vote of this site (Figure 7-11a).
- If the participating site fails waiting for the global decision, recovery takes place as in Figure 7-11b, and the transaction continues.
- Recovery in the final step does not require any actions because the transaction is completed (Figure 7-11c).

The disadvantage of the 2PC protocol is the possibility of blocking sites under some circumstances. Because blocking situations are rare, most DBMSs use this protocol.

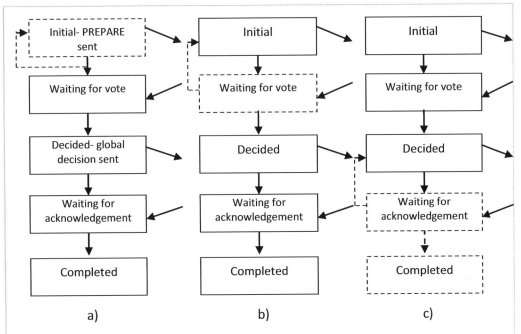

Figure 7-10. Recovery of the managing site during: a) initial step; b) waiting for a vote; c) waiting for acknowledgement.

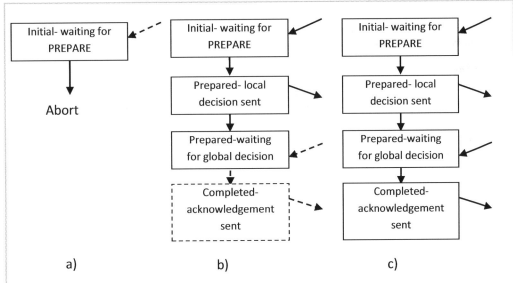

Figure 7-11. Recovery of the participating site during: a) initial step; b) waiting for the global decision; c) completion step.

7.3. *Recovery from a System Failure in a Replicated Database*

Let us discuss the atomicity of distributed transactions that access replicated data. For a read of a replicated data item the transaction can access any replica, while for write of a replicated data item the transaction has to modify all replicas. This is called the *Read-One-Modify-All* (ROWA) protocol. An understanding of the mechanisms of managing distributed transactions is needed to understand the problems of replication.

The goals of replication are better performance and availability (reliability) of the data. Replication can improve the performance of a database with intensive reading activity. Updating replicated data, on the other hand, can diminish the benefits of replication. Any transaction that modifies replicated data becomes a distributed transaction on all sites with the replicas. The transaction will commit only when all sites are available and can commit their part of the transaction. The possibility of unsuccessful completion of such transaction is higher than for non-replicated data and this means that performance and availability of the replicated database can be compromised – replication may work against its primary goals.

To improve performance and availability of the replicated database, different modifications of ROWA protocol are used for modifying queries. For example, *ROWA-Available* (ROWA-A) protocol performs an update of all available copies after the transaction is completed, and postpones updating of the remaining copies of data until they become available. 'Lazy' replication performs updating of the copies of data not by the modifying transaction, but only when these copies are requested by the subsequent transactions. ROWA-A and lazy replication approaches are examples of the asynchronous replication support mentioned in Chapter 3.

7.4. *Recovery from a Media Failure*

The previous discussion of recovery approaches concentrated on securing the content of the volatile part of the database – the buffer – with the help of log files. The stable database can also experience data loss because of a media crash. The stable database can be protected by a *backup* or *dump*. A backup is a copy of the entire database (sometimes, a part of a database) at a particular moment of time. It is a transaction consistent copy, which contains the results of all transactions committed at the backup moment. A backup copy is kept on a special offline storage device, e.g. magnetic tape. If the disk fails, the database can be restored from the backup and log files that contain records of transactions after the backup.

The current database state is defined by the backup and the log files.

A backup of the database should be made on regular basis depending of the updating activity on the database.

Log files play a very important role in recovery of the database from system and media failures. The reliability of the database is dependent upon the reliability of these files. Usually, for reliability purposes the log files are mirrored (replicated on two or more disks). In Chapter 5 it was mentioned that keeping log files and data files on separate disks can improve performance. Actually, storing data and log files separately is necessary to ensure that at least one copy of the data – either from the data file or from the log file – is preserved in case of a disk crash.

7.5. Summary

This chapter explains how a database management system can prevent data inconsistency or loss in case of system or media failures. The database is defined by the content of its stable part (stored on disks) and the database buffer in memory. System failures can result in the loss of the buffer data and inconsistency of the stable database. As a result, the recovered database may contain changes of uncommitted transactions and not have committed changes, which violate atomicity and durability properties of transactions, respectively. Media failures can lead to a loss of the stable database.

The prevention of data loss and the support of data consistency in case of system failures are maintained by the recovery system with the help of recording all database actions in a special stable storage, called the log files. Entries of the log files allow the restoration of the database to a consistent state: write all changes that were committed at the moment of the failure, and erase all results of transactions that were still in processing. The interactions between the database, the transaction management system and the recovery system are handled with the help of special protocols.

The consistency and recoverability of a distributed database are supported with the help of the Two-Phase Commit protocol, which ensures the atomicity of distributed transactions. The support of consistency of modifying actions in a replicated database can reduce such benefits of replication as data availability and better performance because of the necessity to replicate the changes in all replicas.

The stable database is protected from media crash and loss of stable data by periodic backups. The needed state of the database can be restored from the backup and entries of the log file that were recorded after the backup.

Reliability of the database and its possibility to quickly recover from failures are depend on:

- Reliable support of *log files*.
- *Regular checkpoints* (copying the results of committed transactions from log files into the stable database). Setting the interval between checkpoints is important for performance and the recovery time: frequent checkpoints cause overhead, but reduce the recovery time; using longer intervals between checkpoints has less overhead, but makes log files larger and recovery of the database longer.
- *Regular backups*. The time interval between backups determines the time of database recovery in the case of media failure.

Review Questions

1. How are the stable and volatile databases involved in data processing?
2. How can failures endanger the consistency of a database?
3. What is the purpose of log files?
4. What is recorded in the log files?
5. What is a checkpoint? How can it improve the recovery of the database?

6. Describe the protocol of transaction execution with logging.
7. Explain how a database is recovered from a system failure.
8. How are consistency and recovery supported in a distributed database?
9. Describe the two-phase commit protocol.
10. Explain how a distributed database is recovered from a system failure.
11. What is the role of the database backup?
12. How is a database recovered from a media failure?

Appendix 1. Case Studies

Each of the suggested case studies has a description of the user requirements[25] and a corresponding logical data model. In the logical models, the primary keys of relations are underlined, and the foreign keys are in italic; the names of foreign key attributes are the same as the names of the respective primary keys of the parent relations.

The cases can be used[26] for designing the physical data model (including the distributed solution), implementing security measures for both the centralized and the distributed approaches, programming either separate queries or transactions for the described tasks, deciding how to improve the performance of these queries and transactions, and maintaining data consistency.

Manufacturing Company

The company has offices in three cities: Boston, New York, and Cleveland. The database has to support data about departments and employees of the company. For the departments, the company needs to keep their codes, names (names are unique), locations, and types; for the employees – IDs, names, and types (full-time, part-time, or consultant). Each employee is assigned to one department. In addition, each employee has a title, which defines the employee's salary; salaries cannot exceed $100,000.

Departments of the company are located in three cities, and the office in each city needs to support local data, that is, data about all departments located in that city and the employees assigned to these departments. Each office has a database server.

The logical model of this database is the following:

> **Title (<u>titleCode</u>, titleDescription, salary)**
>
> **Department (<u>deptCode</u>, deptName, location, deptType)**
>
> **Employee (<u>ID</u>, emplName, emplType, *deptCode*, *titleCode*)**

The database is expected to support data about 200 departments and 4000 employees.

Users work with an application to manage (insert, delete, update, and select data) data about the departments and employees of the respective location. Such application performs several modifications of the data about departments and several hundred modifications of the data about employees daily.

---

[25] Please note that the case studies are deliberately anecdotal – we are confident that complex concepts of physical design and implementation can be explained and dealt with on such simple examples so that students could focus on these concepts without being overwhelmed with complexities of the case. This nature of the case studies needs to be explained to students.

[26] Assumptions should be made if the supplied information is not sufficient for making decisions.

This application requests the data about employees of a particular department, including ID, name, and title several thousand times per day. Managers of each office also produce quarterly reports about the local departments and the number of employees in each of them.

An additional application is used by managers of the New York office to produce monthly reports about the number of all company's employees of each employee type and the total salary of employees of each title in the company.

Users in each office are allowed to modify and retrieve all relevant data, but they are not allowed to access data about departments and employees of other offices. New York users of the the additional application can retrieve any data for any office. They can modify data about titles only, and perform the transfer of an employee from one department to another.

This case and the following sample tables are used in the book for demonstrations:

Title

Title Code	Title Description	salary
T1	Accountant	10000
T2	Analyst	20000
T3	Programmer	30000
T4	DBA	40000
T5	Manager	50000

Department

Dept Code	Dept Name	location	deptType
001	Computer Center	Boston	IT
002	Budget	New York	Business
003	Marketing	Boston	Marketing
004	Database Support	Cleveland	IT
005	Purchasing	New York	Business

Employee

ID	Empl Name	Empl Type	Dept Code	Title Code
1	John	Full-time	002	T1
2	Adam	Consultant	001	T3
3	Mary	Part-time	004	T4
4	Peter	Full-time	003	T2
5	Scott	Consultant	002	T1
6	Susan	Full-time	005	T5
7	Alex	Part-time	004	T2

Hospital

The hospital has four clinics. The database application has to support data about patients, doctors, and treatments of patients. Each patient is defined by the patient number, SS, name, date of birth, and address. A patient is assigned to one clinic, however, in some special cases, a patient can be transferred to another clinic.; the date when the patient was admitted to a clinic is stored in the database. Doctors of the hospital have an ID, name and pager number; doctors are scheduled for appointments hours in different clinics. Each clinic supports data about the treatments of patients by doctors, including the date of the treatment and the doctor's comments.

Each clinic has a database server. The office of each clinic handles the data about its patients, treatments and doctors' schedules. The central office of the hospital is using the database server of the first clinic; it deals with data about all patients, doctors and treatments of the hospital.

The logical model of the database is the following:

Doctor (<u>doctorID</u>, name, pagerNumb)

Patient (<u>patientNumb</u>, SS, name, dateOfBirth, address, dateAdmitted, clinic)

Treatment (<u>treatmentcode</u>, description)

Pat_Doc_Treat (<u>*patientNumb, doctorID, treatmentCode,*</u> date, comments)

Schedule (<u>*doctorID,* date, clinic</u>, numbOfWorkHours)

There is an application that supports (insert, delete, update and select) data about patients of each clinic, their treatments and the schedules of the doctors. For each clinic, there are several thousand modifications to data about patients and treatments each day. Several hundred times a day users supporting a particular clinic request data about:

- A doctor, including the doctor's ID, name, and number of patients treated by the doctor in the clinic for a given date interval
- A patient, including the patient's number, name, treatment code and number of times the patient had the treatment.

Database users of each clinic are allowed to modify and retrieve data about patients and their treatments in their clinic, but they cannot read or modify data about patients of other clinics. Users in a clinic can also read data about doctors and their schedules in the clinic; they can modify schedules of the doctors in the clinic of their responsibility.

The application in the central office maintains data about doctors. Several times per month users of this application request reports for all doctors, including ID, name, clinic and number of hours worked in the clinic for a given date interval. With the help of this application, the management of the hospital performs transfers of patients with their treatment histories to another clinic.

Car Rental Company

A car rental company has agencies in three cities: X, Y, and Z. Each agency deals with rentals of its vehicles only. The database of the company supports data about vehicles, clients, and rentals of vehicles to clients. For vehicles, the company stores vehicle ID, make, type (truck or not truck), year, and total mileage. The data about rentals include the ID of the client who rented the vehicle, the number of days, and the mileage increase.

The relational model of the database is the following:

Vehicle (<u>vID</u>, make, type, year, totalMileage, city)

Client (<u>clientID</u>, name, address, licenseNumb)

Rent (<u>*vID, clientID,* date,</u> numberOfDays, mileage)

Each agency maintains data about rentals of its own vehicles with the help of a local application, which supports insert, delete, update, and select operations on the data about vehicles and rentals. Each agency has several hundred vehicles and several thousand rentals per week.

Additionally, the agency in X produces a monthly report about all rentals during that month with information about each rented vehicle and the number of days the vehicle was rented during the month.

The office in Y is tasked to produce once a month a report about the rentals of trucks similar to the monthly report of the agency X. Once a month this agency updates the data about the total mileage of trucks based on the information from truck rentals during the month. The office in Z performs similar accounting and updating of the total mileage for all other vehicles.

Database users in each agency are in charge of the support of data about local vehicles and rentals; they cannot retrieve or modify data about vehicles of other agencies (except modifications of total mileage provided in Y and Z). The managers from Y can retrieve data about trucks and their rentals, and can modify the total mileage of trucks. Managers from Z can perform similar functions with the data about all other vehicles.

Department of Health

The Department of Health in New York has four offices for processing immunization records of children. The first office is in charge of records of children from the Bronx; the second office works with records of children from Manhattan; the third office processes records of children from Queens; and the fourth office maintains records of children from Brooklyn and Staten Island. In addition to the basic information about the children, the database includes the data for all immunizations and immunization events, including the immunization code, when it was given, and to which child.

The relational model of the database is the following:

Child (<u>childID</u>, firstName, lastName, dateOfBirth, street, city, ZIP, phone, borough)

Immunization (<u>immunizationCode</u>, description)

Immunization_Event (*<u>childID, immunizationCode</u>, <u>date</u>*)

Each office supports the data for respective children and their immunization events. In addition to all the necessary data modifications, the office daily processes several thousand requests for immunization events of a child (including immunization code and description, and date of the immunization event), given the child's ID or name and date of birth.

The fourths office, in addition to supporting the local immunization information, produces weekly reports about the immunization events of a particular type for all children in New York. This office also maintains (updates, deletes, inserts) the data about immunizations.

The database users in can retrieve and modify all respective data, but cannot access data of other offices. A group of database users in the fourths office can retrieve data about all children and their immunization events.

Financial Company

The financial company ABC provides tax and audit services to its clients. One group of the company's employees is in performing tax services, and the other is performing audit services. Each group provides corresponding services, supports data about them, and produces various reports on them. The database of the company contains data about services (including service type: tax or audit), employees, including the type of service the employee provides, and the company's activities, including service provided, the client served, the date of the service, and the amount charged for the service.

The company has two database servers. The logical model of the database is the following:

Service (<u>serviceCode</u>, description, serviceType)

Employee (<u>employeeID</u>, name, serviceType)

Client (<u>clientID</u>, name, address)

Activity (*<u>clientID, employeeID, serviceCode</u>, <u>serviceDate</u>*, amountCharged)

Employees of each group are allowed to read the data about services provided by their group only. Each of employees supports data about his or her activities and is not allowed to see or modify data about activities provided by other employees. In addition, each employee produces quarterly reports about clients he/she served during the quarter.

Several users of the database are in charge of support of data about clients and services; they can insert, delete, and update data about clients. These employees are also maintaining the changes when an employee is assigned to perform another service type, e.g. an employee who has been performing tax services is assigned to perform audit services.

The company's managers produce monthly reports about activities of the employees, including the number of services the employee provided during the month and the total amount charged for the services. Managers can read any data; however, they cannot modify data.

Appendix 2. Operations of Relational Algebra

Definitions

Relational algebra is one of the data manipulation languages developed for the relational model of data. The relational operations are demonstrated on the following relations Title1, Title2, and Employee:

Title1

titleCode	titleDescription	salary
T1	Accountant	10000
T2	Analyst	20000
T3	Programmer	30000

Title2

titleCode	titleDescription	salary
T4	DBA	40000
T5	Manager	50000
T1	Accountant	10000

Employee

ID	empName	emplType	deptCode	titleCode
1	John	Full-time	002	T1
2	Adam	Consultant	001	T3
4	Peter	Full-time	003	T2
5	Scott	Consultant	002	T1
7	Alex	Part-time	004	T2

The result of each operation is additionally explained by an equivalent SQL statement.

Selection

Selection produces a horizontal subset of a relation. Selection from the relation R by the condition F is defined by a Greek letter σ (sigma):

$$\sigma_F (R)$$

For example, $\sigma_{titleCode="T1"}$ (Employee) returns rows of employees with the title code 'T1':

ID	empName	emplType	deptCode		titleCode
1	John	Full-time	002		T1
5	Scott	Consultant	002		T1

The corresponding SQL statement is:

```
SELECT * FROM Employee WHERE titleCode = 'T1';
```

Projection

Projection produces a vertical subset of a relation. Projection of the relation R on the attributes X (where X is a subset of attributes of R) is defined by a Greek letter Π (pi):

243

$$\Pi_X (R)$$

If the projection produces duplicates (identical rows), they are eliminated from the result.

For example, $\Pi_{titleCode, Salary}$ (Title1) returns codes and salaries of titles:

titleCode	salary
T1	10000
T2	20000
T3	30000

The corresponding SQL statement is:

```
SELECT titleCode, Salary FROM Title1;
```

Set Operations

Set operations on relations include *union, difference, intersection,* and *Cartesian product.* While selection and projection are unary operations (performed on one relation), set operations may be performed on several relations; we will illustrate them as binary operations (performed on two relations). Relations participating in union, difference, and intersection should be operation compatible. That means the relations have the same number of attributes, and the pairs of corresponding attributes have the same domain.

The *Union* of two relations R and S produces a relation with the rows that are included in R, or in S, or in both. If union produces duplicate rows, they are eliminated from the result. Union is defined by a special mathematical symbol:

$$R \cup S$$

For example, Title1 U Title2:

titleCode	titleDescription	salary
T1	Accountant	10000
T2	Analyst	20000
T3	Programmer	30000
T4	DBA	40000
T5	Manager	50000

All SQL dialects contain the UNION operator, and the corresponding SQL statement is:

```
SELECT * FROM Title1 UNION SELECT * FROM Title2;
```

The *Difference* of two relations R and S produces a relation with the rows of R that are not included in S. Difference is defined by the minus sign:

R − S

For example, Title1 - Title2:

titleCode	titleDescription	salary
T2	Analyst	20000
T3	Programmer	30000

Standard SQL includes the EXCEPT operator:

```
SELECT * FROM Title1
EXCEPT
SELECT * FROM Title2;
```

Oracle SQL dialect contains the MINUS operator (the query will be similar to the query with the EXCEPT operator).

If an SQL dialects does not include the difference operation, we can compute the difference either by the query with correlated subquery

```
SELECT * FROM Title1 WHERE NOT EXISTS
        (SELECT * FROM Title2 WHERE titleCode =
             Title1.titleCode);
```

or using the outer join

```
ELECT Title1.*
FROM Title1 LEFT JOIN Title2 on Title1.titleCode =
Title2.titleCode
WHERE Title2.titleCode IS NULL;
```

Intersection of two relations R and S produces a relation that contains the rows that are included in both R and S. Intersection is defined by a special mathematical symbol:

R ∩ S

For example, Title1 ∩ Title2

titleCode	titleDescription	salary
T1	Accountant	10000

The corresponding SQL statement is:

```
SELECT * FROM Title1
INTERSECT
SELECT * FROM Title2;
```

dialects that do not have the intersection operation the corresponding SQL ment is:

```
SELECT * FROM Title1 WHERE EXISTS
        (SELECT * FROM Title2 WHERE titleCode =
            Title1.titleCode);
```

The *Cartesian product* of two relations R and S produces a relation, the rows of which are obtained by merging each row of the relation R with each row of the relation S. The Cartesian product is defined by a mathematical symbol:

$$R \times S$$

For example, Employee x Title1:

ID	empName	emplType	deptCode	titleCode	titleCode	titleDescription	salary
1	John	Full-time	002	T1	T1	Accountant	10000
1	John	Full-time	002	T1	T2	Analyst	20000
1	John	Full-time	002	T1	T3	Programmer	30000
2	Adam	Consultant	001	T3	T1	Accountant	10000
2	Adam	Consultant	001	T3	T2	Analyst	20000
2	Adam	Consultant	001	T3	T3	Programmer	30000
4	Peter	Full-time	003	T2	T1	Accountant	10000
4	Peter	Full-time	003	T2	T2	Analyst	20000
4	Peter	Full-time	003	T2	T3	Programmer	30000
5	Scott	Consultant	002	T1	T1	Accountant	10000
5	Scott	Consultant	002	T1	T2	Analyst	20000
5	Scott	Consultant	002	T1	T3	Programmer	30000
7	Alex	Part-time	004	T2	T1	Accountant	10000
7	Alex	Part-time	004	T2	T2	Analyst	20000
7	Alex	Part-time	004	T2	T3	Programmer	30000

The corresponding SQL statement is:

```
SELECT * FROM Employee, Title1;
```

Joins

The *Join* of two relations R and S is derived from the Cartesian product on these relations – it is a selection with some condition from the Cartesian product. Join is defined by a special symbol:

$$R \blacktriangleright\blacktriangleleft_F S = \sigma_F (R \times S)$$

A join condition can be any valid logical expression. Usually, join conditions are defined on the attributes of the participating relations. In practice, the join operation is applied to parent and child relations, and a join condition in this case is the equality of the foreign key of the child relation to the primary key of the parent.

For example, the equi-join between the relations Employee and Title

$$\text{Employee} \blacktriangleright\!\!\blacktriangleleft_{\text{Employee.titleCode = Title.titleCode}} \text{Title1} =$$
$$\sigma_{\text{Employee.titleCode = Title.titleCode}} (\text{Employee x Title1}):$$

ID	empName	emplType	deptCode	titleCode	titleDescription	salary
1	John	Full-time	002	T1	Accountant	10000
2	Adam	Consultant	001	T3	Programmer	30000
4	Peter	Full-time	003	T2	Analyst	20000
5	Scott	Consultant	002	T1	Accountant	10000
7	Alex	Part-time	004	T2	Analyst	20000

The corresponding SQL statement is:

```
SELECT Employee.*, Title.*
FROM Employee, Title1
WHERE Employee.titleCode = Title1.titleCode;
```

The *Semijoin* of two relations R and S by the condition F results in a relation that is the projection of the join of these relations on the attributes of the relation R. Semijoin is defined by a special symbol:

$$R \blacktriangleright_F S = \Pi_R(R \blacktriangleright\!\!\blacktriangleleft_F S)$$

For example, Employee $\blacktriangleright_{\text{Employee.titleCode = Title1.titleCode}}$ Title2:

ID	empName	emplType	deptCode	titleCode
1	John	Full-time	002	T1
5	Scott	Consultant	002	T1

The corresponding SQL statement is:

```
SELECT Employee.*
FROM Employee, Title2
WHERE Employee.titleCode = Title2.titleCode;
```

Complexity of Operations

Requests to the database are formulated in SQL. While processing SQL statements, the

DBMS transforms a statement into a sequence of relational operations. In many cases, this transformation can be performed in more than one way, and the DBMS tries to produce a sequence with the minimal execution cost or, in other words, with the best performance. Strategies for the transformation of SQL queries into relational expressions are built based on the complexities of relational operations. The complexity of an operation is defined as the order of the number of rows of a relation – n – that have to be processed by the operation. The following table shows the relational operations grouped by their complexity:

Operation	Complexity
Selection Projection (without duplicate elimination)	$O(n)$
Projection (with duplicate elimination) Group operations for aggregation Join Semijoin Set Operations	$O(n*log\ n)$
Cartesian Product	$O(n^2)$

Appendix 3. Architecture of the Oracle Database

Oracle Server and Oracle Instance

Oracle server is an object-relational Database Management System.

Oracle *database* is a collection of physical operation system files.

Every start of the database is defined by the start of a number of Oracle background processes and the allocation of part of memory for keeping and processing database information. Allocated memory is called the System Global Area (SGA). The combination of the background processes and memory buffers is called an Oracle *instance*.

Oracle server consists of the Oracle database and an Oracle server instance. An instance can mount (associate the instance with the specified database) and open a single database at a time; the mounted and opened database does not have to be the same one every time. A database can be mounted and opened by many instances.

The Oracle instance has two types of processes: user processes and Oracle processes.

- A *user process* executes the code of an application program.
- *Oracle processes* are server processes that perform work for user processes and background processes (that perform maintenance work for the Oracle server).

The Oracle *database* is a collection of data that is treated as a unit. The purpose of the database is to store and retrieve related information. The database has *physical structures* and *logical structures*. Because physical and logical structures are separate, physical storage of data can be managed without affecting access to logical storage structures.

Physical Database Structures

The physical organization of the Oracle database includes datafiles with database data and files that support database functionality.

Datafiles

Every Oracle database has one or more physical *datafiles*. Datafiles contain all database data. Data of the logical database structures such as tables and indexes are physically stored in the datafiles allocated for the database.

Redo Log Files

Every Oracle database has a set of two or more *redo log files*. The set of redo log files for the database is collectively known as the database's *redo log*. The redo log is made up of redo records, each of which describes atomic changes of data. Redo log files are used for the recovery of the database from system or media failures. For increased reliability, log files are usually replicated on an additional disk.

Control Files

Every Oracle database has a *control file*. The control file contains entries that specify the physical structure of the database. For example, it contains the following types of information:

- Database name.
- Names and locations of datafiles and redo log files.
- The time stamp of the database creation.

Like the redo log, Oracle allows the control file to be replicated for its protection.

Every time an instance of the Oracle database is started, its control file is used to identify the database and redo log files that must be opened for the database operation to proceed. If the physical makeup of the database is altered (for example, a new datafile or redo log file is created), the control file is automatically modified by Oracle to reflect the change.

The control file is also used in database recovery.

Logical Database Structure

Users or programmers do not work directly with the physical structures of the database; they can address the logical structures of the Oracle database, which includes tablespaces, schemas, blocks, extents, and segments.

Tablespaces

The tablespace is a logical storage unit. Each tablespace is defined on one or more datafiles. The following figure shows the database, which consists of two tablespaces SYSTEM and USER_DATA. The tablespace SYSTEM defines storage in two physical files DATA1.ORA and DATA2.ORA, while the tablespace USER_DATA is based on one file DATA3.ORA.

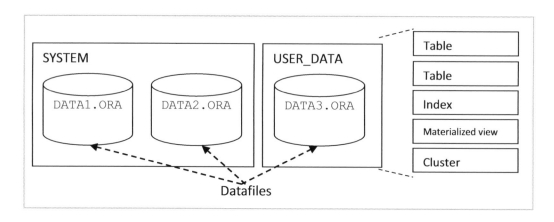

After the tablespace is created:

```
CREATE TABLESPACE User_data
DATAFILE 'Data3.ora' SIZE 20M;
```

users can create objects (tables, indexes, clusters, and materialized views) that occupy storage space in the files of the tablespace, in our case the single file DATA3.ORA.

```
CREATE TABLE Department (
        DeptCode CHAR(3) PRIMARY KEY,
        ....
        )
        TABLESPACE User_data;
```

Users cannot address objects of the tablespace directly; each object belongs to a logical structure called a schema.

Schemas and Objects

A *schema* is a collection of database objects belonging to a particular user (created by the user). *Schema objects* are logical structures that directly refer to the database's data. Schema objects include such structures as tables, views, sequences, stored procedures, synonyms, indexes, clusters, and database links. Objects of the same schema can be located in different tablespaces (see the Figure below).

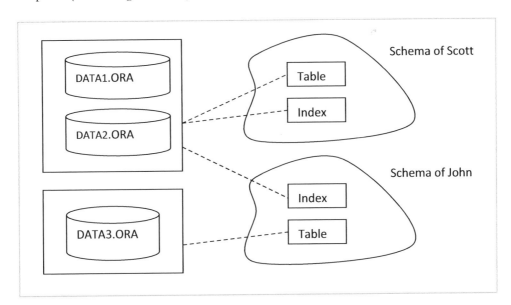

Users can access an object by the object name and the name of the schema, to which the object belongs:

```
SELECT * FROM John.Department;
```

Blocks, Extents and Segments

At the finest level of granularity, data in Oracle are stored in *data blocks*. One data block corresponds to a specific number of bytes of physical database space on disk. A data block size is specified for each Oracle database when the database is created. The default size of the block is 8K. The database uses and allocates database space in data blocks. When data are requested, the server reads the blocks containing the requested records into memory.

Data blocks form *extents*. An extent is a specific number of adjacent data blocks allocated for storing data of a particular type.

The physical objects of the database are stored as *segments*. Each segment can consist of multiple extents, resides in a single tablespace and can occupy space in several datafiles. For example, the table Department of John is created in the tablespace USER_DATA and is stored as a segment of the datafile DATA3.ORA. The index for this table is created in the tablespace SYSTEM and can be stored as a segment spread across datafiles DATA1.ORA and DATA2.ORA.

System Global Area

The *System Global Area (SGA)* is a shared memory region that contains data and control information for one Oracle instance. Oracle allocates the system global area when the instance starts and deallocates it when the instance shuts down. Each instance has its own system global area.

Users currently connected to the Oracle server share data in the system global area. For optimal performance, the entire system global area should be as large as possible (while still fitting in real memory) to store as much data in memory as possible to minimize disk I/O.

Information stored within the system global area is divided into several types of memory structures, including the database buffers, redo log buffer, and the shared pool. These areas have fixed sizes and are created during instance startup.

Database Buffer Cache

Database buffers of the system global area store the most recently used blocks of data; the set of database buffers in the instance is the *database buffer cache*. The buffer cache contains modified as well as unmodified blocks. Because the most recently (and often the most frequently) used data is kept in memory, less disk I/O is necessary and performance is improved.

Redo Log Buffer

The *redo log buffer* of the system global area stores *redo entries* – the log of changes made to the database. Redo entries stored in the redo log buffers are written to the online redo log file, which is used if database recovery is necessary. Its size is static.

Shared Pool

The shared pool is a portion of the system global area that contains shared memory constructs such as shared SQL areas. The shared SQL area is required to process every unique SQL statement submitted to the database. The shared SQL area contains information about execution plans for processed SQL statements. A single shared SQL area is used by multiple applications that issue the same statement, leaving more shared memory for other uses.

Real Application Clusters

Real Application Clusters (RAC) allow the Oracle database to run applications across a set of clustered servers. They provide for the highest level of availability and scalability. If a clustered server fails, the system continues to run on the remaining servers. If more computational power is needed, a server can be added without taking users offline.

Oracle RAC is a shared everything architecture. All servers of a cluster share all storage used for RAC database and cache as shown in the figure below.

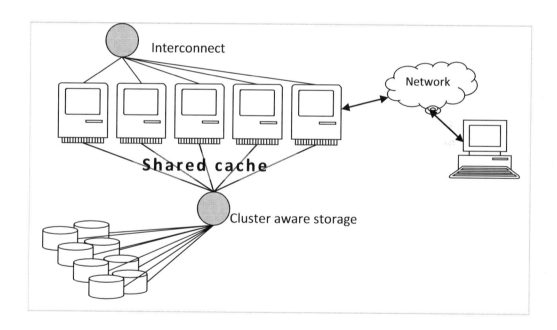

Appendix 4. Oracle Database Vault

Although the Oracle database provides for various *data* security features, these features do not provide for efficient control of the database *environment* and the *context* of database access. The Oracle Database Vault (DV) enhances the database security with the capabilities to *dynamically* secure access to data depending on the context of the access.

DV enhances the database security with the help of realms, factors, and rules. These features of DV build upon the database security and are connected to it.

Realms

Realms are logical groupings of objects/schemas and roles; they provide a means to protect objects from access by users with system privileges, like SELECT ANY TABLE, CREATE ANY TABLE, DELETE ANY TABLE, etc. Figure a) below shows how the users Scott and DBA, both having the SELECT ANY TABLE privilege, can select from any table of the database, in this case – from the table T1 of John. Figure b) shows how the system privilege SELECT ANY TABLE is affected by the realm X that contains the table T1 and user Scott with the privilege to select from it:

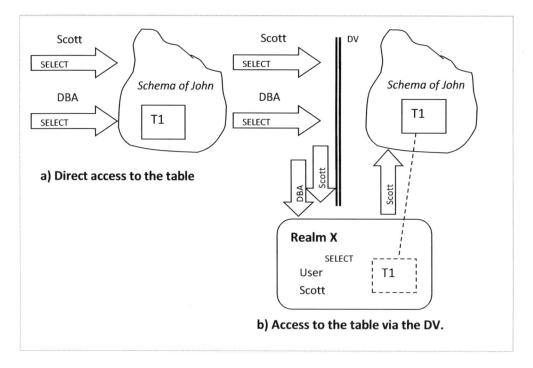

a) Direct access to the table

b) Access to the table via the DV.

- Once a user tries to select from the table, the DV checks whether the user has the system privilege SELECT ANY TABLE.
- If the user has such a privilege, the DV checks the realms that contain this table.
- If a realm with the table is found, the DV checks whether the user is included in the realm with the required privilege to access the table.

- The user Scott is included in the realm and is allowed to select from the table T1, therefore, the DV passes his request to the database. The request of DBA is stopped because the user DBA is not included in the realm.

Factors

A *factor* is a named variable or attribute, such as a user location, database IP address, or session user, that Oracle DV can recognize and use for activities such as authorizing database accounts to connect to the database or creating filtering logic to dynamically restrict the visibility and manageability of data.

In the example of label security (Chapter 4) John can access all records of the table from any connected computer. Factors dynamically provide control of the context of the users' access. For example, we may need to restrict John's access to Public records if he is working from outside the office. This can be accomplished with the help of DV factors:

- Choose the factor Network – one of the supplied factors.
- Create two identities of this factor: Intranet and Remote.
- Associate the identities of the factor with the labels of the table Document: Intranet with the label 'Internal' and Remote with the label 'Public'.
- Associate the identities with the client IP addresses.

When John is working from the outside the office, the DV evaluates the Network factor based on the home IP address and dynamically associates John with the label 'Public'; as a result, John is not able to access all the records he can access when working from the office. Figure below shows the dynamic association of users with security labels based on factors.

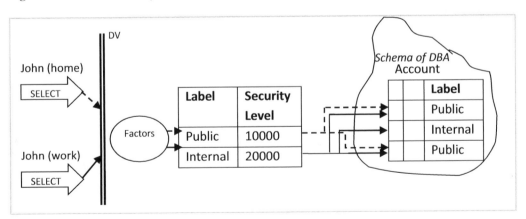

Command Rules

A *command rule* is a rule that is created to enhance the protection of statements that affect one or more database objects through DV rule sets at run time. When such a statement is executed, the realm authorization is checked first. If no realm violation is found and the associated command rules are enabled, then the associated rule sets are evaluated. If all the rule sets evaluate to TRUE, then the statement is authorized for further processing. If any of the rule sets evaluate to FALSE, then the statement is not authorized and a command rule violation is created.

For example, if user Scott who is allowed to access the table T1 through the realm X (Figure 1) should be able to do this only during a defined time range, the corresponding rule may be created, e.g. TO_CHAR(SYSDATE,'HH24') BETWEEN '22' AND '23'. This rule will be evaluated to TRUE only if the operation is performed from 10:00PM to 11:00PM, and only during this time will Scott's access to the table be successful.

Figure below shows how rules provide control access depending on the environment and context in combination with realms.

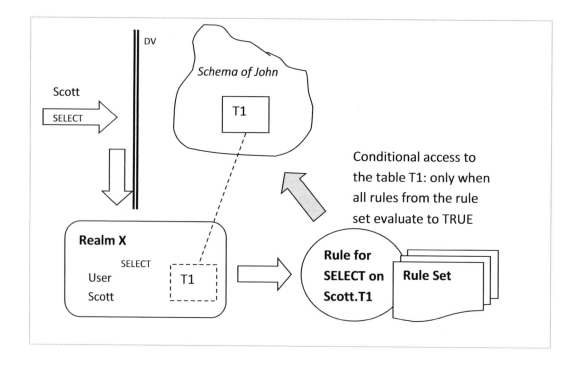

Appendix 5. Analysis of Performance in Oracle

We will analyze the performance of a series of queries on the table T[27](id, object_name, owner) which has several hundred thousand rows and we will examine different ways to improve performance. We will show fragments of Oracle outputs with information about the queries' executions.

To understand how Oracle processes queries we will turn the tracing on:

```
set autotrace on
```

The first query returns the number of rows of the table. The execution plan shows that the query is executed as a full table scan and the statistics of the execution demonstrate that the system had to perform a significant number of physical reads.

```
SQL> select count(*) from t;

Execution Plan
----------------------------------------------------------
   0        SELECT STATEMENT Optimizer=CHOOSE
   1    0     SORT (AGGREGATE)
   2    1       TABLE ACCESS (FULL) OF 'T' (TABLE)


Statistics
----------------------------------------------------------
. . .
        717  physical reads
```

The second query requests the names of objects of a particular owner; the third query requests the list of the objects' owners. For both of them, the system performs a full table scan, however, there are no physical reads – obviously, data is retrieved from the buffer:

```
SQL>  select object_name from t where owner = 'TMALYUTA';
SQL>  select distinct owner from t;

Execution Plan
----------------------------------------------------------
   0        SELECT STATEMENT Optimizer=CHOOSE
   1    0     TABLE ACCESS (FULL) OF 'T' (TABLE)

Statistics
----------------------------------------------------------
. . .
        0  physical reads
```

---

[27] For the purpose of demonstration the table T does not have a primary key and the values of the attribute id are made unique.

Next, we create an index on the column owner, which is often used to access data, and re-execute the second query. The execution plan says that the index was involved in the processing, and the statistics of execution show that there was one physical read – the system read the block of the index.

```
SQL> create index ind_t_1 on t(owner);
SQL> select object_name from t where owner = 'TMALYUTA';

Execution Plan

----------------------------------------------------------
    0       SELECT STATEMENT Optimizer=CHOOSE
    1    0     TABLE ACCESS (BY INDEX ROWID) OF 'T' (TABLE)
    2    1        INDEX (RANGE SCAN) OF 'IND_T_1' (INDEX)

Statistics
----------------------------------------------------------
          . . .
    1  physical reads
```

The next query requests the number of objects that are not owned by user SYS. The index on the column owner is sufficient for the processing of the query, and as the execution plan shows, the system does not access the table. However, the system has to perform numerous physical reads of the index blocks.

```
SQL> select count(*) from t where owner <> 'SYS';

Execution Plan
----------------------------------------------------------
    0       SELECT STATEMENT Optimizer=CHOOSE
    1    0     SORT (AGGREGATE)
    2    1        INDEX (FAST FULL SCAN) OF 'IND_T_1'
(INDEX)

Statistics
----------------------------------------------------------
          . . .
   345  physical reads
```

The next query requests data about the names of objects that are not owned by the user SYS. For the processing of this query the system has to access the table. RBO (Rule Based Optimization) decides that the non-equality condition will return many rows of the table and applies a full table scan. As before, there are no physical reads.

```
SQL> select count (distinct object_name) from t where owner
<> 'SYS';
```

```
Execution Plan
----------------------------------------------------------------
   0          SELECT STATEMENT Optimizer=CHOOSE
   1     0     SORT (GROUP BY)
   2     1       TABLE ACCESS (FULL) OF 'T' (TABLE)
Statistics
----------------------------------------------------------------
              . . .
          0  physical reads
```

We will create an index on the column id and will see if the optimizer decides to use it in the next query. The index is disadvantageous for the query; however, without the statistics the system cannot see this.

```
SQL> create index ind_t_2 on t(id);
SQL> select count(distinct object_name) from t where id >
20;

Execution Plan
----------------------------------------------------------------
   0          SELECT STATEMENT Optimizer=CHOOSE
   1     0     TABLE ACCESS (BY INDEX ROWID) OF 'T' (TABLE)
   2     1       INDEX (RANGE SCAN) OF 'IND_T_2' (INDEX)

Statistics
----------------------------------------------------------------
              . . .
          0  physical reads
```

For the same query, we use the hint to prompt the system not to use the index and the system performs a full table scan.

```
SQL> select /*+no_index (t ind_t1_2) */ count(object_type)
     from t where id > 20;

Execution Plan

----------------------------------------------------------------
   0          SELECT STATEMENT Optimizer=CHOOSE
   1     0     SORT (GROUP BY)
   2     1       TABLE ACCESS (FULL) OF 'T' (TABLE)

Statistics
----------------------------------------------------------------
              . . .
          0  physical reads
```

We compute statistics on the table and one of the indices and re-execute the last query. Based on the statistics, the system decides to use a full table scan without the hint.

```
SQL> analyze table t compute statistics;
SQL> analyze index ind_t_2 compute statistics;

SQL> select count(distinct object_name) from t where id >
20;


Execution Plan

-------------------------------------------------------------
   0        SELECT STATEMENT Optimizer=CHOOSE (Cost=481
Card=1 Bytes=2
          8)

   1    0    SORT (GROUP BY)
   2    1      TABLE ACCESS (FULL) OF 'T' (TABLE) (Cost=481
Card=149107
          Bytes=4174996)

Statistics
-------------------------------------------------------------
         . . .
   0 physical reads
```

Appendix 6. Example of Concurrent Execution of Transactions

This is a slightly modified example of concurrent executions of transactions from Oracle's documentation. It demonstrates the actions of the second transaction while the first transaction escalates the restrictiveness of table locks. The example also demonstrates the READ ONLY isolation level and SELECT FOR UPDATE for explicit read locking.

Transaction 1	Time	Transaction 2
LOCK TABLE scott.dept IN ROW SHARE MODE; *Statement processed*	1	

	2	DROP TABLE scott.dept;
		    *ORA-00054 resource busy
		    and acquire NOWAIT
		    specified
		    (Exclusive DDL lock not
		    possible
		    because of the table
		    lock by transaction 1)*

	3	LOCK TABLE scott.dept IN EXCLUSIVE MODE NOWAIT; *ORA-00054*

	4	SELECT LOC
		FROM scott.dept
		WHERE deptno = 20
		FOR UPDATE OF loc;
		    LOC
		    - - - - - - -
		    DALLAS
		    1 row selected

UPDATE scott.dept
SET loc = 'NEW YORK'
WHERE deptno = 20;
    *(Waits because
    transaction 2 has
    locked the same rows)*
	5	

	6	ROLLBACK; *(Releases row locks)*
1 row processed ROLLBACK;	7	
LOCK TABLE scott.dept IN ROW EXCLUSIVE MODE; *Statement processed*	8	
	9	LOCK TABLE scott.dept IN EXCLUSIVE MODE NOWAIT; *ORA-00054*

	10	LOCK TABLE scott.dept IN SHARE ROW EXCLUSIVE MODE NOWAIT; *ORA-00054*
	11	UPDATE scott.dept SET loc = 'NEW YORK' WHERE deptno = 20; *1 row processed*
	12	ROLLBACK;

SELECT loc
FROM scott.dept
WHERE deptno = 20
FOR UPDATE OF loc;
    LOC
    - - - - -
    DALLAS
    1 row selected
	13	

	14	UPDATE scott.dept
		SET loc = 'NEW YORK'
		WHERE deptno = 20;
		    *(Waits because
		    transaction 1 has locked
		    the same rows)*

ROLLBACK;	15	
	16	*1 row processed* *(The conflicting locks were released)* ROLLBACK;
LOCK TABLE scott.dept IN SHARE MODE *Statement processed*	17	
	18	LOCK TABLE scott.dept IN EXCLUSIVE MODE NOWAIT; *ORA-00054*
	19	LOCK TABLE scott.dept IN SHARE ROW EXCLUSIVE MODE NOWAIT; *ORA-00054*
	20	LOCK TABLE scott.dept IN SHARE MODE; *Statement processed*

	21	SELECT loc
		FROM scott.dept
		WHERE deptno = 20;
		    LOC
		    - - - - -
		    DALLAS
		    1 row selected

	22	SELECT loc
		FROM scott.dept
		WHERE deptno = 20
		FOR UPDATE OF loc;
		    LOC
		    - - - - - -
		    DALLAS
		    1 row selected

	23	UPDATE scott.dept
		SET loc = 'NEW YORK'
		WHERE deptno = 20;
		    (Waits because
		    transaction 1 holds the
		    conflicting table lock)

ROLLBACK;	24	
	25	*1 row processed* *(The conflicting table* *lock was released)* ROLLBACK;
LOCK TABLE scott.dept IN SHARE ROW EXCLUSIVE MODE; *Statement processed*	26	
	27	LOCK TABLE scott.dept IN EXCLUSIVE MODE NOWAIT; *ORA-00054*
	28	LOCK TABLE scott.dept IN SHARE ROW EXCLUSIVE MODE NOWAIT; *ORA-00054*
	29	LOCK TABLE scott.dept IN SHARE MODE NOWAIT; *ORA-00054*
	30	LOCK TABLE scott.dept IN ROW EXCLUSIVE MODE NOWAIT; *ORA-00054*

	31	SELECT loc
		FROM scott.dept
		WHERE deptno = 20;
		    LOC
		    - - - - - -
		    DALLAS
		    1 row selected

	32	SELECT loc
		FROM scott.dept
		WHERE deptno = 20
		FOR UPDATE OF loc;
		    LOC
		    - - - - - -
		    DALLAS
		    1 row selected

	33	UPDATE scott.dept
		SET loc = 'NEW YORK'
		WHERE deptno = 20;
		    (Waits because
		    transaction 1 holds the
		    conflicting table lock)

UPDATE scott.dept
SET loc = 'NEW YORK'
WHERE deptno = 20;
    (Waits because
    transaction 2 has
    locked the same rows)
	34	*(Deadlock)*

(Operation is *cancelled)* ROLLBACK;	35	
	36	*1 row processed*
	37	ROLLBACK;
LOCK TABLE scott.dept IN EXCLUSIVE MODE;	38	
	39	LOCK TABLE scott.dept IN EXCLUSIVE MODE NOWAIT; *ORA-00054*
	40	LOCK TABLE scott.dept IN ROW EXCLUSIVE MODE NOWAIT; *ORA-00054*
	41	LOCK TABLE scott.dept IN SHARE MODE NOWAIT; *ORA-00054*
	42	LOCK TABLE scott.dept IN ROW EXCLUSIVE MODE NOWAIT; *ORA-00054*
	43	LOCK TABLE scott.dept IN ROW SHARE MODE NOWAIT; *ORA-00054*

	44	SELECT loc
		FROM scott.dept
		WHERE deptno = 20;
		    LOC
		    - - - - - -
		    DALLAS
		    1 row selected

	45	SELECT loc
		FROM scott.dept
		WHERE deptno = 20
		FOR UPDATE OF loc;
		    (Waits because
		    transaction 1 has a
		    conflicting table lock)

UPDATE scott.dept	46	

SET deptno = 30 WHERE deptno = 20; *1 row processed*		
COMMIT;	47	
	48	*(Transaction 1 has released the conflicting lock)* *0 rows selected*
SET TRANSACTION READ ONLY;	49	

SELECT loc
FROM scott.dept
WHERE deptno = 10;
    LOC
    - - - - -
    BOSTON
    1 row processed
	50	

	51	UPDATE scott.dept SET loc = 'NEW YORK' WHERE deptno = 10; *1 row processed*

SELECT loc
FROM scott.dept
WHERE deptno = 10;
    LOC
    - - - - -
    BOSTON
    *(Transaction 1 does
not see uncommitted
data)*
	52	

	53	COMMIT;

SELECT loc
FROM scott.dept
WHERE deptno = 10;
    LOC
    - - - - -
    BOSTON
    *(Sees the same results
even after Transaction
2 commits)*
	54	

COMMIT;	55	
SELECT loc FROM scott.dept WHERE deptno = 10; *LOC*	56	

– – – – – – *NEW YORK* *(Read only transaction* *is finished and the* *new transaction sees* *committed data)*		

References

[Churcher] Churcher, C. (2007). *Beginning Database Design. From Novice to Professional. Designing Databases for the Desktop and Beyond*, Apress.

[Connolly 2004] Connolly, T., & Begg, C. (2004). *Database Solutions: A step by step guide to building databases: 2e.* Addison Wesley

[Connolly 2010] Connolly, T., & Begg, C. (2005). *DataBase Systems: A Practical Approach to Design, Implementation and Management: 5/e.* Addison Wesley.

[Coronel] Coronel, C., Morris, S., & Rob, P. (2009). *Database systems: design, implementation, and management.* Cengage Learning.

[Hernandez] Hernandez, M. J. (2003). *Database design for mere mortals: a hands-on guide to relational database design.* Addison-Wesley Professional.

[Hoffer] Hoffer J., Prescott M., McFadden F. (2013). *Modern Database Management: 11e.* Prentice Hall.

[Kroenke] Kroenke, D., & Auer, D. J. (2010). *Database concepts.* Prentice Hall.

[Kyte 2003] Kyte T.. (2003). *Expert One-on-One Oracle.* Apress .

[Kyte 2005] Kyte T. (2005). *Expert Oracle, Signature Edition.* Apress.

[Kyte 2010] Kyte, T. (2010). *Expert Oracle database architecture: Oracle database 9i, 10g, and 11g programming techniques and solutions.* Apress.

[Kifer] Kifer M., Bernstein A., Lewis P. (2005). *Database Systems: An Application-Oriented Approach, Introductory Version: 2/e.* Addison Wesley.

[Manino] Mannino M. (2008). *Database Design, Application Development, and Administration: 4e.* McGraw-Hill.

[Muller] Muller R. (1999). *Database Design for Smarties.* Morgan Kaufmann Publishers.

[Özsu] Özsu, M. T., & Valduriez, P. (2011). *Principles of distributed database systems.* Springer.

[Shasha] Shasha D., & Bonnet P. (2003). *Database Tuning.* Morgan Kaufmann Publishers.

[Silberschatz] Silberschatz A., Korth H., Sudarshan S. (2010). *Database System Concepts: 6e.* McGraw-Hill.

[Written] Whitten J., Bentley L., Dittman K. (2007). *System Analyses and Design Methods: 7e.* McGraw-Hill.

Oracle Database Online Documentation 11g Release Library.
http://www.**oracle**.com/pls/db111/homepage